ONE NATION UNDER PAR

From the Clubhouse...   To the White House?

BY

MARK NEMCEK

PUBLISH TO GO
PUBLICATIONS, LLC

This story is a work of fiction. The names, characters, places and incidents are the product of the author's imagination or are used fictitiously. Any resemblance to actual persons, living or dead, business establishments, events, or locals is entirely coincidental.

One Nation Under Par

Copyright © 2006 by Mark Nemcek

ISBN 0-9745110-6-4

Library of Congress Control Number: 2007928934

All Rights Reserved.
This book, or parts thereof, may not be reproduced in any form without permission. The scanning, uploading, and distribution of this book via the Internet or via any other means, without the permission of the publisher or author is illegal and punishable by law. Please purchase only paper or authorized electronic editions.

Publish To Go Publications, LLC
P.O. Box 272737
Boca Raton, FL 33427

www.onenationunderpar.us
Printed in the USA

10 9 8 7 6 5 4 3 2 1

Acknowledgements

This book is dedicated to my wife Kathy:
My primary editor, the definition of patience, tolerant of my untimely humor
and twisted wit, my biggest fan, and the love of my life

Special Thanks

Hard Rock Cafe International (USA), Inc.

TaylorMade-adidas Golf Company

Hole Number 1
Par 5

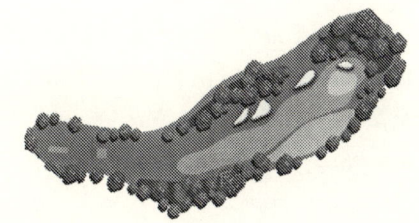

(**Coarse Notes:** "One short putt away from victory and 23 years of misery. This is it. One short putt. That's all I need. Be the ball. Jack, Arnie, Tiger, guide me... Nice Ta-Ta's?")

For over twenty frustrating years, Jeff Taylor pursued his goal to obtain a PGA Tour card. He vowed that this was his final attempt to compete for the card to live the dream of playing professional golf on tour. He didn't remember making a bet with God or the Devil, but somehow, some superior force helped him play the best round of his life.

Wooph. Smack. "Oh baby, that felt good. Goodbye Mr. Titleist." "Goodbye Mr. Driver. That was Sweeeeeet. You got all of me. Man, he really launched me. Okay, Okay, now keep it straight. DON'T TURN RIGHT. Okay. I straightened out and see a good spot to land. Don't turn, spin straight. Okay, I'm running out of breadth. Let's bring er down." Flump, flump, roll. "Okay, roll towards the center of the fairway. AVOID THAT DIVOT. Okay. Okay. Good move. I'm sit'n high in the short stuff, ...maybe a little eight iron away from victory."

Through 17 holes, Jeff, along with his ball and clubs, teamed up and executed long straight drives that repelled the rough, and knocked stiff irons that shook hands with the soft and inviting greens. This resulted in a three under par, one stroke lead in the tournament. He approached his next shot with nervous confidence, selecting an eight iron for distance and a short prayer for accuracy saying, *Lord, please let this be the right club. Please?*

Whack. Jeff looked up to the sky and said "Thank you", while his club, using an Ozzie Osbourne voice said "I am eight iron man."

The Titleist jumped off the sweet spot of the club and yelled "Yes you are, Mr. eight. You crunched me. Now we're doing the backspin. I love digg'n my dimples in the green and spinn'n back towards Mr. Hole. I can do no wrong today." Flump. "Yes. Spin back. I said SPIN BACK. Yes! Perfect. Hey cup. I'm banging on your door. Ready for a little ball action?"

Jeff strolled up to the green and grinned when he saw his ball resting four feet above the cup. His mind was racing while he lined up the putt. *Great shot Jeff. Now, it's birdie time. Knock this in, and you're play'n on tour. It's a routine, downhill putt, so easy does it. You can do it. No spike marks in the way. No confusing bumps. Sink it.* As he sized up the straight putt, a disturbing motion caused the mostly male gallery to stir like a herd of somber water buffalos whiffing an encroaching lioness. He looked up and noticed a well proportioned but unbalanced blonde holding a half-drunk bottle of Corona wobble directly across the green from him.

Meanwhile, the putter said "Hey ball. I'm drooling over this putt. Are you and Jeff ready?"

"I'm ready to roll. My logo is zoned in on the cup and Jeff is,... hey? What's going on over there? Man, that chick is hot. I hope she doesn't distract Jeff. Come on Jeff, knock me in so we can win this thing. Jeff, down here. Focus on me. Jeeeefffff."

Jeff stood over the putt with sweaty palms, unable to breathe. Several practice strokes did nothing to help him calm his nerves. Worst of all, his mind was confined to watching her butt more than his putt. *Come on Jeff. Focus. Knock this thing in the hole. Win this damn thing. Man, her ass is falling out of those shorts. Jeff. Focus. Knock the ball in. Man, her tank top looks like two over filled water balloons ready to burst. Damn it Jeff. Concentrate. Be the ball. Knock it in. OK. Relax. Don't rush it. Smooth. Breathe. OK. I'm ready. Please God, let it happen.*

Jeff regained his composure. With a slow and deliberate action, he drew the club back. Then, just as he was tapping the ball, her chest, with the aid of a cool, quick desert breeze, announced that there was a nip in the air, which nearly caused the gallery to applaud. The ill-timed breeze, coupled with the misfortune of her red high heels getting stuck in the short grass, caused her to tumble over, resulting in a high-pitched, muffled scream from the opposite gallery.

The twenty minute, slow motion fall really lasted just two seconds. Her blonde hair appeared to be on fire in the wind, like a plane plunging to the earth with jets ablaze. Her patriotic eyes displayed a rare surprised, yet not surprised look about them as she fell, reflecting "Oh no, not again." Men from around the green raced in her direction attempting to catch her in hopes of accidentally grabbing a body part other than her arms or legs, but to no avail. She crash-landed on her own, without major injury or breaking a 5-inch heel from her shoe.

While Jeff watched her fall, he also noticed his Titleist travel thirty feet past the hole.

She heard the moan of the gallery during her descent but couldn't see the face of the golfer who had just missed his putt, as it was buried in his hands.

Two more putts later, Jeff's last and fatal attempt to become a professional golfer ended, putting him back in the Las Vegas golf store selling golf shoes to old women with bunions and flabby ankles. He lost by one stroke and was devastated. The gallery departed with the winner of the tournament, except for a few vultures who hovered around the fallen girl like a wounded rabbit.

With the aid of the flock of predators, she resumed her vertical position, displaying a sign of professionalism by not spilling any beer during the turmoil. Even though she removed her shoes, her top-heavy body and Corona-filled cranium minimized her natural acts of balance. She stumbled over to Jeff, knowing that he had missed his shot on account of her. Just as she reached him, imbalance won over balance, and she fell into his arms with teary, apologetic eyes. Jeff had the overwhelming urge to see how far he could shove his putter down her throat, but the sound of her tears and the friction of her body against his melted him into his typical, complacent self.

Without looking at her eyes, Jeff said "If it wasn't for you, I'd be on my way to playing on the PGA Tour right now. I blew a simple four foot putt because of your wipeout. Just one putt away... I can't believe it. I had the card."

With her chest heaving against Jeff's, she said, "I'm so, so sorry. I never meant to mess you up."

Jeff realized they were locked together on the eighteenth green and eventually looked into her blurry eyes. He felt his rage dissolve into disappointment, and said, "Well, you owe me. Big time. You can clean my clubs, or, uh, buy me a few beers to let me play catch up to your Corona state of mind."

The corners of the woman's mouth edged up oh-so slightly and she said, "I'll see you inside the bar. It's the least I can do." She released her grip, regained her composure and walked away while Jeff packed up his golf bag thinking, *I've had worse consolation prizes.*

Several attitudes later, Jeff discovered that Ginger was the sole proprietor of a blossoming start-up business venture in Las Vegas. "I own my own business, specializing in fostering temporary romantic partnerships for the lonely business traveler. I have a web site and everything. I was supposed to meet a client at the golf course bar to negotiate a business transaction when the bartender told me that a golf tournament was taking place, and my client might be watching the event."

Ginger did not tell Jeff that she mostly stumbled over to the 18th green in search of Joe-Somebody and last month's rent. That, however, was when lightning struck.

(In the bar, Bob Marley is whaling in the background, "I wanna love you, and hold you tight, I wanna love you, everyday and every night"...)

No matter what state of mind she was in, Ginger was rather good at sizing up business opportunities, but this tall, blondish, golfing-boy pushing 40-something was somehow interfering with her antenna. *I don't understand it. I feel weird. Is it the fact that I ruined his career by not wearing appropriate golf shoes at the appropriate time? He is kinda cute. Well, this guy will never be a paying client of mine, but why?*

While Ginger provided a non-detailed underview of her work to Jeff, the TV atop the bar boringly blared out a news update regarding the upcoming presidential election. Ginger's focus was disrupted when she heard the name of the candidates, as one name stood out: Sonny Hoag.

She stood up on the bar railing, and leaned toward the TV, nearly suffocating Jeff in the process as her chest engulfed his face like a catcher's mitt smothering a fast ball thrown from the pitcher... except, unlike a catcher's mitt, her texture was soft and warm, and her aroma was exotic and tingling. As Ginger sat back down, she unknowingly and mildly dragged her shirt and chest across his nose, eyes, and mouth. Jeff, now petrified in a horny daze, heard her say, "Hey, I think I know that candidate." But, her 5'4" curvy body teleprompted a soaring erection versus election discussion from Jeff. The uncoiling of his 3 wood, previously concealed in his golf bag-like underwear, caused him to shift around until his only hope of avoiding embarrassment was to create a diversion to his growing concern and turn her attention to the non-sensational discussion on TV.

Jeff was physically well kept, but politically inept. Yet, he filibustered his opinion and said, "You can't trust any of these guys. They really don't plan on fulfilling their pledge promises. They're all liars and they only care about their potential to make money and have power. So many oxymoron's... Military intelligence, happily married, jumbo shrimp, honest president... Instead of a debate, I'd like to have the press connect all of the candidate clowns to lie detectors. Then, let reporters ask them questions about their past experiences and campaign promises. Let the scribbling lines of the polygraph be the judge to show American voters who they can believe."

Ginger, being educated on the psyche of her new found friend, squeezed out the thought that this was not such a bad idea, while also squeezing a fresh lime into her new Corona. She was not, however, distracted from the obvious commotion within the pleated pants. *He's a golf pro,* she thought, *but I'm a love pro, and I certainly know when the love club grows. Hmm... should I play with or without a glove?*

(**Course Notes**: She's a sin waiting to happen. Vote polyTITS, not politics. Do you take this man/woman, and solemnly swear to uphold the prostitution of the United States...)

A masked stranger at the end of the bar transparently joined in on the conversation. "Partner, you played a hellava round today. Let me buy you and missy a round." Jeff turned his head in the direction of the resounding voice. A low tipped cowboy hat and cheap sunglasses concealed most of his unshaven, desert-dried face while his forefinger whirled around to the observant eye of the bartender. Two fresh Corona's appeared while the bartender announced "Courtesy of Longshot."

Longshot's offer to buy Jeff and Ginger a round instantly projected life-long friendship and trust, which was typically the case in a bar and holds more value than a verdict in a court of law. As Longshot soaked in his rum and Coke, he transformed from his spiritual anonymity to fat reality and said "One bad putt. That's all you had."

Jeff said, "Don't remind me." Ginger grabbed Jeff's hand and tried to console him away from the thought of her ill-timed fall.

Longshot continued. "Partner, you have more going for you than you think. Forget about the golf tournament. This might be a good time for you to change your career. I'll call you tomorrow, and we'll chat about it."

With his brain going through a synapse lapse, and his inability to develop one million new cells of logic in two seconds, Jeff scribbled his phone number on a damp napkin on the bar and handed it to Longshot. "At this point, I'll consider anything."

Longshot grinned like he had a Royal Flush in the last hand of a million dollar poker tournament and said, "Partner, how'd ya like to be the next president of the United States?"

Jeff almost fell backwards laughing and said "Dude, I have as much chance of becoming president as I have of being married tomorrow."

The next day at the crack of noon, the phone rang, and Jeff and Ginger woke up together, both wearing wedding rings. In the middle of a black hole in the Milky Way, somewhere between the planets of Mars and Penis, Ginger answered the phone with a barely audible response. Longshot replied, "Hi missy. It's me, Longshot, from last night. Sorry to wake you. I reckoned you'd be up by now. Is Jeff up?"

"Haaagh. Oh my God." At that moment, Ginger screamed when she realized she had a gold band around her finger. In shock and haste, she fell out of bed finding the elusive treasure de jour: a stained marriage certificate next to the box of Crunchy Creams donuts and an empty bottle of champagne.

While Jeff struggled to regain mortal consciousness, Ginger told the disturbing caller that they seemed to have been married. Longshot merely said, "Is that so?"

Jeff pulled his head up from the bed with a quick jerk and thought he was bleeding. He quickly discovered that two jelly filled donuts were used in place of pillows. He used a semi-clean shirt at the foot of the bed to wipe the sugary jelly out of his ear. That's when he saw his ring for the first time. He carefully fondled it and unknowingly said aloud "Man, I sliced, shanked, and duck-hooked balls out-of-bounds before, but I'm going to need a wizard in a hot air balloon to bring me back to the Kansas fairway this time." Ginger handed him the phone and escaped into the bathroom.

"Congrats, partner. How's it feel to be married?"

Jeff replied, "I don't really know yet. Who is this?"

"It's me. Longshot. We met in the bar yesterday after the golf tournament. I offered you a chance for a new career, and you gave me your phone number. I want you to come down to a local radio station where I work to talk about the future. I host a radio show about gambling called 'Up Your Odds.' Ever listen to it? I discuss strategies and reveal tactics to gamblers on how to improve their odds in betting. Hell, I'm right up there with Jim Cramer's TV stock show and Howard Stern's adult comedy radio. Millions tune in for a chance to up their odds. My show airs bi-weekly on the radio and Internet broadcast, and I expect to be on Satellite radio by year's end."

Jeff caught about every third word and said, "So what does that have to do with me?"

"Come on down to the station and find out."

Jeff agreed to meet Longshot at 4 p.m., scribbled down the address, and hung up the phone.

Ginger emerged from the bathroom wearing the only clean towel she could find. It was frayed at the edges and had one gaping hole in the middle, yet it still provided her naked and sexually bumpy body some shelter. She jumped back into bed and draped the sheets around her. Jeff appeared to be reviewing the marriage certificate for authenticity but really wanted to find out the name of his wife, which was buried deep in his sand trap like memory. He looked at Ginger, and the only thing that came out of his mouth was, "Good morning, Mrs. Taylor." This resulted in playful smiles that seemed to lessen the hurt of the headaches. "How bout some breakfast and aspirin?"

Ginger felt like a virgin bride. She smiled a sweet, coy smile and said, "Okay, Mr. Taylor."

Jeff jumped out of bed and quickly put on some shorts to cover his endowment. Ginger grabbed the remote and put on the TV, pretending not to watch Jeff. She liked what she saw. With just a few remote clicks, she discovered *Gilligan's Island*, which was the easiest show to mentally digest for the moment.

Jeff returned with a pot of coffee, four aspirin, and two Jethro Bodine-sized bowls of Cocoa Puffs. He served up the cereal deluxe and jumped back under the covers saying, "Well, Mrs. Taylor, this is the best I can do for our honeymoon breakfast. Hey, I love *Gilligan's Island*. I think they have a twenty-four-hour marathon going on. How many shows can you watch in a row?"

Ginger was unaccustomed to such playful conversation in the morning and just shrugged her shoulders while she poured the Cocoa Puffs into her empty belly. After several cups of coffee and watching Skipper harass his "little buddy," Ginger said, "What do you remember from yesterday?"

Jeff looked at her and said, "Well, I remember losing the golf tournament. I watched you wipe out on the putting green and smacked my ball to kingdom come. After that, it gets really cloudy. I sort of remember the wedding, and think Longshot was the best man. Oh yeah, we were married by Elvis. Does any of this ring a bell?"

Ginger nodded. "A little. What do we do now?"

The eye wall of the booze-induced mental hurricane was passing for Mr. and Mrs. Jeffery Taylor. As the mind debris cleared, Jeff and Ginger clearly realized that their lives were basically pockets with holes, so neither was completely upset with the current situation. As in hurricanes past where the government was on vacation, and FEMA was not an immediate option, they independently concluded that their options were limited.

Jeff seemed to read Ginger's mind and said, "Well, I don't mind being married if you don't. You're welcome to move in to my place."

Ginger sat there in thought for a moment with a grin on her face and said "Well, I think if we do this marriage thing, it might be a good time for me to change my career. You only have a queen size bed, and my clients and I might keep you awake during business matters."

Jeff snickered and replied in a warm tone, "Yeah, besides, I don't know how much action this old bed can take. It's probably got just enough life for the two of us."

Ginger appreciated his comical yet indirect remark, and was glad to hear that he was not open to sharing his wife with others.

Then Jeff rolled over on his side, looked straight into Ginger's soft blue eyes and said "Well, let's try out this marriage for a while and see what happens? What do we have to lose?"

This was not Ginger's idea of an after-wedding proposal, but it was the best she'd heard in years, coming from someone whom she was attracted to with no good reason. She rolled over on top of Jeff and said, "I'm sorry, but I don't remember if we consummated our marriage. Why don't we start there?"

It was the best round of bedroom golf they ever played, redefining the meaning of "hole-in-one." They missed the next three episodes of Gilligan's Island.

(**Course Notes:** What a difference a day makes. Lights, Camera, Action. Change is good? Interact – Interlude - Interlock - Intertwine – Interface – Intercourse – Internet. I'm right, you're thong.)

Jeff showered and dressed for his meeting with Longshot. Ginger dressed and headed back to her apartment to pack her stuff for the official "move in" to Jeff's apartment. While packing up her belongings, she was relieved to abandon her current profession, as it was not physically or monetarily rewarding. It was a career that chose her, not by her own choice. Her sexy looks, lack of teen guidance, and desperate need for cash could be blamed as the culprit. While she examined her mental resume to develop other possible job options, she haphazardly packed her meager belongings into boxes, and stealthed her way to her car to stay below the radar of her landlord.

Moving into Jeff's apartment was a barely a step up for Ginger, but at least it wasn't a step backward. She hoped that he would tolerate her pet parrot. Blabs was a colorful double-yellow headed Amazon who was very used to strangers, based on the steady traffic of unknowns that frequented Ginger World. She was quick to repeat most anything she heard, but her greatest accomplishment was her ability to repeat the tone, phrases, grunts, and moans of Ginger's house guests with unbelievable clarity. Upon request, Blabs could recreate the sounds of many of Ginger's clients, who included notable politicians, businessmen, clergy, and many other horny pillars of the community. Ginger often thought of entering Blabs on Letterman's Famous Pet Tricks, but she couldn't quite figure out how to get David Letterman to moan without being censored on national TV.

She dumped several dresser drawers into a cardboard box, and took a long look at the contents. She turned to Blabs and said "Boy, look at all this shit. I think I have more love toys, potions, lotions, thongs and high heeled shoes than clothes. Hmm. Should I take the whips, handcuffs, and leathered paraphernalia? They were mostly props anyway. What did Jimmy Buffett say in that song? Oh yeah. Indecision may or may not be my problem. Well, he got that right." It took no time at all for Blabs to run down her repertoire of Buffett tunes, and instinctively started singing "Why don't we get drunk and screw?"

Ginger picked up Blabs, gave her a kiss on the beak and said, "Honey, that's exactly why I'm married now." She placed Blabs back on her perch and continued to pack while Blabs serenaded her with other appropriate Buffett classics.

The last items to move were Ginger's extensive photography equipment and laptop computer, both of which were used primarily for her business. Marketing was a key component for any business to sustain and grow, and she felt the Internet could be an ideal marketing medium. Several months earlier, when she had passed her neighbor's apartment, she could see and hear young girls laughing while sitting in front of the computer. One day she stopped by to see if they'd like to get paid to teach her some computer basics, and they eagerly agreed, knowing they could use the extra cash to shop on various web sites. She bought a new laptop, and within weeks, she had her own web page and one personal and one professional email address.

She was also a member of several chat groups that catered to lonely men who travel frequently. (Yes, there are such sites, and no, the neighbors did not know.) Her site targeted a very niche group of potential customers who were looking for dinner companions while attending trade shows and conferences in Las Vegas. Many lonely businessmen, some of whom were unhappily married or simply desired some female companionship, felt awkward going to a show or dinner by themselves while traveling in Sin City. Ginger made her clients feel attractive, confident, interesting, and protected while enjoying a night out on the town.

She always felt that the safest sex was no sex, and that was reserved for only the rarest and wealthiest of clients. Since she hated actually going to bed with strangers, she set a pricing structure that made it somewhat affordable to rent her companion time for an evening of legal fun. Her fee for anything more than a good night kiss was far more than her typical clients could afford, thus relieving her of between-the-sheet activities, while forcing them to look for personal enjoyment in their own hands, so to speak.

Her site gave the impression that hundreds of women were available through her escort service, and it was voted a "Safe Bet" in several of the raunchy Vegas tabloids. Ginger used stock photos of women on her site to protect her identity. When she received emails or phone calls to reserve a specific escort for a certain day, she'd respond that a convention had depleted her complete talent pool, and she was the only escort available. Her voice, and even her emails sounded sexy, and she'd usually booked the date. Her fee would typically be

$450 for a dinner and a show. This way, she could actually eat a good meal and enjoy decent Las Vegas styled entertainment.

Her level of flirting had a direct relationship to her tip. Of course, her level of flirting was also dependent on her client. She did need to employ acting skills on many occasions. In most cases the men who hired her were unattractive, rather boring, married middle-aged men looking for some companionship and romance that had been lost over the years.

What made her service stand out from the other escort services was her "Night on the Town" package. During her free spirited career, she had developed solid, business-only relationships with many of the hotels and restaurants that provided free or discounted meals and theater tickets. For $850, her rent-a-date would be picked up in a luxurious black limo. An attractive and sensual Ginger greeted them with a warm kiss and a chilled bottle of bubbly in the spacious back seat. After a scenic tour of the Strip with hand holding and suggestive banter, their love coach would eventually arrive at a fabulous four-star restaurant for dinner, followed by an entertaining Las Vegas show. At the evening's conclusion, Ginger's date would then be delighted with a no-sex good night kiss, along with a complimentary souvenir t-shirt, and best of all, a coupon for 15% off their next escort service. Her web site provided a la cart services, giving them the choice of available shows and restaurants. When the client was billed through her web-based store front, the credit card statement indicated A+ Marketing Services, making it a little easier for clients to lie to their spouses or to pad their travel expenses.

Her growing knowledge of the Internet overlapped with her mastering the art of undercover photography. She planned to sell video clips of her exotic experiences on adult Internet sites. She also figured that visual evidence might come in handy to protect her from any dissatisfied customers. As a result, she set up an impressive filming studio that secretly stored her escapades directly to a computer server in Omaha. The Internet Service Provider supplied her with unlimited storage capacity, in exchange for live viewing of her activities. She thought she got the better end of the deal, but they begged (literally) to differ. Since she was not fond of paid-for sexual romance, her film collection was not extensive, but she would have had a good chance of winning erotica film awards if she entered.

With the car radio blasting "On the road again", she drove her bulging 1997 red Camero convertible down the road. In her rear view mirror, she saw her landlord running after her screaming for rent money. No money was a good reason to not stop. Besides, someplace in Omaha, she had him digitally stored with her, sexually bartering her monthly rent, a negotiation that his wife might find intriguing.

Meanwhile, Jeff awkwardly entered the radio station, which was located a block beyond the pyramid at the Luxor hotel on the Las Vegas strip. Longshot greeted him in the lobby. "Howdy partner. Come on in. We'll go into my office. You look a hellava lot better than when I dropped you off at home. I'm glad you could make it".

Jeff said, "Well, I'm supposed to be at work filling plastic bags with golf tees. But based on the last twenty-four hours, that task was far too challenging, mentally and physically." So I decided to take a sick day."

Longshot replied "Good move. Besides, I know you'll be interested in what I have to say. Now follow me." Longshot gave Jeff a brief tour of the radio station while they walked to his office. While Longshot rambled on about uninteresting points of interest, Jeff thought, *His voice sounds memorable, but his face ain't too clear. Should I be sippn' on a margarita? I think I need one. What the hell am I doing here? Well maybe Slingshot, or Longshot, whatever his name was, had something better to offer.*

Longshot's office was foreign to most household cleaning products. The dingy walls were covered with pictures of Longshot with famous celebrities, as well as an assortment of framed winning gambling tickets. While Longshot described some of his biggest gambling accomplishments, Jeff looked at Longshot for the first time. His gray thinning hair was well past the help of Minoxodril. He wore the most expensive sunglasses sold at 7-Eleven, concealing his eyes and years of lost bets. His three-day unshaved face matched his urban cowboy look, even without the black cowboy hat. He guessed that Longshot had probably gone through several wives, or most likely, they went through him. Longshot then started to fill in a few potholes regarding the evening past. *Ouch.*

"I love to gamble and bet Raul, the bartender, $25 that you and Ginger would be married within three hours. I thought this was easy money, as most drunken losers are easy prey for advice, leadership, and acts of stupidity. No offense."

Jeff just shrugged his shoulders and said, "You might as well give me the details."

"Well, partner, after four or five hundred beers, you and Ginger had conveniently discovered each other's mouths, with a common yet unusually wet paradox."

As Longshot spoke in his now elegant radio voice, Jeff spun off into a dream world...

"Ginger assumed the role of the Stingray, similar to those found in Stingray City in Grand Cayman. A 35-foot boat takes you out to peacefully warm and calm turquoise waters where 5-foot stingrays are found. You enter the water wearing your snorkeling mask and fins and holding squid in your hand, a delicacy for stingrays. Humans equate this to things such as caviar, Reese's cups, an open bar, sex with disease proof strangers ... The stingrays circle your nervous existence. Their tingling, thick velvet fins tickle your body, overwhelming you with emotions of being afraid, excited, unnatural, elated, apprehensive, and just generally glad to be where you usually aren't. When you hold out your hand with the bait, they swarm in and *suck* up the squid, leaving your hand shivering as you wonder if a finger is missing. Think of it as an underwater orgasm without sex. You and the stingray share the experience, but smoking afterwards is not an option, as you are underwater. Instead, you're almost guaranteed to slug down several beers afterwards to equal the beers you downed prior to jumping in the water. To be honest, no one quite knows what actions the stingray does after this human interlude, but sources believe that the University of Florida marine biology department is currently researching this phenomenon."

Longshot continued, "Jeff, you weren't nearly as eloquent. You were a Shop Vac. Plug it in, turn it on, suck it up."

Jeff phased out into another of his own dreams as Longshot spoke. "The difference in this scenario is similar to two different golfers: a short, yet precise hitter versus a long ball hitter. Both have the same goal but display different approaches to achieve it. When you and Ginger used your oral skills in this match play event, a new style of music was created unknown to MTV, VHS, and cable or satellite TV. Best of all, there was no loser in this event. The stingray and Shop Vac are harmoniously independent, yet each reached the suck face summit during their passionate plummet at the same time."

Longshot could see Jeff slipping in and out but persisted with the accounts of last evening. "The result of this beautiful yet disgusting act of behavior further improved my chances of winning the bet. As the bar was ready to close for the evening, I suggested taking the party to a new level that included great entertainment, booze, and a lifetime of memories that you probably won't ever remember (or don't want to remember). Even stingrays and Shop Vacs need to come up for air at some point, so you mutually agreed to follow me, your new leader, to Phase Two, not knowing that you were the entertainment. You and Ginger saying 'I do' seemed easier than breathing."

(**Course Notes:** Hunk of Burning Love. You have nothing to fear but fear itself...and a triple bogey. Looking for Love in all the Thong places. The only thing more blind than love is remembering your memory. HIM: A beer, and a girl's mouth, seems to always taste better in a bar. HER: If I wake with a stranger, and I don't puke, there's a good chance that he's still cute.)

Jeff was too hung over to say anything and let Longshot continue filling in all the holes of his wedding. "It was a first rate service. And yes, I was the best man. The King was the minister, flaring his white-spangled jump suit and cape. His perfectly timed hip and pelvis thrusts throughout this uniquely acclaimed Las Vegas wedding event should be, somehow, showcased in Graceland. After the ceremony, he performed his encore rendition of 'Love me Tender' (thank you, thank you very much), which has often been heralded as a 'best bet' in the Vegas Wed and Bed weekly gagazine. The Crunchy Creams (used in place of wedding cake) and Dom Juan champagne were delivered from the store conveniently located across the street from the Now or Never Chapel of Love. The wedding rings were purchased at Lucky Louie's pawn shop and bridal boutique, which is conveniently located next to the Now or Never Chapel of Love. By the way, Lucky Louie offers you a two-day, money back guarantee on the rings, less 20% cleaning fee, if you and Ginger mutually agree that your spur of the moment decision to wed was wrong. Lucky Louie said that his returns, although few, are typically based on sex, drugs, rock-and-roll, alcohol, temporary insanity, lust, religion, gender preference, or other natural acts of God. There may be a few others I forgot. In addition, with an hour's notice, Lucky Louie can also arrange to have your divorce papers prepared with the help of Ellen Spackler, Divorce

Attorney, whose office is conveniently located on the other side of the Now or Never Chapel of Love. Ginger opted against flowers, but if she wanted some for the nuptials, guess where the store is?"

Jeff again nodded his head, knowing a florist was located somewhere in the immediate vicinity of the chapel.

"Raul provided transportation services in exchange for his gambling debt to me. He chauffeured you, the blissful entourage, to the chapel, and then to your honeymoon apartment. He poured your nearly comatose bodies into bed, along with your parting gifts of donuts, champagne, and legal documents. This was a truly Kodak moment, but neither of us had cameras."

Longshot withheld the last leg of the journey from Jeff for no good reason. Raul had ended up at Longshot's office at the radio station. This known hideout was where Longshot often crashed due to circumstances beyond his control. It was here that Longshot detailed Jeff's political polygraph bar room idea, pitting him against all odds. Longshot, although confronted with his ball deeply buried in twelve inch rough, knew he had a great chance of making an eagle with a little luck, timing, and persuasive distortion.

Jeff, at this point, didn't even realize he was in the game.

Hole Number 2
Par 4

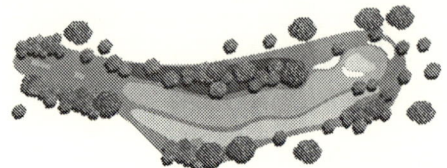

(**Course Notes**: Look out, incoming. Honesty is the best odd icy. What do you get when you mix politics, booze, absurdity, sex, and human stupidity – an eclectic official. If I had a million dollars…)

"**I bet you $100 that I can make you a millionaire.**" Longshot's comment made Jeff feel as though he had been hit on the side of the head with a golf ball while standing on the tee, only to hear "Fore" ten seconds after the direct hit. Jeff thought, *Where did that come from?* After hearing the foggy recap of his drunken wedding, a bet to be a millionaire sounded as confusing as blowing a 10-shot lead on the final three holes at the Masters.

Jeff's a naturally sharp guy, good sense of humor, polite, almost boring. Worst (or best) of all, he's brutally honest and doesn't even know it. But the last twenty-four hours have depleted him of common sense and wisdom, leaving him, at least for the moment, as sharp as the golf ball that symbolically hit him. He sat in wonder. *Why would anyone make such a bet? If I win, I make $100, and if I lose, I make a million bucks less $100. Big deal. Oh those Coronas. I wish Forest Gump's mother could offer me some insightful words that would make this situation easy for me to understand what the hell is going on.*

Jeff sat back into a spongy, fake leather chair across from Longshot's warped oak desk to digest this bet, but he couldn't conjure up any questions or answers. *Maybe I need a hair-of-the-dog, or possibly the entire tail.*

Longshot read Jeff's mind with ease and poured two glasses of Jack Daniels for himself and his new gambling buddy. Longshot then asked Jeff, "Do you remember your comment regarding the lie detector test for presidential candidates?"

Jeff hazily recalled the remark but didn't think it was something really worth remembering. "Vaguely," Jeff replied. "It was just barroom bullshit."

Longshot had profited from such ridiculous remarks in the past with his ability to feast on poor unfortunate souls, a.k.a. Jeff. "I think it was a brilliant idea, and I have a plan in place to make it happen."

Jeff couldn't figure out his role in this dream scheme and didn't know if Longshot had enough Jack Daniels to explain it to him.

Longshot continued. "Let me ask you a few simple questions. Have you ever been arrested?"

"No."

"Have you ever stolen anything?"

"Yeah, a dozen golf balls and golf glove from my store, a six pack from my buddy's fridge, a couple of Playboys from a 7-Eleven when I was a kid... All petty stuff."

"Have you ever cheated on a girlfriend or wife?"

"Actually, no, although I'm new to the wife thing."

"Have you lied to your boss?"

"Yes, I did today just to come here."

"Have you ever used drugs?"

"Sure, smoked some pot. Where is all this going?"

Longshot poured Jeff another drink and said, "I had a gut feeling that you had only a few skeletons in your closet of no significant value. I also had a buddy in the Las Vegas Police Department do a quick search on you this morning to confirm my intuition."

Longshot's next comment mirrored the sensation of a perfectly struck one iron crushing the dimples of the ball into Jeff's skull. Jeff saw the stray ball coming in his direction but couldn't react fast enough to get out of its way...

"I'm going to announce on my radio program that none of the presidential candidates would pass a polygraph test of truth, and I'm going to bet, up to a million dollars, that a semi-pro golfer from Las Vegas named Jeff Taylor has more honesty and integrity than any of the current candidates, and that you're a better choice for running the country."

Jeff spilled his drink as he fell over laughing in voice, "Me, a drunken semi-pro loser who just married a hooker, President of the United States. Dude, you don't have nearly enough Jack Daniels to get me involved in something like this. It's insane."

Longshot was also laughing aloud and said, "Jeff, you're right. It is insane. It's absurd. Yet, it's so stupid, it's a sure bet. The goal here is not to get you elected. The goal is to win my bet with you and make you a millionaire. Several million gamblers listen to my show as regularly and religiously as Southern Baptists attend Sunday service. Demographics prove that 40% of my followers are golfers, and 70% of my fans are sports nuts. They'll jump all over this bet. In addition, I have some contacts and clout with a variety of magazines, newspapers, racetracks, and sporting venues. Best of all, I have connections with some of the wealthiest bored people on the planet who are eager to risk parting with, or piss away, their easily earned or inherited cash in exchange for absurd entertainment."

Jeff felt as though he were standing in the middle of a driving range while professional golfers took aim at him.

Longshot went on, "I'll announce on my weekly show that I have a new presidential candidate who challenges all other candidates to a polygraph test. I'll bet even money to the first 10,000 registered gambling voters that my Independent candidate will beat the top Democratic and Republican candidates in the polygraph test. We'll figure out a way to design the test questions and get them to my media contacts. There is a $100 cap on the bet per voter. I'll work out the bet with one of the casinos, as they'd love to get in on this action. I know all the managers in town. The polygraph showdown will take place in 60-90 days, allowing enough time to get you placed on the ballot. During this period, you and your charming new wife will get to travel around the country, playing golf with the media and camera hungry dignitaries. Not a bad gig, Jeff, and you have nothing to lose."

Jeff loved the idea of playing golf on good courses for several months, but he was confused. "I still don't see how I can make $1 million and lose the original bet, and who will pay for this two month vacation?"

Longshot said, "We won't collect fundraising dollars as you're not really campaigning. But you are eligible to keep any dollars generated by endorsements, book deals, speaking engagements, or virtually any celebrity-focused activity, less 40% to me as your agent. Once I make the announcement and the media catches wind of it, companies will line up to be involved with you in some financial way. Best of all, these endorsements occur whether you win, lose, or drop out of the election. Just think, free golf, a three-month vacation, and a risk free chance to end up a millionaire. How could you say no?"

Jeff was spinning, but not from the Jack Daniels. *How could a guy that I met in a bar roughly twenty-four hours earlier, get me married to a girl I just met, do a complete credit and background check on me, come up with such an elaborate plan to make me a millionaire while mostly drunk, and become my business agent and campaign manager to get me nominated for President of the United States based on my own stupid idea of using lie detectors to determine who is worthy of becoming the most powerful person on earth? All based on a bet? To drink, or drink a lot is the only question that remains.*

Jeff came home in time to help Ginger bring in Blabs' birdcage and load some of her surveillance equipment into his apartment. Ginger was somewhat embarrassed when Jeff looked at the video equipment and said, "I used to take pictures of my clients sometimes, but I never did anything with the videos." Jeff didn't really even notice the equipment or her attempt to hide her past. He was still in shock, and nothing could faze him right now.

Ginger looked at his blank expression and asked, "Are you okay? How did your meeting go with Longshot?"

Jeff sat down next the birdcage and said, "Based on my last two-hour conversation with Longshot, I could find out that Osama Bin Laden was living in the White House after 9/11 as the president's gay lover, and it would be of no surprise to me."

Ginger said, "What happened? What did he say?"

"Do you remember my comment in the bar yesterday about hooking up presidential candidates to a lie detector?"

"Yes, I thought it was a good idea. Why?"

"Well, Longshot bet me a hundred dollars that he'd make me a millionaire if I answer some questions while hooked up to the polygraph. Oh yeah, he's going to announce on his radio show that I'm running for President of the United States, but first, we're going on a free, three month golfing honeymoon. That about sums it up."

Ginger fumbled with the bottled water she was holding, totally confused.

Jeff continued. "I told Longshot I wanted some time to think about the bet and needed to discuss it with you." Jeff added a little detail to the conversation.

Ginger reflected on the facts for a moment and decided to add a little scotch to her water to help her think more clearly and logically. After she posed him a few questions he could not answer, her one-person jury deliberated a guilty verdict of being drunk in the right bar at the right time and sentenced him to spending the next few months enjoying sex and golf on his potentially winning jackpot tour to the White House. She said, "Jeff, it sounds like you have nothing to lose, as long as you can quit anytime. Worst case, you'll make $100 for losing the bet and end up back in the golf store, but you might make a million bucks while on vacation."

Jeff grabbed a plain bottle of water and chugged half of it, and then asked Blabs, "What should I do, go to work or take the summer off?"

Blabs looked at Jeff, flapped her wings, and stunned Jeff by singing, "School's out for the summer…"

Jeff said, "Oh my God, that's amazing. Well, Ginger, I guess I'm going to run for president while on vacation."

Ginger hugged Jeff while humming the song along with Blabs.

Jeff called Longshot and said, "Let's golf for the presidency."

Longshot smiled on the other end of the phone, as he had just made a quick $100 on two bets with the station manger and sound engineer regarding Jeff's decision to enter the race. "Great," he replied, "I'll get things rolling and will be in touch."

Jeff hung up the phone and smiled at Ginger, and said, "We're on," and then, "Let's do it." Just then Blabs shouted out, "Let's do it," but it had a strikingly familiar, muscular Austrian accent. Then Blabs screeched in the same accent, "I'll be back." Jeff smiled a confused smile, while Ginger pushed Jeff into the bedroom and leaped for lust before Blabs could continue the conversation.

Their encounter of afternoon delight was wonderfully shared by each of them. Jeff's only real relationship had been with a female golf pro from Baltimore twelve years earlier. But the long distance relationship, coupled with her ability to out play Jeff, reduced his desire and ego.

Ginger, on the other hand, had had many suitors, but it was difficult to mix business with pleasure, and business, due to bills, typically came first. She felt something special in Jeff, but two days of marriage can hardly evoke love. Ginger thought, *I always expected to marry a rich guy, so the opportunity that Longshot presented to my new hubby is intriguing. Since we're legally married, I'm entitled to any fortune that may come our way. If our marriage doesn't work out, and his financial situation does, I might be able to earn several years of on-my-back and leg-spread donations in a few short months. I might as well enjoy the ride and see where it goes. Love may or may not happen, but if bucks end up in my bank account as a result, let the good times roll.*

(Course Notes: I bettcha $10 I can quit gambling. Arnold the Pig may be a good running mate – He's cute, smart, and has the ability to cut out the pork spending in D.C.)

Longshot's radio show had been on the air for almost ten years. It aired on Monday and Thursday nights for two hours. Typically, the first hour focused on a specific aspect of gambling such as playing poker, horse racing, or sports betting. It aimed at developing techniques that could increase your chance of winning. On the second half of the show, listeners called in to discuss sports or general gambling topics. Often, Monday callers discussed their successes or failures of the past weekend and looked for remedies to improve their past performances. Thursday callers were eager to develop confident tips that would assist them on their upcoming weekend gambling binges.

Gambling was a disease that Longshot possessed himself and couldn't treat. But subconsciously, he hoped his advice might minimize the losses of other hardcore gamblers and prevent them from betting the farm on "a sure bet" that would, in almost all circumstances, result as a sure loss. If not for his radio broadcast job, his financial situation would be equal to or less than that of the common loser.

He did, however, believe that hunches were an important aspect of gambling, whether it's investing in real estate, buying a fish for your aquarium that won't die in five days, picking a horse to win, or getting married (again). His hunch on Jeff for president sickened him to ecstasy. He was ready to bet the farm, which he vehemently told listeners never to do. Yet, he felt that a supreme power, a power higher than the Las Vegas mafia, presented him with an opportunity that even Oliver Douglas would bet the farm on. ("Green Acres is the place to be…")

Longshot was short on funds but high on perceived knowledge. And he hoarded a bit of knowledge on something that he'd never share. A truly sure bet. A good attorney should never ask a courtroom question without knowing the answer in advance. A good gambler, who finds someone stupid, drunk, or desperate enough to bet that time will stand still for ten seconds, was sure to win, unless God intervened. Although he wasn't in the same class with God, his listeners believed he could walk on water and would take his advice to the grave, or bankruptcy, typically the latter, followed soon afterwards by the former. When he debuts his new presidential candidate to his loyal fans, dollars would roll in like the winning roll in craps. But, he knew he was going to need some help.

The next day, Longshot detailed his betting scheme with Bob, his sound engineer and close friend. After listening to Longshot's plan, Bob felt a weird tingle rustle through his spine and said "You've come up with some crazy ideas before, but this one, well, it's the most ridiculous thing I've ever heard. I love it."

Longshot replied "Wait until you see Ginger. She's hot, and this will significantly increase the odds to get Jeff elected when any male voter sees her reach down to pick up her husband's golf ball wearing a snug halter top. Do you think I should have her wear a tasteful wrap or sweater to add a touch of morality and class?"

Bob replied "No way. Sex sells, always has, always will. Vegas wouldn't be here without it. If we're forced to watch a president and the first lady on TV for four years, we might as well enjoy it, and possibly look forward to it."

"You're right. With the right clothes, hairstyle and makeup, I'll bet she could seduce both genders, and possibly be a trend setter in fashion. Hmm, this might be another way to make money. Just think, a presidential line of clothing and perfume – what to call it - First Lady, Politislut, Capital Scents, DCXTaC". In addition, Jeff's no slouch himself. I think he's got gleam hidden somewhere under his golf hat that will attract the female voters."

Jeff was beaten down from many aspects of his life, but a million dollar smile did exist, which had been seen on some of his better days on the golf course. Although Longshot didn't know it, Ginger saw the smile for the first time on the morning of their honeymoon when they consummated their marriage. It remained on his face for almost two hours, and made it very difficult for him to eat breakfast without oral spillage.

With Bob nodding his head in agreement thinking about Jeff and Ginger's sex appeal, Longshot asked him "What do you think about our current list of presidential candidates?"

"Pathetic, as usual. No charisma, Category 3 hurricane blow-hards with enough wealth and political clout to buy their way to the election playoffs but in need of a boost to get them a win in the World Series Presidential election. Kinda like most any NY Yankee team. My only concern is Jeff's' lack of experience. He's got zip."

"You're right, but, I'd wager that Jeff, instilled with a sense of confidence, would boast a hallowed-like glow that would overshadow his opponents like a spicy black pepper seasoning. The biggest challenge is getting Jeff to overcome his inability to address the hoards of reporters. If he chokes, the campaign trail comes to the end of a cliff.

"Longshot, he's a golfer, not a senator. He talks to golf balls. Hell, I won't even talk into a mic here at that station. I'd shit my pants if I had to address the media."

"Well, I've got a plan. He won't do any formal press conferences, at least initially. Instead, we'll invite three reporters to play several holes of golf with Jeff. While on the golf course, they could ask Jeff questions regarding his candidacy. Few, if any reporters will be able to match his golf ability, thus increasing his confidence. It minimizes the barrage of questions that often occur at political events and will provide a relaxed and casual atmosphere on camera.

"Where does Ginger fit in?"

"She'll join the foursome with caddy-like intentions to tend the flag and have the choice to professionally and graciously bend over at opportune moments to retrieve sunken putts. Her participation will probably receive most of the media coverage. She's a perfect diversion to mask Jeff's inabilities and help defray the most serious questions away from our newest presidential hopeful. Of course, I'll be riding shotgun, protecting my candidate and betting opportunity. I'll need your help organizing this thing and will cut you in for a piece of the pie.

"Count me in. This action sounds delicious."

(Course Notes: Dress for success, but expose some chest, to express and impress, and achieve more with less. Then Say Cheese. The camera doesn't lie, so don't sweat it.)

Jeff and Ginger spent most of the day shopping, with Ginger hoarding most of the time and wardrobe expense money. Jeff was a breeze. Beige golf slacks, white tennis shoes, and a solid navy blue golf shirt. A custom embroidered logo was created and stitched to the shirt pocket. Two golf flag pins crisscrossed, and the clearly visible flags were, of course, our American Stars and Stripes.

Ginger, on the other hand, was on a mission. With Longshot footing the bill, Ginger raced between Sachs, Gucci, and her personal favorite, Victoria Secrets. After she purchased several outfits for the photo session, she and Jeff went into the Sands Salon for haircuts, makeovers, manicures, waxes, facials — the works. Jeff was unaccustomed to the treatment but settled down after accepting a glass of Pinot. Ginger acted as though she belonged there but actually needed some wine to repress her excitement of newness. When they emerged, they looked fabulous.

They taxied over to Kyle Matico's for the photo shoot. Kyle was a professional photographer whose office was conveniently located kitty corner to the Now or Never Chapel of Love. Longshot met them there with a beer in his hand. Kyle introduced himself and said "Ginger, I'd like you to try on a few outfits. We'll take a few pictures, and see what looks best. Let's have fun with this."

After awhile, Kyle said, "Ginger, you look fantastic in everything you've modeled. It's hard to believe that you never went into modeling. The camera loves you." Ginger blushed, knowing the camera was fooled, like virtually everyone else she met. Ginger was gifted with the fountain of youth, being twelve years older than her perceived age. Since the camera didn't ask Ginger her age, she didn't give one, and let the pictures snap without question. After she modeled all the outfits, they all agreed that the leather tennis outfit matched Jeff's sports look, and she went back into the dressing room to change.

Longshot jumped on the phone to make sure final preparations were made regarding the website and the casino wager. He also called the Viva Las Vegas Country Club to make arrangements to hold a press conference there, as well as reserve several starting times as part of the press conference. Kyle was playing with lights, backdrops, meters, and ice for his gin and tonic. With nothing to do, Jeff decided to help Ginger with her outfit. When he entered the room, she was wearing the red bra and thong purchased at Victoria Secrets. As good as she looked, his eyes magically removed the lacey garments, and they floated to the floor. They spent twenty-six minutes rehearsing positions that could be captured on film for *Sex as Sport Magazine*, but alas, Kyle was not aware of the missed photo opportunity.

When they emerged from the dressing room, the spark in their eyes was only upstaged by Jeff's smile. Ginger, although professionally used to such situations, looked childishly shy. Longshot and Kyle were somewhat jealous of Jeff at that moment. But Kyle, being a professional, hurried them to the red, white, and blue backdrop to capture the moment. Although he took hundreds of pictures with different poses, the first picture out of the gate was the best. Jeff and Ginger complemented each other better than lobster and butter, steak and potatoes, peas and carrots, or corn and flakes.

Ginger epitomized a conservative sports slut. She was wearing a tan with red trim leather tennis outfit, substituting red high heels for tennis sneakers. The skirt length was modest enough to exude class but short enough to squirm male voters regarding their delightfully dirty thoughts. The Christmas-red bra strap was barely visible underneath the cleavage-enhanced leather tennis top. The shirt fit like a wet suit, yet, it somehow, didn't look overly gaudy. The image of high-sports-fashion and wealth was emitted, similar to that of a model advertising an expensive perfume in an upscale Beverly Hills magazine. She tied a blue sweater around her neck, a color matching Jeff's golf shirt. She had that girl-next-door Playboy look, ready to satisfy the male's subconscious fantasies.

When the shutter snapped, their flushed, sex happy expression reeked in the air and on camera. Several small, natural beads of quick-sex sweat appeared on Gingers face that added realism to the sports look. Yet only this small cast of characters knew of the actions taken to achieve such a perceived planned picture. The feeling of fresh exercise, bodies moving and intertwining, lungs gasping for air, the heart pumping blood and real romance in the game of sex that included three periods, foreplay, middle play, and scoring in the final seconds, were all captured digitally.

What made the picture so natural was that Jeff stood tall and erect, yet relaxed and peaceful. His million-dollar smile was real and unable to leave his face. He was holding his putter with one hand between his legs. Ginger was leaning against him, bending over slightly, unknowingly advertising her clout, while holding his putter with her right hand.

A picture perfect picture was captured of the new President and First Lady, happily screwed and ready for prime time. This was the picture that would be displayed on the Up Your Odds web site. It was also included on the press release and media kit that Longshot sent via FedEx to all the national television news stations. Stars were about to be born, and they didn't even know it.

Hole Number 3
Par 4

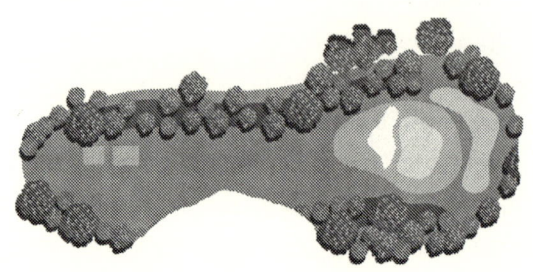

(**Course Notes** : "On the Radio," sing Donna sing. WKRP in Cincinnati, Harry Chapin's WOLD, Dr. Dimento, Howard Stern, Radio Free America. You can run for office or run for the hills, but for God's sake, Run Forest Run. Is a gimmie a sure bet? If I win, I lose – If I lose, I win. Glory Hallelujah, I'm gonna screw ya.)

At 8 P.M., Kenny Rodgers' song, "The Gambler" began to play. At precisely ten seconds after 8, "Welcome to Up Your Odds" was announced by Longshot. He used his radio voice, which was a warm yet confident resonant projection over the expensive and professional radio microphone. It was a full octave lower than his normal sounding tone. The music of the Gambler slowly phased out, and a simple instrumental version of "Glory, Glory Hallelujah" started playing subtly in the background. Music adds a tremendous amount of emotion, and Longshot parlayed this element into his broadcast, which he expected to cause turmoil similar to the original radio broadcast of Orson Wells' "War of the Worlds" but with less panic.

"We, the Gamers of the United States, in the next few months, will be placing bets, and hopefully voting, for the most important position in the world, President of the United States. As you all know, the current list of presidential contenders are lightweights in a heavyweight match. They are like amateur golfers playing in the final round of the U.S. Open. This position should be held by a person who doesn't lay up, but instead, beats the odds, goes for the green, and makes the shot; a person you can trust, above all odds, to never interfere with the sanctity of American sports and the U.S. Gaming Association. "

"Fellow gamers, tonight's broadcast is like no other. Tonight, you have the chance to be part of gaming history. Tonight, you'll be given the first opportunity to place a bet that could determine the next Commander in Chief. Tonight, I'd like to endorse and bet that newcomer Jeff Taylor will be our next President of the United States."

At this, the Glory song blared triumphantly with trumpets and drums, bombs exploding, crowds cheering, a certain monumental radio event, courtesy of Bob's imaginative sound engineering. You could actually hear the tears of emotion sliding down the cheeks of any true patriotic gambler. Slowly, the sound subsided and changed over to a classical-country version of the song, "Hail to the Chief."

"Fellow gamers, as you know, I offer you advice on methods to reduce risk and up your odds when betting on events, but I've never actually initiated a bet on the air. Tonight is earmarked as a betting extravaganza never before placed in the world. I'm going to wager to the first 10,000 gamers that Jeff Taylor will be our next American President. Yes, you heard correctly. Jeff Taylor will be the next oval office king. Would you like to take this bet?" On cue, Bob increased the energetic hoots and howls of the prerecorded crowd.

"You can only bet once, up to $100, and the odds are even. Just think of it. You'll be betting against me, Longshot, your mentor, regarding a candidate that you've never heard of. Jeff Taylor has no political background and agreed just yesterday to be placed on the ballot. If I were in your shoes, I'd take the bet. This is the type of bet I've been telling you to look for. Now, I'm handing it to you on a platter, almost like betting on a one-horse race. If I lose, I stand to lose one million dollars. What a gamble. High stakes gambling at its finest.

"No fellow gamers. I'm not crazy. I'm poised to put an unknown, inexperienced, common everyday Joe in the White House, and yes, I'm betting the farm. Eagle's Nest online gambling has proudly joined us to accept your bets in this prestigious of all games. We're going to take a quick break, and then come back to answer your questions. Yes, gamers, we're going for a White House hole-in-one."

Bob brought the Glory song back into full gear, pushing the needles on the sound equipment to speaker breaking levels. This was the most fun he'd had in years.

What the adoring fans didn't know at the moment was that the Eagle's Nest online gambling site was taking bets on both sides of the fence. Obviously, the radio show was going to generate a tremendous amount of traffic and gambling revenues, and it would increase for some time, unless the news polls dissuaded the voters in the upcoming weeks. Eagle's Nest believed that typical non-betting voters were sick and tired of the traditional parties running for office and would consider placing a bet to match their vote in hopes of getting some new blood in office. Longshot also made an arrangement with the casino to receive a percentage of those bets to reduce his perceived risk and make him eligible to purchase protection insurance, which he did.

In addition, Longshot was careful to not provide all the details of his plan in the first phase of his program, particularly the lie detector event. Like other candidates, aspects of the campaign had to remain confidential until the right moment. Longshot wanted the momentum to rise for several days, along with the bets. On his next broadcast, he'd invite all the candidates to the polygraph showdown within ninety days. He didn't feel that he had to be hardnosed regarding the offer, as the press would have a field day with this unique method of developing candidate legitimacy.

The Up Your Odds switchboard hit a new level of callers, and Bob, now acting as the switchboard operator, could not keep up. The busy phone lines prompted callers to attempt to contact Longshot via email. As a result, thousands of emails poured in, in less than 45 minutes. Everyone wanted to know more about Jeff, his background, the bet, simply everything. The Up Your Odds web site had 50,000 hits within the hour. Jeff and Ginger were prominently displayed on the home page, with the caption "Bet on Jeff Taylor for President." Clicking on the picture automatically linked the surfer to the Eagle's Nest web page for options on betting for Jeff.

(Course Notes: Jeff and Ginger, standing on the tee, about to share a new fantasy: First comes beer, then comes marriage, then entertain the media in a golf cart carriage.)

Jeff and Ginger decided to listen to Longshot's broadcast in their apartment. Since neither of them had ever actually heard his show, they wanted to get a true feel of the broadcast outside the studio. They didn't recognize Longshot's voice, as he was far more professional sounding on air. The background music and broadcast hype was far more inspirational and motivational than they could imagine.

They were aware of the Jeff for President web site, but they were in the dark regarding the response, as well as Longshot's press releases and media kit distribution. Longshot minimized their participation and knowledge of his marketing endeavors, as he didn't want to scare them off before he had a chance to get things into full swing.

Toward the end of the broadcast, Jeff's phone started ringing. And ringing. And ringing. Local golf buddies, work associates, everyone it seemed, called to see if it was him, Jeff Taylor, running for president. They were also surprised to find out he was married.

While he was on the phone, Ginger started watching TV out of boredom. Except for email, no one knew how to contact her. She had left no forwarding address in order to escape former bill collectors. Her landlord had disconnected her phone, and her cell phone was terminated for bill paying avoidance. She couldn't check her email, because Jeff was tying up the phone line. She added that to the list of things to talk to her new husband about: get a high-speed Internet connection. A presidential candidate's wife shouldn't have to wait for a free line. It didn't matter now, since most of her contacts were probably at home with their wives in other parts of the country, not likely to send her an email unless it was work related. She switched to the local news station, and saw, with eyes bulging in disbelief, the picture of her and Jeff taken earlier that day. She screamed for Jeff in an excited frenzy, and he came charging into the room like a rhinoceros with the phone still glued to his ear. She turned up the volume while Jeff said goodbye to his latest caller and disconnected the phone, as it started ringing immediately.

In the media kit that was sent to local TV stations, Longshot had provided embellished bios of Jeff and Ginger which were basically read, word for word, as a favor to Longshot by the TV station managers:

Jeff Taylor, Las Vegas Presidential Hopeful, and Ginger (Holiday) Taylor Biography Brief

Jeff Taylor is an aspiring and successful golf professional and retail manager at one of Las Vegas' finest golf shops. Jeff is known and respected throughout the community as golf's guiding light, helping those to improve their swing without commercial golfing gimmicks; just pure and simple golfing advice to improve their game and love of the sport. Little is known of Ginger Holiday, Jeff's new bride. She came to Las Vegas to enter the world of modeling, but ended up working independently in social services, providing guidance, direction, and a "caring heart" for those inflicted with immense feelings of loneliness and personal misfortune.

Meeting Ginger is like winning the jackpot, except her warmth, sincerity, and her delicious attempt to make you feel good about yourself are the winnings you receive. Spending time with her can take your breath away and will make you feel like new, a quality she has selflessly provided to so many. (Her picture, alongside of Jeff's, added a huge amount of credibility to her description profile.) *When Jeff and Ginger met, it was love at first sight. Without question, this relationship will stand the test of time.*

During their brief marriage, Ginger became fully aware of her husbands' discontent of presidential hopefuls, along with his sincere desire to improve the welfare of U. S. citizens. "Just think," he told her, "how good it feels when you help someone improve their golf swing and see the smile on their face when they hit a good shot. Just think of that good feeling multiplied by 300 million, helping fellow Americans with their most troublesome issues." Overwhelmed by his patriotic intensity, she encouraged him to consider running for office, as any political contender could not match his honesty and integrity. Although he did not take her comment seriously, she did, and she was willing to thrust her new husband into the arms of America for the betterment of the country. Their accidental meeting with Longshot, national sports columnist and popular radio broadcaster, created a volcano that quickly exploded into hot patriotic lava that can only be distinguished by putting honesty back in the White House. Longshot offered to be, at least initially, Jeff Taylor's campaign manager and to help True-Blue American citizens do something that has not been accomplished in many years: Elect an honest President.

Las Vegas is as American as apple pie and baseball (both of which can be bet on in some form or fashion in Sin City but not mentioned here). It's the place to go when you're ready to enter the gambling world of High Stakes. What better place than this to launch America's new presidential candidate? What stakes could be higher than electing a public servant, who, in fact, controls the world? Can a golf pro, with common sense and honesty, have better skills to run the country than lawyers, real estate developers, or actors? Tee off with Jeff Taylor, and make a Hole-in-One for America. No gimmies, no winter rules, just an honest scorecard. Jeff Taylor, Las Vegas' own hopeful for President.

Jeff and Ginger sat and stared at the TV as though they had just witnessed a jumbo jet crash into an ocean liner. And to think they thought that getting married was a big deal; it's like taking a crap and finding out there's no toilet paper by comparison. This TV broadcast of Jeff and Ginger hit them in epic proportions like an Indiana Jones movie.

At the end of his radio show, Longshot headed outside his studio to meet and greet the local media that was waiting for him. In preparation of their anticipated arrival, he had set up a makeshift podium to more easily address their questions and improve film opportunities. He also set up a small bar outside the radio station offering refreshments to the late night media crews, with Bob gladly doubling as a bartender.

"Welcome everyone, and thanks for coming. For those of you who did not hear my radio program, I officially announced that Las Vegas' own son, Jeff Taylor, will be placed on the presidential ballot. Jeff's a local golf pro who believes that honesty has been absent in Washington for some time, and if elected, would bring an honest breath of fresh air to the White House. A press conference will be held at Viva Las Vegas Golf and Country Club at 3 P.M. tomorrow. Make sure you bring your clubs. At that time, you'll be formally introduced to Jeff Taylor and get to play some golf with him. I'll address all political questions at that time. Any questions on the bet?"

One reported shouted, "Do you think you'll win?"

Longshot replied, "Well, I'm ready to bet the farm on it."

After a few ill-thought-out questions, Longshot concluded the mini press conference. "Well, if that's it, thanks for coming out. By the way, I commend you on scooping the major networks (although he planned it this way). Stop by Bob's office before you leave for a refreshment. Thanks again and see you tomorrow at the golf course."

The low-paid media personnel raced over to Bob and consumed anything and everything he had. In a few short minutes, the bar was depleted, and the now woozy media departed in time to get the story on the 11 o'clock news. Bob turned to Longshot and said "You do realize that this thing is going to blow. How are you going to manage this?"

Longshot was having the same thought as he was getting into his car to drive over to Jeff's apartment. Then, without warning, a young, African-American woman with baggy clothes, oversized glasses, and her hair pinned back into a face-hurting bun, tapped him on the shoulder and pressed a cassette recorder to his mouth.

"Hi, Mr. Longshot. I'm Jade Tomsay, a news reporter for a local, Christian rock station. I wanted to find out if the new presidential candidate is a Christian?"

Longshot replied, "Does it matter?"

She looked sweet, innocent, and confused by his remark.

Then he asked her, "How long have you been in radio?"

"Two weeks," she replied. "I recently graduated from UNLV with a degree in communications. I'm interning at the radio station while looking for a real job."

Longshot tilted his head up towards the sky thinking, *Thanks for the gift.* Longshot felt that this was the perfect person to manage the press for Jeff and Ginger while he took care of more important matters. "Well, little missy, I believe that God works in mysterious ways. How would you like to work as press secretary for the new president to be?"

Jade couldn't believe her ears and said yes without negotiating salary or even asking for one. No discussion on benefits, 401k's, vacation, dental, and she hadn't even met Jeff yet.

"Welcome aboard, Jade. I'm sure you'll enjoy the ride to the White House."

Jade was weak at the knees and couldn't believe her good fortune.

"Can you start right now?"

Jade replicated her confused look once again and asked, "What do you want me to do?" in a skeptical voice.

Longshot replied, "Go home, and pack some clothes and any needed toiletries. Then, go over to the Hard Rock Hotel and ask to speak with Stanley Curila, the night manager. Tell him I sent you, and confidentially tell him a new presidential candidate is moving in tonight for several days to announce his plans to be president. Have him prepare three rooms, one of them being the penthouse or presidential suite if available. Fill the suite with flowers and a champagne welcome basket along with a congratulations card with Jeff and Ginger's name on it. Add any other goodies you and Stanley can think of. You'll need the rooms for four nights. You and I will be sleeping in the other two rooms. Ask him to bill me for everything. Next, tell him you need a business casual wardrobe, and that it's an emergency. He'll arrange to get you some clothes from one of the hotel's upscale clothing shops. Make sure it fits, not to baggy, not to tight. You're the new press secretary, so look professional. Any questions?"

By good luck or accident, Jade conveniently let the tape recorder record to capture his list of instructions. Good thing, as she was still fumbling over the fact that she had a real job, and the list of responsibilities went through the temporary wind tunnel between her ears. She asked "What do I call you?"

"Longshot, next question," he replied.

"Why the Hard Rock?"

"We will be on the campaign trail for ninety days nationally. If we play our cards right, we can stay at the Hard Rock chain of hotels for free in exchange for free advertising. Our budget is tight, so one of your primary responsibilities will be to create a media campaign with exceptional exposure on a shoestring budget. Are you up for the challenge?"

Jade replied, "You bet. Your prayers are answered."

Longshot mentally agreed with her reply, as he couldn't believe his good fortune. Although Jade would be working behind the scenes, Longshot hoped her religious convictions would be conveyed somehow during the campaign. This could certainly address the huge group of Bible Belt voters who otherwise might not be sport fanatics or approve of the First Lady to be. He felt as though he had just been dealt the 4th ace in a game of poker. "Yes Jade, my prayers are answered. We'll meet you at the hotel lobby within the hour."

Longshot drove over to Jeff's apartment and simply walked in to find Jeff and Ginger still in a sobering stupor watching a now blank TV screen. Longshot's short press conference with the local media was already being shown on the 11 o'clock news.

Longshot said, "The response was remarkable. We should be on national TV by morning. Oh, by the way, I hired a new press secretary named Jade. She'll manage all of your affairs as you travel around the country playing golf with the media."

Jeff shook his head in disbelief and said, "Man, how can you arrange so much in such little time?"

Longshot laughed. "Partner, I don't know. Law of Attraction? Let's just roll with the punches. It might be fun. By the way, we're moving the party to the Hard Rock Hotel and Casino. Pack some bags and be quick."

They threw some items in a duffle bag, put some fresh seed in Blabs' cage, and left with Longshot. While en route, Longshot decided to massage the media story somewhat. "Listen, for the time being, the two of you are still going to travel around the country for ninety days or so, except it will be for the perceived primary purpose of honeymooning. During your trip, you'll continue to play golf with reporters, but you'll invite average voting citizens to join your golfing entourage to obtain feedback on their most pressing national and local concerns. This will give America a chance to meet you up close, while improving your understanding of voters' issues. In addition, planned footage of the presidential hopeful playing golf with voters will provide ideal press clips, as good as or better than kissing ugly babies. On my next radio broadcast, I'm going to announce the polygraph test. We'll see how the media and other candidates respond to the test, but I expect the media to have a field day with this." Jeff and Ginger listened with great intensity, trying to absorb their future.

"Now listen closely. During this time, you're free to accept gifts, endorsements, and any celebrity perks that arise. Jade will arrange your schedules, hotel accommodations, flights, and so forth, and will accompany you on your tour, although she doesn't know that yet. As previously discussed, you're not to participate in any press conferences, debates, or interviews away from the golf course, at least initially. Any questions?"

Ginger quickly chimed in, "If we do get any endorsements, who will handle the money?" This raised a good question that pitted Ginger's raised eyebrows against Longshot's when Jeff stepped in. "Longshot, why don't we get the attorney who was involved with our marriage to handle all financial aspects of the partnership? She'll keep everything clean and legal."

Longshot agreed, and called Ellen Spackler right then. "Ellen, it's Longshot. Sorry for the late call. Are you awake?"

"Absolutely. Most of my business occurs from midnight to 3 A.M. What's up? Wait a second. I saw the news. Does this have anything to do with your bet and Jeff running for president?"

"Exactly. We need to have you set up a partnership between me and Jeff Taylor and his wife, Ginger. We expect to be getting some endorsement fees in the near future and need bank accounts, or anything else you can think of."

Ellen replied, "I'd be glad to help. I'll take care of your legal and financial affairs. I'll call the bank in the morning to set up preliminary accounts and then meet you there to finalize everything. I'll call you in the morning with a time. I have to run now. I'm finishing a pre-nup for a blissful couple waiting in line to be married at the Now or Never Chapel of Love. Until tomorrow." In the background, Longshot could hear the Elvis minister singing, "I'm in love, I'm all shook up."

Longshot drove his car to the entrance of the Hard Rock Hotel and Casino, and the valet dashed over to park the car. As usual, there was an electric buzz in the air that the Hard Rock always generates. The bellhops attended to the bags, following Longshot, Jeff, and Ginger to the hotel lobby where they met Jade, along with Stanley, the hotel manager.

Stanley had caught the 11 o'clock news and was well aware of the exposure his hotel would incur during their stay. Stanley said, "Hi Longshot, good to see you again." Then he turned to Jeff and Ginger and gushed, "Welcome Mr. and Mrs. Future President. It's a pleasure to meet you. Jade and I have taken care of everything for you. My hotel is your hotel. Let's go up to your suite."

As Longshot finalized introductions, Jade and Ginger examined each other. Jeff and Ginger were wearing scraggly jeans and t-shirts, and Jade was having second thoughts about her new position, as they did not look like they belonged in the White House. Ginger mentally questioned Longshot's choice of press secretary, as she wasn't even old enough to fill out her baggy clothes. Jeff was too tired to even care.

Stanley guided them to the private elevator and said, "You are very lucky, this is the last and only penthouse suite available. A visiting Egyptian sheik and his wives already occupy the other presidential suites. They flew in last night to attend the Brotherhood Concert starring the Allman Brothers and the Doobie Brothers. Those were his favorite bands while he was a teenager growing up in Cairo, although he confided in me that his father, the Sultan, was displeased over his choice of American music. Personally, he picked two of my favorites."

The main foursome was quite exhausted and said little as Stanley escorted them up the private elevator. When the doors closed, ZZ Top could be heard from the elevator speakers. Not your typical elevator music, but then again, this *was* the Hard Rock Hotel. Stanley sensed their tiredness and warmly entertained them with a rundown of the famous people who had stayed in the room, while rock and roll serenaded them as their elevator glided upwards to their suite. "You'll be sleeping with the stars tonight. This room has been graced by the likes of Elton John, Johnny Depp, Michael Jordan, and dignitaries from around the world. I'm proud and excited to include you on the list."

Jeff looked at Ginger, and they both rolled their eyes, as they couldn't imagine being associated with the celebrities he described.

When the elevator doors opened, they needed sunglasses to reduce the rich glare of decadence this excessive suite emitted. The only things brighter than the elegance of the flower-laden room were the smiles on the honeymooners' faces. As they entered the castle-sized suite, a quintet of violins and cello, located next to the Baby Grand piano in the suite's mini ballroom, delicately played "Here Comes the Bride."

Stanley announced, "The Las Vegas Hard Rock Hotel and Casino is very proud and honored to have Jeff and Ginger Taylor as our guests. I hope your stay here is just the beginning of a long and happy life together. Happy Honeymoon."

Jeff and Ginger reentered the awake state, and Jeff impulsively carried Ginger over the threshold and into the room. Ginger's clients could never afford such luxury, and Jeff never stayed in anything better than half-star rated hotels. The music purred them into a rich and peaceful existence as they wandered around the suite. The quintet smoothly transitioned to the Beatles' songs "Here Comes the Sun" and "Lucy in the Sky with Diamonds." The angelic music in the background, coupled with their high-rise suite overlooking the Vegas strip, had Jeff and Ginger literally feeling like they were floating while the quintet melodied into "Stairway to Heaven."

Jade and Longshot each had adjoining rooms that were equally excessive, combining for a total of over 4,000 square feet of sadistic luxury that none of them had ever encountered. Best of all, Stanley said their stay was "On the House," which produced a sigh of relief and near-bowel movement from Longshot.

The penthouse butler and maid entered the room from their guest quarters, bowed and curtsied while handing Jeff and Ginger welcome baskets of gifts that paralleled gold, frankincense, and myrrh, and gracefully said, "Monsieur and Madame, I am Helmsford, and this is Sasha. We welcome you to our hotel. It is our pleasure to attend your needs and wishes, anytime, day or night, as it is our wish to surround you with the comforts you deserve."

Jeff was ready to pass out from all the attention. His idea of receiving courteous attention was having a customer who didn't have stinky feet while fitting them for golf shoes, which was a rare occasion.

Stanley continued showing them around the suite. "Helmsford and Sasha are at your beckon call. We encourage you to summon them by using any one of the dozens of buttons located throughout the suite. Again, they are available to you at any time, day or night, for virtually any request. Tomorrow afternoon, Felipe and Lolita will assume these key roles."

As he was speaking, a man emerged from the west wing, displaying the combined traits of middle linebacker and secret service agent. "Good evening. I'm Johnson, your personal penthouse security. We have a series of hidden cameras that maintain security but also privacy for our penthouse guests. My staff and I are also available to you 24/7. Please let me know if there is anything I can do to make your stay enjoyable and safe."

Ginger's ears perked up when she heard "hidden camera" and wondered if she could get some professional surveillance tips from Johnson.

When the introductions were completed, Helmsford uncorked the Dom Perignon and poured two glasses for the newlywed couple. Jeff was still Jeff, and couldn't perceive anyone in the room being beneath him (which they weren't), so he grabbed additional champagne glasses from behind the bar and poured the bubbly for cast and entire crew in the room, much to the horror of Helmsford. The hotel staff was reluctant to partake in the toast, but Jeff comically said "Listen. Right now, my best friends are in my room celebrating my marriage. I'm sure I can find better accommodations elsewhere if you don't join Ginger and me in a toast."

That comment and gesture broke the pungent smell of stuffiness in the room. Everyone smiled and lifted their glasses while Longshot announced, "To the new Mr. and Mrs. Jeffrey Taylor, our next President and First Lady of the United States of America." Glasses chinged while the band kicked it into high gear by playing Bruce Springsteen's "Born in the USA." Afterwards, Jeff embarrassingly poured more glasses for the band, which they accepted, along with his apology for not including them in the toast. He added that their music swept him away along with this splendid moment. He reached into his wallet to tip them, along with the staff, but realized he only had $20 from his last ATM visit.

At that moment, everyone in the room knew Jeff would never become president. He was too real, too nice, too normal, too poor. He was them, and people like them do not become president.

To avoid further embarrassment, Stanley stepped in to explain that a 20% tip would be added to the overall bill with equal distribution to the current staff members and musicians in the room, again courtesy of the hotel. Jeff was speechless, but Jade said, "That's okay, Mr. President, save your speeches for the campaign." They all laughed. The band played on until 2 A.M. providing opportunities for all to become better acquainted.

Hole Number 4
Par 3

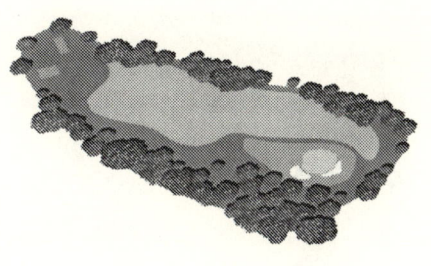

(**Course Notes:** Snatch a picture, for all to see, you have nothing to hide, on national TV. Does she, or doesn't she. If you rub the club, will a golf genie appear, or will your ball just be happy?)

At 7:30 A.M., the sounds of ocean ripples and sea gulls whispered over the Bose entertainment system in the master bedroom while the window shades electronically and automatically opened a quarter of the way to encourage the sun to peak in and say good morning. In front of the window, piping hot gourmet coffee, organic tea, freshly squeezed orange juice, and several varieties of newspapers were already positioned on an antique looking table with fine linen, eloquent china, and silverware. His and her monogrammed robes were placed at the foot of the king sized bed, with steam sneaking in from the wash area where a bubble bath had been just drawn. Helmsford and Sasha were ghost-like in preparing for the presidential-to-be couple's awakening.

After each produced a good morning smile and kissed cheeks to avoid morning breath, Jeff and Ginger slid into the robes, poured coffee, and wandered into the wash area for their morning bath. The Roman-styled tub was large enough for a party of six, but not quite large enough to do laps. The tub was elevated, offering a wet and bubbly view of the Vegas foothills. A hot pot of coffee appeared beside the tub, again, in ghost-like fashion. After a second cup, they discovered the dial to turn on the Jacuzzi jets and proceeded to bask in the warm, Caribbean-like moving waters while soapily cleansing each other to joyful extremes.

Soon after they were thoroughly cleaned, inside and out, the waterproof, tub-side phone started playing "Splish Splash, I was taking a bath". Longshot good morning-ed Jeff and requested their presence for breakfast on the patio to discuss today's agenda. While Ginger concluded her morning bathroom business, Jeff entered the bedroom and was again surprised to find the bed already made and their clothes neatly pressed and hanging in the open wardrobe. With all this attention, he was expecting someone to dress him and zip up his fly upon request. He wondered, *How far do they go to service me? What happens when I go to the bathroom? Is Ginger being attended to and in what way?" Man, I never felt so uncomfortable getting dressed before.* He proceeded to put on his pants while looking out the corners of his eyes for a ghost hand to appear. *Would it be Helmsford or Sasha's hand?* He felt relieved when he zipped up his own fly.

The hotel salon staff provided in-room styling and restoration services to Longshot and Jade at 6 A.M. including attire assistance. For the first time, Longshot did not look like a typical Vegas bookie, but exuded the flare of professional sports promoter, on the same level as Don King but without the high hair. Custom-fitted trousers and blazer jacket, matching leather belt and shoes, and a Polo golf shirt to leisure out the ensemble, were complemented by his prized wardrobe accessory: 2 pairs of Italian designer sunglasses. They hugged his face like a Ferrari racing on a tight curve.

Jade was transformed from a stodgy, Bible-selling college geek into a confident, organized, and almost unapproachable presidential press secretary. Her hair bun was released to allow blood flow to her face, revealing a concealed ebony beauty that was magnified by a conservative yet stylish $200 haircut and makeover. Contact lenses, which she owned but rarely wore, were substituted for her Groucho Marx specs at the request and pleading of the head stylist. Jade's naturally beautiful eyes and smile actually rivaled Jeff's after sex glow. In addition to removing her mask, Jade's new attire emulated that of a high paid Nike executive, complementing a previously hidden physique that exposed her love of tennis, hiking, and volleyball. Longshot practically fell out of his chair when she joined him on the patio, thinking of the money he would have lost if he bet she couldn't look any better than she did last night. He picked a winner without knowing it, and he attributed his success to his internal experience.

Likewise, Longshot's new and improved look instilled a higher feeling of confidence in Jade's decision to accept this job, although, for the first time, she did wonder when she would get paid, and how much.

Longshot and Jade prepared the day's activities, along with a list of to-do's required to begin their political adventure that included website editing and speech writing. Unknown to Jade, the original goal of this endeavor was to make money through betting and endorsements, and not necessarily winning the election. Without knowing the true intent of the campaign, Jade initially had a difficult time understanding some of Longshot's recommendations.

"Remember, Jade, no campaign posters will be used as they litter the country and kill helpless trees with no obvious gain to mankind. No badges, hats, banners, or signage of any type. We're going to the White House in an untraditional fashion. Honesty will triumph over advertising. This also means no staff initially, except you. In fact, there is to be no initial mention of 'Jeff for President.' What I propose is that the American public 'Vote for Honesty.' Convey that message to the media over the next few months. In fact, all contributions that are normally donated from individuals and corporations for campaign promotions and advertising are requested to be donated to charities in Jeff Taylor's name. Any questions?"

"Not at the moment, but I'm sure I'll have many later." Jade wished she'd taken a dictation class in hopes of catching all of Longshot's "to do's." She thought that this method of electing a president was noble and followed his lead without question, especially when she realized that millions of dollars wouldn't be wasted on TV ads bashing political opponents, but would instead be donated for the good of the country and the world. She circled a line item in her notes, *Jeff's only type of advertising will be free publicity through media coverage of his golf honeymoon.* But she asked herself, *Can this really work?*

Just as she completed transcribing her last note, Jeff came out to the patio. He, quite simply, couldn't believe his eyes, which was a feeling he'd had to deal with regarding just about everything over the past few days, and said, "You guys look fantastic. I hate to say it, but I almost didn't recognize you."

Jade and Longshot gleamed with his compliment. They also recognized that they were hours ahead of Jeff as far as mental comprehension and decided to wait for Ginger to discuss today's agenda.

Ginger, still wearing her bathrobe, created a foursome on the patio. She, too, was shocked by the transformation of her team members and voiced her approval. "Longshot, you look like you hit the jackpot. You look fabulous. And Jade, well, you're stunning. I might have to keep a close eye on Jeff when you're around."

Jade was embarrassed but appreciative of Ginger's remarks. The intercom interrupted their morning chat. "Good morning. This is Sasha. Breakfast will be forthcoming. In addition, the Salon staff will be in your suite after breakfast to treat Jeff and Ginger."

Jeff was not a happy camper and acted like a little boy who was told to get dressed up to visit some ancient aunt. "Oh man, do I have to get poked and prodded by these salon chicks? Can't I just shave and brush my teeth? I'm already dressed. I'll have to undress, have them make a fuss over me with creams and gels, and get dressed again. I can't take this."

The others were silent for moment, then bust out laughing while Ginger said, "Oh, poor baby has to have strangers make him look pretty. Poor, poor president."

The warm aroma of the breakfast buffet, which included freshly baked breads and croissants, varieties of eggs, assorted meats and seafood, flapjacks, and items unknown to this inexperienced group of food connoisseurs, preceded the buffet itself as it was delivered and served by Helmsford.

During their international breakfast, the day's agenda was discussed, and Jeff already showed signs of nervousness regarding the press conference and the thought of speaking in front of a group of unknown reporters, cameras, and microphones. Longshot attempted to calm him and said, "Jeff, remember, this won't be a media zoo. It will be a small group of reporters from local news teams who'll join you and Ginger for a casual round of golf. It will be fun and relaxing, plus, you get to play your first free round of golf."

Jeff was already thinking vodka and OJ to calm the nerves but knew it was much too early for that.

Then Jade stepped in. "Jeff, Longshot's right. It'll be low key. I'll make sure that everything runs smoothly, and I'll protect you from any embarrassment. Have you played golf in a tournament where you had lots people surrounding you?"

Jeff answered, "Well, yes. I didn't mind it. On those past occasions where I played golf with a gallery, I was comfortable being in a small limelight and actually enjoyed it. This experience, however, raises the bar to new heights, similar to playing in the final round of the U.S. Open."

Longshot said, "Don't worry, Jeff. We'll make sure everything is under control. Your job is to go play some golf, be yourself, and have fun. Both you and Ginger."

Then without any notice, a helicopter came swooping down from out of nowhere with a camera aimed at the breakfast club on the patio. A local news station, using inside information from a hotel employee, wanted to be the first to capture a live preview of the new presidential candidate. With the precision and timing of a surprised Navy SEAL attack, they succeeded, leaving Johnson's security team helpless to intercede. The whooshing sound of the helicopter blades scared the livin' crap out of them as it hovered outside their patio. Even in this time of bewilderment, Jeff fully expected a ghost hand to appear and clean the mess in his pants if it truly did occur. It did not, as far as he could tell.

Longshot calmly yelled to the group, "Smile and wave, and then one-by-one, casually proceed into the suite."

Based on their sitting positions, Jade and Longshot exited first, followed by Jeff and then Ginger. When Ginger rose from her seat still waving and smiling, the hurricane force winds of the helicopter swirled a small tornado-like wind on the patio and raised her robe like an opened parachute above her head. She had yet to exercise the right to wear underwear and frantically fumbled with her robe for what seemed an eternity, but with no results. Her backside bottom was naturally caught and posed along with the rest of her bouncing birthday suit. The force of the wind kept the robe in full flight. Johnson finally grabbed her arm and yanked her inside the suite as though she was rescued from a passerby before colliding with a beer truck on a street corner in Manhattan. This Marilyn Monroe extreme pose was not planned or rehearsed, and it displayed the potential of what voters could encounter over the next four years. The cameraman nearly fell out of the chopper when he realized what was being shown on local and live TV. Without realizing it at the moment, Ginger debuted her complete body waxing for hair removal during her makeover yesterday. It safeguarded her blonde (or not) haired secret from viewers and voters.

Within the hour, all the major networks aired the censored version of Ginger's plunge into notoriety, each attempting to outdo the other with clever captions. CNN: "Future First Lady Up for Grabs?" FOX News: "True Blonde, Brunette or Red Head?" MSNBC: "Candidate's Wife Bares All." CBS: "Honeymooner Moons the World." Just Fore Golf: "Wind Gust Tees Off Candidate's Wife." What seemed a catastrophe, though, turned out to be the most exotic – not to mention erotic – publicity stunt that could ever have been imagined for a presidential candidate.

A sense of calm finally crept in once several Mimosas were consumed by all, courtesy of Helmsford's attention to detail and brisk professionalism, but several more were needed while watching CNN a mere thirty minutes after the first batch of drinks. The entire team, including Longshot, who was in broadcasting, was amazed at how fast news travels. Ginger was in a state of shock, watching her blurred nude body parading around the patio in front of the world. She switched to vodka and orange juice on Sasha's recommendation.

The Hard Rock Hotel had to deploy a security team to manage the throng of reporters that flooded the lobby. Johnson headed up the security team and also arranged for security at the press conference and golf outing that was to take place later that afternoon. It was easy for him to assemble a team, as many of his colleagues were anxious to protect Mrs. Taylor after watching the news. Although no one, at least at this point of time, would consider taking a bullet for Jeff. Maybe a stray golf shot, but not a bullet.

Just as calm settled in, the salon personnel arrived to prepare Jeff and Ginger for their "official" television debut, not to be confused with their "unofficial debut" currently being aired. The salon staff treated them as celebrities and even asked for their autographs once they completed their beautifying tasks. One of the salon girls, Crissy, couldn't control her mouth and spilled out her emotions as they were leaving. "You guys are hot. I mean, awesome. And Jeff, you rock. You got my vote, and if you weren't married, anything else you wanted."

Ginger saw Jeff smile while she overheard the comment, and she let it slide, although, for the first time, she felt an unusual sense of jealously come over her.

During the salon treatment, Jade was reviewing the Vote for Honesty website, newly created by a local Web design company based on Longshot's direction. The site was basic and needed more patriotic punch, so Jade word-smithed the text using the suite's top-notch PC with high-speed Internet connection. Jade set up email addresses for the team, and sensed that the site would be overwhelmed with hits once it became publicized.

The message light on the suite phone flashed for some time, yet no one had the responsibility to retrieve the messages, so Jade undertook that task as well. Johnson instructed the switchboard to dump all calls into voicemail to protect the newlyweds' privacy. Hearing that there were over thirty messages, she began transcribing the important ones. She was surprised at the number of interview opportunities already coming in, as all the major TV news stations wanted exclusive interviews. In addition, sponsors were calling for endorsement opportunities including local auto dealers, other competitive hotels, restaurants, and even Lucky Louie's Pawn shop and the Now or Never Chapel of Love. She called down to the front desk, and asked them to have callers fax inquiries to the suite fax machine, or have them visit the newly created website for email contacts in order to save her hand from writer's cramp.

When she showed Longshot her notes, he said, "Prioritize the opportunities based on projected dollars. But, be sure to conceal this activity from Jeff and Ginger, at least for the time being. We can't afford to scare the pants off of them, although Ginger already underwent that activity for the camera this morning."

While Jade nodded her head, Longshot couldn't even imagine what would occur by the end of the day. He felt overwhelmed by the unaccustomed barrage of activity.

The presidential foursome met Ellen Spackler in their hotel suite at 11 A.M., and she agreed to be legal counsel for Jeff in exchange for a small percentage of any proceeds gained from campaign business venture. She had never worked on a percentage basis before, but developed this method of payment after watching the CNN news prior to their meeting. She was not accustomed to legal meetings so early in the morning but was surprisingly awake and was well prepared to handle this new legal quest. She'd already set up bank accounts and contracted the Finch and Finch Accounting Firm to monitor the account to ensure that all monetary transactions were properly and legally handled. She also reviewed the U. S. election web site to follow the guidelines to make sure Jeff was properly entered as a candidate for president. Based on his late entry, he'd be entering the race as an Independent write-in candidate, which simplified the registration process.

During this meeting, Jade prepared speeches for Longshot and Jeff regarding their first press conference at the country club. It was also her first test to use her degree without receiving a grade. Longshot's speech was short, and Jeff's was even shorter. The goal was to explain how the media could interview Jeff during his golfing honeymoon. In Longshot's speech, she indicated that she was the contact person to set up golf outings, starting times, and round robin interviews with Mr. and Mrs. Taylor. In addition, his speech directed any and all endorsements to her email address for review. Jade was really quite amazed with herself, as she organized a plan to manage the campaign of a presidential candidate without really knowing what to do. She still didn't know how much or when she'd get paid. Jade kept telling herself, "Just be cool, girl. This could all end by tomorrow. Enjoy the show today."

With that line of thinking, and not being sure she'd have a job after the press conference, she called room service to order lunch. "Yes, I'd like the cracked crab salad and lobster bisque soup for lunch. And what do you recommend for dessert...chocolate fudge rum cake... yes, that would be perfect." While she finalized last minute items and waited for lunch, she silently prayed, "Lord, I can't make heads or tails of this presidential candidate, his wife, manager, or my role in this scheme. Please guide me, and please let the fudge cake be huge."

On Longshot's request, Jeff made a quick phone call to Dave Vargo, the head pro at the Viva Las Vegas Country Club to make sure they were prepared for the news event that was about to take place there. Dave and Jeff were friends, and Dave was glad to set things up for him, knowing his club would get some good publicity as a result. Dave had seen the news and also heard about Longshot's bet, and asked Jeff what was going on. "Two days ago I saw you miss a putt for your card, and now you're married and running for president?"

Jeff shrugged his shoulders while on the phone and said, "Dave, to be honest, I ask myself the same question. Things are moving pretty quick, and I'm just trying to keep my head above water. All I know is that I'm going to be playing a lot of golf on some great courses over the next few weeks, so I'm just going with the flow."

Dave said, "Well, we're ready for you, but keep an eye out for unseen hazards. You know how they can come up and bite you in the ass."

"I'll do my best. See you soon."

After Jade devoured her lunch, she sped over to K-Mart and purchased all the American flags they had in stock, along with a CD called *Patriotic Music for the 4th of July*. She then violated several traffic laws en route to the golf course, and, with Dave's help, placed flags of different sizes throughout the course. They set up a small stage-like area outside the clubhouse overlooking the 18th green. Here they tied larger flags to the desert palm trees. The Sunset Strip print shop, which had the ability to create large banners and posters, along with wedding invitations (which was conveniently located down the street from the Now or Never Chapel of Love) delivered several "Vote for Honesty" banners just at that moment. Jade contacted them earlier that morning. These would be the only campaign banners created, based on Longshot's original direction of no advertising signage. They also decorated a golf cart with flags and "Vote for Honesty" posters. It was 2 o'clock, and, already, the line of television trucks and news personnel were fighting for position to cover this anticipated mega news story. They created a backlog of traffic around Las Vegas equal to a major prizefight event.

Jade called Longshot to give him a quick update. "Longshot, I have the golf cart and areas around the course patriotically decked out. It looks fitting of a presidential press conference, if I do say so myself."

Longshot was ecstatic. "Fantastic. I just donated $300 to St. Mark's Catholic School for their participation in sending the children's choir to the course to sing "Glory, Glory Hallelujah" as Jeff and Ginger enter the media session. I also arranged to have the Vegas Sky Writers provide some aerial advertising over the course with captions such as "Vote Honesty" and "Bet on Jeff. This is melting together perfectly. We'll see you there shortly."

When he got off the phone, Ginger approached Longshot and said "I'm concerned about Jeff. He seems unusually calm and cool. He's sitting in front of the TV watching a girl's softball game on Japanese station drinking a vanilla milkshake. We both have only known him for two days, and it's difficult to get a reading on him. Will he lose it? Will he be able to speak? Will he shit his pants without any cleanup assistance from Helmsford?"

Longshot returned the concern. "I don't know what to expect, and it's making me friggin' nervous. But no matter what, don't let Jeff know we're uneasy. Besides, it's only a couple of cameras and few bumbling reporters. What is there to worry about?"

Little did they know that over thirty major and minor television news teams were already hunkered down and waiting to professionally assault the latest, high-profile national news story, a story filled with politics, sports, sex, and intrigue.

Johnson prepared for the worst situation. He had a team of security officers in route to the golf course while he prepared the limos at the hotel for their departure and arrival. All security personnel had concealed radio transmitters for direct connection to each other and Johnson. He had several routes planned to the golf course and would disclose the route to the driver and team upon entry to the course. He also had emergency routes created based on "what if" scenarios. He was very adept at crises management. Managing the reporters on the course was a major undertaking, as the golf course was wide open, so he planned to position security officers at strategic locations to maintain security integrity. He wasn't really concerned with any violent attacks on Jeff, but he was worried that the loony bin of perverts who normally prowl Vegas in the evening hours may decide to escape their vampire rituals based on the news casts and seek opportunities with Ginger prior to the moon's rise. In fact, he figured that your basic lap dance aficionado might become aggressive for the chance to see an encore performance of Ginger on the course and cause security breaches. With that in mind, he started to wonder if he had enough security personnel.

With the invisible assistance of the butler and maid tag team, Felipe and Lolita prepared Jeff and Ginger for their gala news event. Jeff's attire made him look like a golfer running for president. Honest, trim, wealthily athletic, poised, and groomed. Ginger attempted to dress more modestly, but her body would not allow it. Her legs and chest just seemed to draw attention, even in a rather plain $300 tennis outfit.

Johnson secured the penthouse floor area and proceeded to transport Jeff and Ginger down the elevator to the hotel lobby. Johnson would have preferred that they leave the hotel in a less conspicuous place, but Longshot wanted the exposure.

When the elevator doors opened, the sun fell on the earth, as camera lights flashed and shutters snapped like a major Hollywood movie event. Luckily, Jeff and Ginger had donned sunglasses, otherwise, they probably would have been permanently blinded. Johnson said "OK guys, remain calm, smile, wave, and follow me. Johnson's security team did an admirable job creating a path to the limo, but several reporters and onlookers had to be physically restrained from breaking the human security fence.

Once inside the limo, Jeff and Ginger experienced the same deja vu feeling that occurred when they woke up and found they were married: complete shock and disbelief. Only this time, they weren't hung over and were aware (or so they thought) of what they were getting into.

Longshot entered the presidential party from the other side of the limo and said "Yee Haa. What a party. I feel like we're riding a bucking bronco in a rodeo. Hey, looky here." He pointed his finger in the direction of the refrigerator and wet bar. They collided heads like the Three Stooges as they swooped in to grab any form of alcoholic relief. The limo sped quickly away from the hotel for the short fifteen-minute ride to the golf course. Not knowing of the firing squad ready to squeeze the trigger when "fire" is shouted, the news gallery, roughly fifty times larger than the hotel lobby crowd, awaited their arrival at the golf course.

The short ride to the golf course lasted over an hour due to traffic. The LVPD did their best to maintain open passage, but the country club entrance and surrounding streets were not prepared for a last minute spectacle like this, which caused a flash flood-like effect in traffic. Longshot's radio broadcast bet and Ginger's "X-rated on prime time" newscast generated a media explosion not seen since the Beatles invaded America. As the limo finally made headway into the country club parking lot, Ginger noticed the wedding bells on the front of the limo and questioned Longshot, who assumed it was Jade's doing. The driver overheard the question, and said "The wedding limo was courtesy of Stanley Curila, the hotel manager. Congratulations, love birds."

As the limo moved into position, reporters and voting fans immediately swarmed it. Johnson's security, along with the police riding horses, pushed the wall of people back far enough so Jeff and Ginger could exit the vehicle. Several drinks helped them overcome the fear of being trampled. The cheering crowd screamed out multitudes of chants, "Jeff for President," "Vote for Honesty," "Ginger for President," "Ginger, get naked," and so on. Many comments were very crude regarding Ginger, but the police were diligent in maintaining peace and removing any potential threats away from the blissful couple.

The limo party was whisked inside the country club for a temporary safe haven. Jade was inside waiting, looking as though she had just delivered triplets, twice, wondering if more might spill out. Johnson entered first, along with the rest of the party. Dave Vargo was there as well, along with the country club manager who welcomed Jeff, Ginger, and Longshot. The area where the podium was set-up was more secure than the parking area, so mayhem could be minimized from intruders and waves of people.

Ginger was feeling the effects of the liquid stress reliever and was quite relaxed, knowing she didn't have to actually do or say anything except smile and be herself. Jeff, on the other hand, was mentally terrorized. She was concerned for Jeff, but didn't know how to help him. "Jeff honey. Relax, Breathe. We're going to play some golf." Jeff smiled at her like he was preparing for brain surgery. Longshot was holding back a heart attack, but his gambling experience carved an expressionless poker face. He motioned to Jade to speak with her without Jeff's knowledge. "Jeff's scared out of his mind. Let's relax in here for a few minutes before we head outside. I also think we should scratch Jeff's original speech."

"But he has to say something! Everyone came to see him and Ginger. What if I shorten his speech?" She wrote a few words on one cue card and asked Jeff to read the text.

"Hi, I'm Jeff, and this is my new wife Ginger. Let's play golf." That was it. He read it aloud several times.

Jade asked him, "Can you read or say this at the podium?"

He regained his composer and said, "Yes," although his hands were shaking.

Ginger asked to speak with Jeff in private, and Dave escorted them to his office. Behind closed doors, Ginger said, "Jeff, you don't need to go through with this. We can return to the limo, and have the driver take us away from here." Then she whispered, "I'll even give you some in the back seat if you like?"

Jeff smiled his million-dollar smile at the thought of her being naked in the back of the leather-trimmed and fully stocked limo. Her gesture relaxed him and, somehow, even provided a sense of confidence. He said, "Now that's an option worth considering. But, let's try this thing out and play some golf with these media fools. If it sucks, we'll pack it up and I'll take you up on your offer."

They kissed and rejoined the group. Jeff said, "Let's do it." Jeff and the patriotic golf chariot were recharged and ready to roll.

Johnson directed them through the pro shop to the waiting golf carts outside. Jeff strolled through the golf shop, gaining a sense of belonging and home. When they went outside, Jeff took a look at the patriotic cart and rolled his eyes, but noticed something in the back: a brand new set of TaylorMade golf clubs, a carton of Titleist golf balls, and an assortment of golf goodies such as gloves, hats, and shirts.

Dave said, "I received calls from several local golf product sales reps who offered you the gifts along with an invitation to meet with them afterwards to discuss endorsement opportunities. You have some great stuff in there. Check out those new TaylorMade's!"

Jeff was like a kid in a toy store who couldn't wait to try out everything. He fondled and caressed the 7 iron and became more excited and anxious to get the show on the road.

Johnson radioed the security team. "The eagle's on the move to the podium. Take your positions." He and Longshot rode in the first cart, followed by Jeff and Ginger in the rocking chair, and then Jade and another guard caboosed behind. Everyone was wondering what Jeff would say or do at the podium. All Jeff could think about was hitting those new clubs and seeing how far he could crunch a golf ball down the fairway.

The St. Mark's children choir starting singing right on cue when the golf cart entourage was in sight. Their majestic little voices squealed out Glory Hallelujah, which made this golf-focused press conference rather warm and religiously cozy. Instinctively, Jeff and Ginger parked in front of the choir and sat and listened until the song finished. They were supposed to head right to the podium, but they gave the children's choir their five minutes of nationwide stardom. When the last verse "Truth is marching on" was completed, Jeff and Ginger approached the podium with Longshot, who was still applauding the choir.

While still applauding, Longshot adjusted the mics and said in his adjusted radio voice, "Aren't they wonderful? The St. Mark's Children's Choir, simply fantastic."

Johnson helped remove the choir inconspicuously as the cameras focused on Longshot. At that moment, Jade pointed at Bob, who was co-producing the music with the assistant pro. They started playing the patriotic CD she previously purchased. The sound level was preset to provide a relaxing undercurrent of favorite American songs while Longshot entertained the press corps.

"For those of you who don't know me, I'm Longshot, and I host a biweekly radio show that helps gamers improve their odds in games of chance. A few short days ago, I was watching a golf tournament at this very course, the Viva Las Vegas Country Club, and accidentally found myself speaking with a near winner of the event. His name was Jeff Taylor. A fortunate, yet unfortunate circumstance occurred that sadly caused him to overpower a short putt to lose the match. But, the fortunate outcome was that he met his new bride as a result of that missed putt. Sometimes, God closes a door but opens a window, and this certainly turned out to be true in Jeff's case."

"I met up with Jeff and Ginger in the clubhouse afterwards to chat about the round and his missed opportunity. For someone who just lost a dream, he was very positive and upbeat, displaying sincere signs of sportsmanship and courage when personally challenged. Very stoic. Very presidential. A TV temporarily interrupted our conversation with a newsflash update regarding the current race for the presidency. We all soured on the current choice of candidates. Jeff said that's it sad when the most influential and democratic society in the world has such a difficult time finding candidates you can trust and believe in. He indicated that he felt that most people tend to vote for the lesser of two evils, or vote, not to elect a president, but to keep another out of the office. Honesty and integrity have been replaced with money, power, and political candidate bashing. What really struck me as refreshingly absurd is that Jeff doesn't want to vote for a candidate who will change the world. He would, however, like to vote for someone who doesn't really mess it up any worse than it is now, and he felt that even he had the ability to accomplish that."

At that point, Bob turned up the music just a notch as many of the reporting gallery clapped and cheered at those words. Jade beamed with pride of her speech thus far and hoped that Jeff wouldn't mess up Longshot's professional delivery.

"I was very impressed with Jeff, and suggested that he run for the position of President of the United States. Jeff laughed and said that if for some reason, Americans believe that he can do a job as good or better than the incumbent or challengers, and vote for him as a write-in candidate, and he wins, he'd accept the job. It was these inspiring words that persuaded me to make such an unusual bet on my radio program. I believe, in my heart of hearts, that Jeff Taylor could do no worse than any other politician in office, and, quite possibly, do better, as he's as American as they come. So, Jeff Taylor is not running for President of the United States. Yet, I'm betting that Jeff will become our next President anyway." The media looked completely perplexed, yet cheers were heard around the course.

Longshot continued, "Ladies and gentlemen of the press, before I bring Jeff up to the podium, I'd like to add that we've already been approached by various groups regarding campaign contributions. Since Jeff is not officially running for office, we ask that all potential contributions be donated, instead, to your favorite charity in Jeff Taylor's name. Jeff believes that millions of dollars are wasted on campaign signs that kill trees and litter the roads, as well those horrible TV ads that politicians use to bash their opponents. Jeff would like to see those dollars put to good use such as disease research, natural disaster relief, or any charitable organization. Now isn't that a great way for political donations to be spent?"

The crowd cheered at the thought of this, except some TV news teams cringed at the lost advertising revenue for their stations.

"Jeff and his new wife, Ginger, will be on their honeymoon for the next few months. During that time, and starting today, Jeff invites the press and select voters to join him in rounds of golf around the country. You can contact Jade Tomsay, Jeff's traveling social director, to arrange to play a round of golf with him and ask him questions, such as why he's not running for office. Jade has business cards available to pass out with her contact information. And now, I'd like to introduce to you a man who's not running for office, Jeff Taylor, honeymooner, and our next President of the United States." Bob cranked up the volume as the "Star Spangled Banner" soared, and the reporters were lulled into excitement and cheering.

Jeff and Ginger held hands as they tentatively approached the podium. Jeff took a deep breath, unsure what to do or say. He pulled out his cue card and, desperate for help and assistance, looked at Ginger. On cue, she secretly reached from behind, slipped her hand under his pants and lovingly took a passionate grip on his personality as though she was holding a 5 iron. He twitched in surprise and dropped the cue card while she whispered in his ear, "Don't lay up, go for the green." Hitting the ball cleanly, she released the club and gave him a tender kiss that invoked warm moans for the gallery.

This stroke cleared his head (the one with the brain), and he naturally smiled his million-dollar smile while cameras flashed and video rolled. "Hi everyone. I'm Jeff Taylor", speaking with a puberty like crack in his voice, "and this is my new bride, Ginger." The reporter's unprofessional enthusiasm resulted in rowdy version of applause with wolf whistles and lustful moans as she waved and jiggled nervously to the delight of the cameras.

"Thanks for coming out today. Longshot is right. I'm not running for president. I am going on my hornymoon, I mean honeymoon, and looking forward to see how many holes I can get in as I love to play with my wife, ah, er ... I mean golf." Jeff's Freudian slips caused the crowd to howl in laughter. It not only broke the ice, but also melted some polar caps. It was a perfect mistake. Jeff's face emitted a red glow, and he laughed like a little boy while Ginger forked her elbow in his ribs for the cameras to see. Then she affectionately pecked him on the cheek while America began their love affair with this new dynamic duo.

"Longshot asked me about running for president. I told him that I don't think I can mess up the country any more than the guys in office or running for office, so maybe I should consider it." There was hint of laughter from the crowd. "But then I told him that people would be crazy to vote for me. But if Americans want to vote for me, they can be my guest," he said, broadcasting his lotto winning smile.

He continued, "Folks, I'm looking forward to spending some time with my new bride and playing some golf. Our stay at the Hard Rock Hotel was the perfect place to tee off our honeymoon. Best of all, not too many brides would let their husbands take their clubs along on their honeymoon. I am a lucky guy. But, I was upset, and Ginger was embarrassed by the event that took place outside our honeymoon suite this morning. Without a doubt, there is sense of comedy regarding this mornings' event. Yet, invasion of personal privacy is something Americans should not tolerate. Compassion, humility, honesty, and human dignity are aspects of our American culture that are often forgotten, instead of fostered. With this in mind, I trust that you, the media, and the American public, will treat our vacation with respect and dignity."

During Jeff's impromptu speech, Longshot and Jade were ready to pass out, simultaneously thinking, "What past presidential spirit possessed Jeff, and thank God he showed up." Ginger was also amazed at his newfound composure and sincerity. She'll grab anything, anywhere, more often if that's the type of verbal response that would occur.

Jeff continued, "Ginger and I look forward to our honeymoon, and thank you all for coming to wish us congratulations. Now, in this cart, I've got a new set of TaylorMade golf clubs that are just dying to be hit. Anyone want to play some golf?" With that, the crowd again cheered. A tidal wave of reporters rushed in to ask questions and get on the playing list. Bob turned the music volume up, but switched the CD to "American Girl" from Tom Petty. It was a political miracle of success, and Jeff didn't even remember what he said.

Johnson's security team dove into the tidal wave of reporters like a floodwall, holding them back from crushing his entourage. They swooped Jeff and Ginger into the golf carts and quickly paraded them back to the pro shop. Jade stepped up to the mike and announced, "I'll be glad to arrange for the media to play a few holes with Jeff and Ginger. Our courteous security team will instill order and set up a single file line so I can accept your requests in an orderly fashion."

The reporters, particularly those from the major networks, were stunned that they couldn't parlay their news clout to move to the head of the line, but the security wall was already in place. Jade then passed out tickets with numbers to the reporters based on their position in line, similar to ordering cold cuts at a crowded deli. She said, "We'll announce the numbers so you don't have to stand in line. While you're waiting to hit a few shots with Jeff, feel free to help yourself to our food and beverages."

During her announcement, tables of hors d'oeuvres and an open mobile bar splashed into the center of the party. Jade had arranged this with the country club manager prior to the press conference. Bob switched the music in order to mellow out the crowd and decided to play some classic jazz cuts, thinking he might like to switch jobs and become a disc jockey some day.

The golf cart motorcade sped back to the pro shop for reentry to a temporary safe haven. As soon as they entered the pro shop, Ginger tackled Jeff and planted a big kiss on him. The manager and Dave smiled and pretended not to watch. Ginger said, "Darling, you were fantastic out there in front of those reporters and cameras. I'm so proud of you."

Jeff had never had a woman say words of such importance and sincerity to him before. His emotions started to come out like he'd just won the PGA championship, and he almost started to cry. Ginger's exuberant remarks, coupled with the tension of speaking in public started to hit him. Yet, he was very glad with the outcome. He realized that her brief round of pocket pool at the beginning of his speech was the inadvertent reason for his success, and he said, "Baby, I couldn't have done it with you. Let's continue the game of pocket pool later tonight." Ginger smiled and shook her head in approval.

Just then, Jade burst into the pro shop saying, "It's a zoo out there. At this rate, you'll be playing golf for the next two years." Jeff didn't really care. He and Ginger were hitting a new level in their relationship, and it felt as good as a perfect drive. Jade saw the expressions on their faces and brought them back down to earth. "Okay, Jeff, I've got a corral of wild horses out there wanting to play golf. Are you ready?"

Jeff's mind quickly turned to those new clubs in his new golf bag, and he said, "Let's tee it up."

Johnson and Jade coordinated the golf outing with the media. Dave Vargo had golf carts prepared with rental clubs for the media, along with golf balls, gloves, and even new golf shoes in a variety of sizes. Jade reminded Johnson that the goal was for Jeff to have a relaxed round of golf with reporters, switching foursomes every three holes.

Cameramen connected with the reporter in the foursome were allowed to follow behind but not film ahead of the golfers. Ginger would tend the flag and retrieve the balls if she wanted to. Jeff was going to keep his score, with the reporters' total score competing against Jeff's. Jade leaked out the challenge, "Can the press beat Jeff?" Film at 11, no doubt. Longshot wanted to get some bets going, but he didn't want to make any enemies with the hands that would eventually feed him, so he curbed his gambling temptation.

Many of the reporters grumbled over this method of interviewing, but once the round was underway, they actually enjoyed it. Security would transport three new reporters every three holes to play with Jeff. Dave tagged along, offering pointers and club selection to the players. Reporters who were scheduled to play on the back nine with Jeff were originally pissed due to the long wait but realized that they now had an opportunity to go to the range and hit some practice balls. They hoped their improved play might open some interview opportunities with Jeff in the future.

On the first tee, Jeff was given the honor to hit first. The driver he pulled out of the bag had an oversized club head so large that it could be used as a space shuttle fin, yet its sleek, high tech, titanium based, low center of gravity design gave Jeff a feeling of confidence and superiority as he caressed the club. Since the clubs were new, however, he wasn't quite sure what to expect when he hit them. He decided to just follow John Daly's advice: Grip it and rip it. And he did. He was filled with so much adrenalin that he clobbered a soft fade over 320 yards that landed in the first cut of rough.

The gallery of reporters applauded, knowing that the combined score of hackers would never beat Jeff, even if some type of handicap were implemented.

The rest of the players in the first group demonstrated extreme levels of play, though none of them were used to playing golf while cameras rolled. Longshot's plan was working. Jeff was confident and in control on the course, while forcing the reporters to now be in front of the camera with mostly awkward swings, putting them at a disadvantage.

This first group of reporters didn't have ample time to down many drinks and were rather aggressive in interviewing Jeff. Longshot, who was busy speaking with reporters and golf club manufacturers regarding endorsements, caught up to Jeff after his drive on the first hole and helped subdue the over-zealous reporters and divert many questions to golf. Jade stayed at the clubhouse with a radio to organize the pairings for the rest of the round. Thus far, all things had gone much smoother than planned, thanks to Johnson and his security team.

Phase two of Longshot's plan worked even better. Once the reporters were averted to golf and honeymoon questions, Ginger kicked in her charm and sex appeal. Her ball retrieval and pin tending techniques caught more camera footage than Jeff's golf game. She congratulated a good putt from a reporter with a high five or a slap on their ass for a great putt. By the next hole, they were putting with the intensity to win the British Open just to gain some interaction with her. The press was able to ask Jeff some questions regarding his views on the country, and he was honest yet evasive at pointing fingers, especially since he didn't know the names of the vice-president, cabinet members, or most other elected officials. He mainly expressed his perception of the country, which was pathetic according to recent news sources, so his comments were not off target. His game, however, was very much on target, maintaining Jeff's high level of confidence and comfort on the course.

As new groups of reporters joined Jeff and Ginger, many of the same questions were asked. Jeff started to refine his responses and included words and phrases that added more substantial meanings. Also, the reporters were getting noticeably more drunk as the day went on, which made it even easier for him to respond to their questions. One reporter from an independent TV news station in Arizona was very tipsy by the time he joined Jeff's foursome but asked a very sober question while strolling down the eighth fairway. "Mr. Taylor, how would you rate our current president?"

Longshot knew a question like this, answered incorrectly, could severely damage Jeff's image, and he slugged down a beer in anticipation of his response.

Jeff looked at the reporter and said, "Well, that's a good question, but you already know the answer."

The reporter looked confused and said, "I do?"

Jeff said "Sure. Is your life better, worse, or the same now than it was when our president took office?"

The other reporters eased in with their tape recorders to hear the response. "Well, my salary hasn't changed, my wife lost her job to someone overseas, and I can't afford to pay my health insurance."

Jeff turned to the other reporters and asked them, "Are any of you better off today then you were several years ago?"

They all shook their heads no, almost in shame.

Jeff said, "Well, I hate to say it, but I'm much better off." Everyone, especially Longshot, was stunned by his response. He was endorsing the current president, but he quickly followed up his remark with "I married Ginger, and she lets me play golf. How could I not be better off?"

Ginger walked up and gave Jeff a peck on the cheek while the golfing press corps cheerfully agreed. Longshot couldn't believe it. He had the press disparage the current administration for him, and he came out smelling like a rose.

With a smile on his face, Longshot lagged behind Jeff and the press crew and called Jade on her cell phone. "You won't believe it. Jeff has them eating out of his hand. This plan is actually working. How's it going on your end?"

"Good and bad. I can't prioritize the endorsement opportunities and interview requests, 'cause it's too long. Just about every golf equipment manufacturer wants to speak with Jeff regarding endorsements. But that's just part of it. The list of non-golf offers is even larger. Financial companies, clothing companies, restaurant chains, the list goes on. I need a computer to sort it all out. In addition, everyone wants to interview Jeff and Ginger. Larry King, Oprah, Lettermen, CNN, MSNBC, Fox, Just Fore Golf, and dozens of others I've never heard of. It's a zoo here."

Longshot was radiant with the news and said, "Jade, we need to generate some working capital ASAP in order to continue this party."

She finally asked, "You mean so I can get paid?"

Longshot replied, "Yep, among a long list of other things. Try to get a handle on endorsements that can generate the fastest cash flow. I think we'll all need a day off tomorrow to recover from today. We'll use that time to review the list and determine who we should speak to and where to go next."

Jade agreed on the plan and hung up, as everyone was still bombarding her for something.

While Jeff was finishing the back nine, the evening news on the east coast was already airing segments of the adventures of Jeff and Ginger. Since Jeff did not actually announce his running for office, he was not considered a serious contender for the presidential throne, and the media basically decided to play this newsworthy event as a public interest story. Ginger's morning dance with the chopper was aired, followed by a brief clip of Jeff's speech. Although the media downplayed the story, Jeff and Ginger captured the hearts of America in many different ways. Their looks, sex appeal, love of sport, and true American Pride hit a home run with the viewers. TV and website surveys were already showing that voters would consider Jeff as a presidential candidate. Basically, the surveys of American voters revealed that if famous entertainers can get into politics, why not let a golfer try giving it a whiff.

Jade had set up a private reception in the clubhouse that included reporters from major TV news stations, but no cameras were allowed. She also invited the sales reps from several golf product manufacturers, as well as several endorsement-interested organizations. The assistant pro helped Jade determine what golf companies should attend. The overall attendance did not exceed thirty invitees, so as to not overwhelm Jeff. At the end of the round, Johnson's security team brought the final foursome into the bar.

When Jeff and Ginger entered, they glanced at each other, knowing that this was where the fireworks started just a few short days ago. The unplanned but perfect entrance song by Bonnie Raitt "Something to Talk About" purred in the background. The invitees were very warm and cordial, slowly introducing themselves to Jeff and Ginger and offering them congratulations on their wedding. Jeff and Ginger approached the bar and remembered Raul the bartender, much to his joy and satisfaction. Jeff said, "No matter what happens tonight, under no circumstances are you to drive us anywhere except our hotel room."

Raul smiled and said, "No worries, Jeff. I'm on your side," and he gave Jeff a thumbs-up vote of confidence. Without hesitation, Raul uncapped two icy Coronas and squeezed in some fresh lime.

Jade totaled up the scorecard and revealed the results. "Attention everyone. I have a brief announcement. Jeff shot a 1 under 71 on his round today, and you, the press, had combined scores of 99, 112, and, hmm, this score looks more representative of a bowling score."

Jeff said, "I'd be glad to offer you a rematch."

One of the invitees said, "Mr. Taylor, I'd like to set up a rematch with you now, as you may be too busy to play once you're in the White House." A vivacious combination of cheers, roars, and hollers echoed around the bar.

Unlike their original encounter, Jeff and Ginger minimized their beer love affair. They were too busy socializing. Jeff's discussions typically hovered around golf and sports in general. He dabbled lightly about politics but with little emotion. Ginger was used to men making a fuss over her and leveraged her socializing skills by using the fine art of casual rubbing, touching, and talking too close to her intended audience. Her actions were not vulgar, but, instead, projected a slightly teasing persona of shy warmth and affection. The mostly all-male contingent ate it up and, like the final song at a concert, wanted more.

Longshot and Jade were also busy entertaining the mostly business aspects of the conversations, although, men, being what they are and being in Las Vegas, became overly friendly to Jade when word spread that she was single and available. They assumed Ginger's role, reversing the touchy-feely talents that Ginger had mastered. Yet Jade had matured dramatically over the past twenty-four hours and displayed no signs of interest to any advances made to her. She did realize that many of the people present could help her with her communications career in the future, so she decided to be professionally courteous, but did some extra mingling with specific invitees as well, much to their approval.

By around 10 P.M., the original political golfing party realized they were running on fumes and used mental telepathy to signal Longshot to end the bash. Longshot called out to get everyone's attention. "Hey partners… It's time for us to ride off into the sunset. I'd like to thank you for coming out today to wish Jeff and Ginger congrats on their nuptials."

Jeff quickly chimed in, "Yes, we'd like to thank you and hope you enjoyed our little round of golf. I invite you to join me for another round anytime."

Jade made sure that business cards were exchanged and most of the guests said that they would be in contact with her in the next few days regarding their offers and requests. Johnson radioed the limo into position and dragged everyone inside. They took advantage of the limo's peace and quiet while gazing at the spectacular lights of Las Vegas. Ginger was starving and said, "Why don't we call the hotel and arrange to have dinner brought to our rooms. I'm starving." They all agreed and ordered the most extravagant array of food the menu offered. In desperate need of personal intimacy, each ate alone in the comfort of their own suite, with no specific time for wake up calls. All four deserted dessert for sleep.

Hole Number 5
Par 4

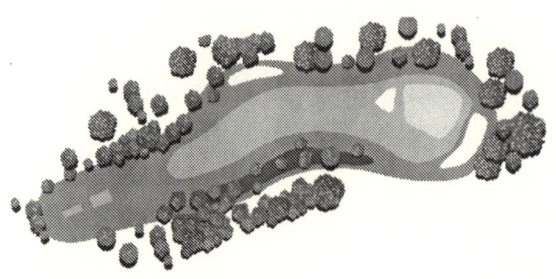

(**Course Notes:** Air Force One is traveling at 41,000 feet over the Atlantic Ocean while his putter taps balls on the practice green toward the hole. Turbulence creates new hazards uncommon to a typical putt. Down the hall, the Secret Service is busy with the on-board computer, downloading the satellite pictures taken of the famous Arubii golf course along with the original designer's drawings of the course. This perk of reviewing courses digitally, prior to play, cut at least 2 strokes off his score. When the 42-inch plasma TV monitor is ready to display the course layout in high definition, they call for him, Mr. President…Mr. President. But then one of the agents starts kissing his ear like a lizard. Is this what goes on high in the sky? To hinder confusion, he opens his eyes, as Ginger finishes massaging his ear with her tongue. Thank God it's not a marine, as he was enjoying it…)

This was certainly a wet dream but in the wrong place. He said to himself, "No problem mon", as he'd gladly take this wake up call daily. Seeing Ginger first thing in the morning was good and bad. You wanted to wake up, but you didn't want to get out of bed.

Once again, the hotel ghosts haunted their room with coffee and other pre-breakfast treats, teasing them to depart from the covers. Jeff and Ginger were more trainable than Pavlov's dog. After only one day, they began their ritual of moving from the bed, to the coffee, and onward to the bath. How could they ever have managed without Helmsford and Sasha before? As they had both passed out after dinner, Jeff decided to take advantage of Ginger's social service skills once again. Neither the bubbles or Ginger put up a fight.

The Hard Rock was completely booked, as anyone who needed to be near the new presidential candidate not running for office booked every available room. Several of the nearby hotels also decreased their vacancies substantially. The patio was deemed the conference room, but Johnson added new levels of security to avert chopper intrusion. Since there was no scheduled meeting, the presidential foursome waived the bathroom prep option. The guys didn't shave, and the girls' hair was disoriented. No one cared or noticed.

Jade and Longshot had arrived on the patio about an hour earlier, since they didn't have desired company in their bathtubs. This gave them time to review the list of endorsements. After Jeff and Ginger sat down, and steaming hot coffee had been poured into the fine china, Longshot turned to business. "We have great news. Several golf companies want you to sponsor their products to the tune of $400,000. In addition, $850,000 is already pledged to charities on your behalf."

Ginger said "Almost a million dollars for charities after playing golf for one day? That's incredible.

Jade went through the list of opportunities, but Jeff's mind went off course. He was starting to get used to his daily dose of shock treatments, but today, the strike seemed to come off the toe of the club. He was certainly glad that his two days of fame had generated goodwill and dollars to charities, especially since he had probably only donated $100 of his own to charities over the past few years. But, he focused more on the endorsement prospects thinking, *Based on some quick math, subtracting fees to Longshot, Jade, Ellen's legal and accounting guidance and incidentals, I stand to make more money right now than what I earned in the last four years combined.*

Ginger's mental cash register was also on the prowl, and she was amazed at how fast she could think of ways to spend the invisible money potential.

Jade could see that Jeff and Ginger were playing different courses and brought them back to her game. "Earth to Jeff and Ginger. Guys, you need to hear this. I'm going to contact all the potential quick-cash endorsement opportunities and have their contracts sent to Ellen Spackler's office for review. After that, I'll analyze the long and diverse list of offers. It includes hair removal creams, adult branded cereal, toothpaste, patriotic condoms, and new flavors of passion punch, just to name a few."

Ginger giggled, "Will Jeff have to model the condoms?"

Jeff refocused from his money-focused slumber when he heard the question and said, "What? Model condoms, with the U.S. flag on them? That's sick. And unpatriotic. Pass on that one."

Jade said, "Okay, ax the rubbers. I also received requests from over a hundred golf courses around the country, inviting Jeff to play their links. Jeff, I'll need your help in selecting the courses."

Jeff took a quick look at the list of courses. "I can't believe it. I can play some of the best courses in the country, many of which are sites for the U.S. Open and PGA tournaments. Man, this is awesome." Jeff converted from banker to little boy and quickly developed two golf course lists: must play and love to play.

Jade said, "Pencil in the state location of each course. That will help me map out a travel itinerary."

While going down the list, he noticed an invitation from the TPC at Sawgrass in Florida, home of the famed 17th island green. He imagined hitting a full 9 iron to the green and was ready to climax for executing a perfect shot, based on a hole of no relation to Ginger yet with no worry of breaking his wedding vows. He concluded this brief romantic golf interlude, and converted from the little, horny golf boy to a Fortune 100 project manager and laid out a travel plan to minimize travel time and expense, while maximizing golf playing options.

Jeff said, "Here's our initial plan. We'll begin our tour in South Florida, playing nine courses in just over 14 days. We'll travel north through the state, allowing for some time to visit theme parks, beaches, and tourist traps. Ginger, I'm assigning you and Jade the task of arranging the none-golf related itinerary. From there, we'll travel through the South, with stops that include Pinehurst. I don't see an invitation from Augusta National and, quite frankly, don't expect to receive one. From this point on, the itinerary will be flexible. We'll most likely move the tour on a path to the Northeast, Midwest, maybe some Rockies golf, concluding the honeymoon tour in California before heading back home to Las Vegas. I don't see a Pebble Beach invitation, but we might allude to the reporters during this mini tour that that would be a great place to end the tour. Jade, call the Florida courses first to set up a playing schedule"

Everyone at the table was in awe of his ability to set up the itinerary with such organized precision. Longshot said, "Partner, slow down on the java. You'll get a headache with all that thinking and organizing."

Jeff let the remark flow through him like the wind, as he was mentally playing the courses.

Jade said, "Okay, Jeff, I'll start calling the Florida courses today. I'll also post the itinerary on the web site so the media knows your location and can arrange to join you. Next, we received an assortment of requests for TV and magazine interviews. All golf magazines were interested in interviews but requests were made from virtually all other types of publications as well."

Longshot smirked while he announced, "A request from La Pussay, a new adult web site, would like to have an interview with Ginger. I've seen this site. Bob, our sound engineer, has memberships to all these sex sites. This one offers tabloid-styled trash news, but includes XXX rated pictures, and it has grown to over 6 million subscribers in just one year."

This caught the ear of Ginger. Longshot continued, "They would do the interview for free and post it on their web site within days, but they would be willing to pay Ginger over $500,000 for some pictures."

Ginger quietly wondered how much they'd pay for several hours worth of video but decided to keep that to herself for the time being. She said, "I'd agree to the interview for now, but I'd consider the picture shoot *after* we make it to the White House." They all laughed and decided to consider it for the future.

While Jade scheduled the tour and checked her email, Best Bet Transport, a private, Vegas based travel service, offered them air and land transportation services. The owner was even willing to paint "Vote for Honesty" underneath his company logo on the sides of the jet and limos. After reviewing their web site for legitimacy, Jade called them and accepted their offer. As a special honeymoon gift, Best Bet arranged a sightseeing trip over the Grand Canyon and Hoover Dam on one of their smaller planes. Since nothing else was planned for the next day, Jeff and Ginger accepted.

It was a long morning of business, and Jeff decided to retire to the bedroom to catch up on sports. The ghost butler used spiritual ESP to turn ESPN on the big screen, along with a vanilla milkshake at bedside. Jeff expected no less.

Ginger and Jade independently shared the urge to shop. Both were excited about spending money they had never had, and collided while attempting to sit down for some cyber shopping. Ginger said, "I was going to shop online for some clothes."

Jade said, "Me too."

They both stood up, feeling a new bond of sisterhood, and smiled. Ginger rolled a cushy chair over to the computer and said, "Please sit down. It's time to spend. Where shall we shop?"

Jade said, "Anywhere." Jade was anxious to get to know Ginger better, and Ginger, who had never had any real girl friends, or any long lasting friends for that matter, was glad to have a shopping companion. They both knew that they'd need each other to continue this journey to the unknown. Meanwhile, Longshot headed downstairs to find out how his bet was going, and he couldn't believe what was transpiring.

The casino manager pulled up the current numbers regarding Longshot's bet to his radio audience, but it just didn't make sense to him. Longshot said "Two thirds of gamblers are betting for Jeff, not against him. People think Jeff can become president. People want him to become president. Over 1,800 bets have been placed worth $200,000 in wagers. Even though I'm a betting expert, or supposed to be, my plan backfired, but in a good way."

The manager said, "Your foresight to take a cut in either side of the bet could potentially end up in his favor. Look at the local newspaper. A poll revealed that if the election were held today, Jeff would receive 11% of the vote. Can you imagine this, 11% of the vote, coming from a candidate who's been on the election market for less than forty-eight hours. And he's not even officially running for president."

Longshot laughed. "God bless America, golfers, voters, and gamblers."

"Now," he whispered to himself, "Let's set up the polygraph test."

Switching temporarily from a golf tour to a Grand Canyon tour was a wonderful escape for the new celebrities. As they flew through the center of the canyon, with late afternoon shadows casting majestic 3-D images on the North Rim, Jeff could not get golf out of his mind, comparing the canyon as the most formidable hazard in golf. *Slice it right, and your ball travels 1,000 feet into the Colorado River. Do you take the mules down the cliff to look for the ball? Can your white water rafting guide help you locate the missing cluster of tough dimples? It sure would make you think twice about slicing.*

While Jeff looked for interesting pin placements and tried to determine club selection for the next shot, Ginger, for a change, assumed the role of a little girl. She had few fond memories of family vacations, and witnessing the Grand Canyon from a bird's point of view reassured her that marrying Jeff, at least for the first few days, was a blessing rather than a mistake. As the pilot weaved and curled through the multi-colored canyon walls, Ginger held Jeff's hand in a roller-coaster like fashion as the plane descended and then rose, tickling her tummy from an internal perspective.

Returning to the hotel required Johnson's tough security. This new king and queen of romance rivaled the electricity that Charles and Di originally displayed. New admirers, would-be voters and the press lined the doorways for glimpses, pictures, and autographs of this regal like couple. They retired to the suite, preparing for one more afternoon of media golf. They also prepared their minds and suitcases for the next round of golf in Florida.

The short break from media bombardment provided Jade with time to improve her organizational skills. She had starting times reserved at the courses around the country, news media foursomes lined up, and brief descriptions of each foursome including their names, media association, and handicap if available. She also had the majority of the Florida swing itinerary scheduled, expecting her updated email in-basket to solidify plans.

Her emailing was interrupted when Longshot volunteered her assistance to edit the commentary for his upcoming radio show. He planned to announce the polygraph test to "real" presidential candidates. Jade suggested that they give this test a name, and called it "The Honest Scorecard," which caused Longshot to smile like the Grinch. They felt "The Honest Scorecard" should intensify the press coverage during their romp in the Sunshine State.

While they were preparing for the next phase of the tour, Ellen Spackler called to deliver some good news. "Several short term contracts to endorse golf products were signed, and the fee should be electronically transferred into our bank account by the end of today. I'll email a statement to you showing the balance, less my legal fee percentage, accounting fees, 10% business expenses and Jade's salary. I'll have check cards available for all of you by tomorrow, giving you monetary access to your personal accounts."

Longshot easily negotiated Jade's salary, which included a $600 per week salary, and 2% of product endorsements. This also included meals and hotel accommodations for the next few months, although she was basically on call 24/7. Ellen arranged to have the accounting firm handle her payroll and bonus dollars, and also provide automatic transfer into Jade's personal bank account biweekly. Longshot wanted all transactions to be legal to keep the ultimate king of dealers, the IRS, happy and uninvolved.

The next day's golf outing went smoothly with Johnson's protection. Ginger decided to start putting with the foursome, which added a new dimension of excitement to the event. The media reversed rolls, tending the flag for her, while she bent over the short club to address the ball and strike at will, much to their enjoyment. Within a few holes, her stroke actually improved, due to some pointers from Jeff. In the middle of the round, a new group of playing partners joined them. After brief introductions, the group prepared to tee off.

Ginger was standing off to the side of the tee while Jeff was preparing to hit when one of the new players nudged alongside her and whispered, "Do you remember me?"

Scratch Delacantos was introduced to the golf party as press corps liaison. No one took much notice of him, as the titles and names of players were merged into one muddled media cloud. Jade had entered him into today's golf pairings based on his offer to donate $10,000 to a children's charity, but she was too busy to find out if the donation was ever made.

Scratch didn't have any official title, and he didn't work for any specific company. He was self-employed and leased his talents to anyone who needed to have something done that was typically not legal or moral. Most of his activities were achieved at or below the sewer level. But, he was decent enough to draw the line when contracts were issued to permanently remove an individual from existence as the last resort to resolve a situation. He would, however, gladly subcontract this service if requested for a reasonable, tax-free, cash-only fee.

Scratch was well known in many political circles for being results oriented, affordable, and discreet. In fact, his resume (potentially legal evidence that was never printed or distributed) would proudly display his accomplishments with numerous business executives, local and state governmental officials, congressmen, federal judges, and even a U.S. president. In fact, Sonny Hoag, the North Carolina congressman who was currently running for president, had unofficially hired Scratch just over four years ago to act upon a variety of unethical and unreported tasks that had aided his election to Congress. That was when he and Ginger crossed paths.

Sonny was in his junior year, attending a no-name university in North Carolina, successfully achieving a C- average. He worked part time in the administrative office. One night while removing trash from the office, he stumbled across the president of the college giving his dicktation to a college freshman who didn't really know shorthand, but was in the process of learning on-the-job. The freshman ran out of the room before all the notes were transcribed while the president stood there, physically and criminally exposed. Sonny, knowing that his poor grades and lack of learning abilities could keep him in custodial services permanently, presented an option to the president in exchange for secrecy: adjust his record to show him graduating at the conclusion of the current term with at least a 3.4 GPA.

The biggest lesson Sonny learned there was that knowing of or having critical information can be leveraged into a huge amount power. According to school records, he graduated with honors that semester, and entered the workforce with the goal of finding out "things" about people or companies. In professional circles, this is termed research analysis via networking. He parlayed this work ethic into the promotion of his own interests that propelled his career through business, and eventually into politics. He used his spider web to catch unsuspecting business and political kingpins with skeletons in their professional or personal closets, and promised not to devour them in exchange for some personal or monetary gain. He thought this skill was unique, but he found out over time that many successful business and political leaders had honed this talent to some high degree.

When Sonny ran for congress four years earlier, he had been invited to attend a seminar at Regal Corporation, a Las Vegas-based land developer who was in the process of purchasing tracts of land nationwide for high-end housing projects. Regal had major projects underway in many states including North Carolina, and their corporate president was interested in meeting Sonny to discuss how they could mutually benefit from joining forces. Sonny knew that he needed some information on Regal to leverage his opportunity and called Scratch Delacantos to help him obtain some informational clout. Prior to Sonny's visit to Vegas, Scratch interviewed several escort services in search of a candidate who could assist him in obtaining vital documentation while rendering romantic services if required.

After several interviews, Ginger was found and temporarily employed. Scratch portrayed himself to her as an independent undercover agent, employed by a land conservation group to uncover any illegal aspects of Regal that could be used to stop them from building on sensitive land areas such as the Florida Everglades and the North Carolina coastline. Ginger was skeptical but convinced herself that she was on an honorable mission that paid well. With Scratch's help, she infiltrated the higher tier of executives at Regal. Within a few weeks, they obtained a wealth of illegal documents and unethical information that Sonny could leverage during his discussions with Regal. With such information in hand, Sonny's meeting with Regal was successfully short and lucrative. Regal agreed to provide him with millions of fundraising dollars, in exchange for his secrecy regarding their shady business activities. In addition, if he was elected, he'd also receive a bonus from Regal while promoting their promising land development activities in the great state of North Carolina.

At the conclusion of the meeting, Sonny had over-partied in celebration and called Scratch to arrange a meeting with Ginger to express his thanks and indulge in some parting favors. Scratch told Ginger that the leader of the land conservation group wanted to thank her personally, and that it should be an honor for her to meet with him. Scratch did not, however, reveal Sonny's name, which was considered proper etiquette in both of their lines of work. Ginger's gut feeling was similar to being kicked in the stomach by a jackass, but she agreed to meet Sonny at her apartment. The taxi cab driver delivered Sonny to Ginger's front door. He was roaring drunk when he arrived, and that was his best quality.

When Sonny entered her apartment, he said, "So you're the hooker who'll help get me elected to Congress?"

She did not respond well to that title, or his cigar-smelling fat-laden body and thought, *I won't let this sleaze lay a hand on me, but how can I excite him without contact and get him the hell out of here? To think I might have helped this pig get elected to some office. It makes me sick.*

Sonny swaggered past Blabs perch, noticed the parrot flapping her wings and mumbled, "Hello widdle birdie. Polly want a cracker?" Blabs looked at Sonny and sang, "Oooh Oooh that smell, can't you smell that smell?" Sonny just shrugged his shoulders, turned to Ginger and said, "Come on sweet ting, let's get the party started." Ginger realized that she was playing a Lynard Skynard CD earlier that day, and poor Blabs wasted her talent on this unappreciative bum.

"Relax lover boy. Let me get you something to drink while I prepare myself for you." She poured some cheap booze into a plastic cup with no ice and handed it to him. She left the bottle in the room. Sonny was already excited at the sight of Ginger. She admitted him wearing a tight LA Lakers t-shirt with no bra, cut-off jean shorts that exposed more ass than material, and black high-heeled shoes. She came back into the room twenty minutes later wearing a skin-tight black leather vest, gloves, mask, and matching leather thong. She looked like Cat Woman except far more skin was visible. She tied Sonny's hands and feet to the bed, blindfolded him, and slid his pants down to his knees. Sonny was smiling in a drunken blissful state of anticipation. Ginger wasn't sure if Sonny realized that he'd been handcuffed and blindfolded. He just smiled without saying a word. Either he was too drunk to notice, or he'd done this many times before and was used to it. She turned on her stereo, and started playing a Rolling Stones CD, wishing that Mic Jagger were in the room with her rather than this pompous fat ass.

Next, she grabbed a bar of soap and thoroughly cleansed his manhood, although its size was directly opposite to his huge ego. Nonetheless, he enjoyed the bathing, with the warm water and gentle rubbing caressing him into a peaceful dream, one notch above sleep. Next, she proceeded to turn on three hidden cameras, positioning them with the skill of a famous Hollywood director. While she was setting up the cameras, Blabs decided to join the party. She tipped over a package of Tweet Treet bird seed from her perch. The seed cascaded down like a waterfall and bounced off of the stand, coming to rest on Sonny's moist body. He smiled and said, "Oh baby, are you gonna grind me with love crystals? I haven't had that done in years." Blabs didn't know or care what he was talking about. She did, however, float down to the mountainous, jelly fish-like body to savor and devour the delicious blend of seeds, nuts, and organic ingredients while being very careful not to clip any skin. Blabs' tiny beak, tongue, and claws roamed over Sonny's body enjoying the smorgasbord.

With the cameras adjusted, Ginger came back into the room, gasping at the sight of the beauty and the beast buffet. Although she feared for the health of her pet, she decided to let the meal continue. Blabs, however, decided that this meal should be accompanied with a show and started singing along with the music, "You can't always get what you want." Sonny's hands and feet moved along with the song, and before too long, he joined in with Blabs, singing, "But if you try sometimes, you might find, you get what you need…"

Ginger couldn't help to laugh at this buck-naked rich fool who was all tied up and singing a Rolling Stones classic while getting a parrot BJ. Blabs nibbled and sang, causing Sonny to hum the rock and roll melody in moan-like delight.

Blabs instinctively moaned back to Sonny, who smiled even more thinking Ginger was enjoying this as much as he was. It was the most erotic feeling he'd ever experienced prior to passing out completely.

Ginger's smirk continued, knowing that she caught a Hoag making an ass of himself on video, but she prayed that Blabs wouldn't catch anything from Sonny. She never used Blabs in her work, and felt guilty as she flirted with bestiality using her own pet. As a result, Ginger did something she never did before. She gave herself a bonus, courtesy of $100 she found in Sonny's wallet. This bonus was to be used for a vet visit for Blabs to make sure no congenial diseases were transmitted to her prized Amazon. She also viewed Sonny's name on his driver's license and scribbled it down in her black book along with the date and time to cross-reference the video being currently streamed to Omaha Internet servers. Ten minutes later, Blabs was full, but she couldn't descend from the large, over-inflated belly on her own. Ginger helped Blabs return to her cage.

Then, under the watchful eyes and ears of the cameras, Ginger decided to disclose the identity of her love slave. She removed his mask and kissed Sonny on the lips. She was proud that she could do this without puking while thinking; *I must have some acting blood in my veins after all.* Sonny groggily opened his eyes and smiled when he saw Ginger standing above him. Ginger affectionately tilted his head up in full view of the cameras and said, "Sonny Hoag, you're quite a man and quite a lover. "How did you like getting your pecker pecked?"

All Sonny could do was smile and say, "I need this type of therapy on a regular basis. I wish you lived in North Carolina. I'd be a regular customer."

At that, Ginger turned off the cameras, changed back into normal attire, then dressed and untied Sonny for his cab ride back to his hotel. As the taxi driver hoisted Sonny off the bed, Blabs purred as they departed past her cage. Sonny, in a drunken, satisfied and disoriented state, turned to Blabs with blurred eyes, and slurred in song "My, my my, I got what I need". Oh baby, that was the best BJ I ever had."

The driver stopped and looked at Blabs who said, "Bye, lover boy."

Sonny said, "Bye, Baby," and kissed the cage. The driver then turned back around and looked at Ginger, who simply shrugged her shoulders looking confused. The driver said, "Okay?" and dragged Sonny back to his hotel. As the driver assisted Sonny through the hotel lobby, Sonny kept scratching his stomach and groin, leaving a trail of husks and seeds that led all the way to his room.

The next day, Scratch called Ginger and asked if she was available for another meeting with Sonny. Ginger lied, responding that she was completely booked for the next three days due to a convention that was in town. Besides, she was out of birdseed. Sonny was disappointed but vowed that they would meet again, and took the next flight back to North Carolina, still trying to figure out how a bird feather ended up in his underwear. Scratch had never attempted to contact Ginger again, until now.

Ginger turned her head while the crack of a driver ignited the golf ball down the fairway. It took her a moment to place the face, but the actuators of her mental storage device quickly located the proper sector of her brain and realized that she had been hired by Scratch years earlier to perform some romantic investigative services. Suddenly, the name Sonny Hoag roared into her head like a freight train, causing her to slightly tremble from being too close to the tracks. More ingredients were added to the kettle as she remembered hearing Sonny's name on the TV on the same day that she had met Jeff in the bar. Obviously, she attempted to forget the names of these characters, but she never completely emptied the recycle bin, and these names floated in her mind until this current involuntary request occurred to resurface the past.

At that moment, Jeff turned to Scratch and said, "You're up."

Ginger knew that her past was bound to catch up to her during her marriage to Jeff, but she didn't think it would happen so quickly or with the sleaziest of clients. Scratch addressed his ball and hit a worm burner that didn't quite make 100 yards past the ladies tee, but fortunately for him, Jeff was cordial enough to indicate that kimono golf rules were not in effect.

(For those of you primarily male golfers who are not familiar with kimono golf, this was a tournament where, if you **don't** hit your ball at least 100 yards past the ladies tee, you must wear a kimono for the remainder of the hole. The kimono is typically a tight, Hawaiian themed skirt laden with exotic flowers that extends from your waistline to your ankles. Unfortunately, one size fits all. The skirt is very tight, restricting normal athletic movements, causing those wearing it to walk down the fairway in a Geisha girl like fashion. In addition, your golf stance is so narrow that it's almost impossible for you to hit any of your next shots further than 100 yards. Best of all, the other golfers on the course can see you a mile away, advertising your inability to hit your drive 100 yards past the ladies tee, and causing your fellow golfers to play in absolute glee. The only saving grace is, when walking down the fairway wearing your chic kimono, most likely in a drunken stupor, you can look across the fairway to see many other tournament players in similar apparel. Rest assured, though, that you don't look any fatter wearing the kimono, and it might actually accentuate your eyes, but no golfing buddy will ever tell you that, as they might be wearing a kimono on the next hole if they drink enough, and they, too, would be afraid of hearing any non-manly remarks.)

Scratch smiled after the hit, as he had worn the kimono before, and he knew his black golf shoes and gray golf shirt would not have flattered him wearing the kimono. His smile was weaved into his desire to chat with Ginger regarding her new role and find out how challenging her husband's presence would be concerning his boss's ambition to become president. Sonny Hoag had the clout, financial backing, southern charm, enough perceived governmental accomplishments, and media popularity to have a great shot at becoming president. He hired professionals like Scratch to improve his odds at becoming president. Maybe Sonny should have hired Longshot, but he didn't understand that the same psyche was needed to be successful in rolling craps or running for office. Sonny was arrogant enough to think he knew what was needed to succeed, and he hired people like Scratch to affirm his arrogance with law bending undercover intelligence.

After the foursome teed off and pleasantries had been exchanged, Scratch inconspicuously walked down the fairway with Ginger, as the other reporters initially targeted Jeff for their forty or so minutes of newsworthy questions. Scratch asked Ginger, "Who are you working for?"

"No one!" she replied. "I married the guy."

Scratch said, "For love? Come on, Ginger. I've seen you work. Someone's paying you for this charade. This guy isn't a contender for the Oval Office. What's going on? I saw you on TV, all of you literally, and heard about your nuptials to the newest of presidential candidates. Awesome PR. I had to come and find out for myself. I think someone is throwing Mr. Taylor into the election fire to shake up the outcome. Who is it?"

The veins in Ginger's neck bulged as she asked, "Who are you working for?" But she already knew the answer.

Scratch replied, "Baby, I work for no one, and I work for everyone."

Ginger tried to remain cool, but her voice didn't know it, and she exclaimed "Don't call me baby."

Two security personnel closed in on the pair and asked, "Is everything all right, Mrs. Taylor?"

Ginger said, "Keep an eye on his ball. We wouldn't want anyone to cheat." She quickly walked up to Jeff and stayed close to him for the next few holes.

Scratch mingled with the other reporters, and finally asked Jeff his one and only question. "What made you decide to enter the race now, Mr. Taylor?"

Jeff sensed Ginger's apprehension toward this reporter and simply responded, "Sir, remember, I'm not running for office." He responded sternly, but the other reporters took it as a joke, and laughed it off while they hit their shots.

Ginger was not her usual congenial self, as she was thinking what to do about Scratch. She did her best to entertain the media, but she already decided that she must let Jeff and Longshot know about today's meeting and her past events with Scratch and Congressman Hoag.

When the round concluded and they returned to the hotel, Ginger jumped on the computer while Jeff showered. She wanted to make sure that the "Sonnyblabs" video was saved, and she accessed the Omaha server with her user id and password. Once she was logged in, she did a keyword search on Sonny Hoag. In a matter of moments, three files appeared on the screen dated roughly four years earlier. She clicked on the first file, and voila, the video started the playback of her encounter with Sonny. She watched the three videos she had recorded from the three different cameras in her room and was relieved that each camera had clearly recorded the evening's activities from different angles. Best of all, she was not recognizable, but Sonny and Blabs sex duet were clearly identifiable from three distinct and pungent (or rather putrid) angles. Ginger thought, *This might be a good time to put Blabs in protective custody, and announce this non-eventful but potentially historical event to Jeff and Longshot. Poor Blabs, she might have to encounter a wrath of media exploitation.*

Earlier in the day, Jade suggested that the foursome meet at dinner to discuss their move from Las Vegas to Florida and cover any open issues. At 7:30 P.M., the group convened in the main suite for dinner. Jade presented them with the itinerary details over specialties such as Duck La Grange, prime rib and fresh seafood, exquisitely served in a less-than-ghost-like fashion by Helmsford and Sasha. The conversation swirled over jets, hotels, golf courses, media, and blah, blah, blah. After dessert was served and the servants departed, Ginger filled the group in regarding her current and past association with Scratch and Sonny. She also decided to divulge her interests in video and the Internet. Jeff's skeletal closet was quite empty, but Ginger's closet was large enough to seat an average Super Bowl crowd, forcing her to store her skeletons digitally.

Longshot grinned an evil grin after Ginger related her escapades, much to the surprise of the group. "Sonny thinks he has valuable information about his new political adversary. But, Ginger, well, you're the casino, and in the long run, the casino always wins."

Longshot removed his sunglasses and looked at Ginger. "Don't worry about this. "There's a good chance that your past will surface and become public knowledge. No offense, but your business involved you with people who might like to comment on their association with you now that you're a public figure. But my dear, you're holding a royal flush compared to Sonny's full house. Sonny has everything to lose, and you have everything to gain." What he didn't say was that Jeff and Ginger had no career, no future, and nothing to lose, but he wanted to be more eloquent and positive. The fact remained that Sonny still had everything to lose.

Longshot continued, "Jade, please develop a list of potential media questions regarding Ginger's profession, as they might be forthcoming. Then, work with Ginger to use your imaginations and develop loving, humorous, witty, yet honest responses for such questions, and rehearse the responses. If the media catches wind of her background, I want you to be verbally prepared to attack back with confidence. Ginger, arrange to have backup DVD copies made of the 'Sonnyblabs' video and have them shipped to my office tomorrow. Sonny's web goes beyond the Internet, and backup copies can certainly help protect our odds as this circus continues. Once it arrives and is viewed for accuracy, the original files should be deleted from the server."

Without any hesitation, Ginger jumped on the Internet and contacted her Omaha Internet Service Provider to copy the "Sonnyblabs" videos on one DVD and mail it overnight to Longshot's office address.

While Ginger was typing and accepting confirmation of her request, Jade mentally brainstormed questions and responses. *"This could be a long list: How long have you been a hooker? What's the largest size you've seen? Who else have you entertained? Will America accept you in the White House? Too many questions. Too many skeletons."*

To reduce the possibility of wire tapping, Scratch called Sonny's paging service from a public telephone and left the phone number. Sonny, with a roll of change, found a public phone and returned the call. As you would expect in the boardroom of a Fortune 500 company discussing a hostile takeover of a business on the brink of bankruptcy, they discussed Ginger's encounter with Sonny and her association with Jeff Taylor.

Scratch said, "I think it's too coincidental for Ginger to be involved with a presidential candidate. It makes no sense. Are they being paid to be independent candidates to possibly bash or damage you or the other candidates?"

But Sonny's ego loomed, and he saw no cause for alarm. "I'm not worried. A hooker, masquerading as a presidential candidates' wife, exceeds all the boundaries that are essential for a candidate to be considered a serious contender for running for president. Just keep close to the situation for now."

After he hung up the phone, Sonny pulled out and lit an illegal Cuban cigar, one of many he received from a General stationed in Guantanamo Bay in exchange for some political favors. He walked down the street, puffing away to the delight of his unknowing cancerous prone taste buds, contemplating Ginger's involvement. He knew it wasn't unusual to marry for votes. He himself had married a favorite daughter of North Carolina to project and protect his moralistic and down home public perception. Just prior to announcing his intentions to run for congress, Sonny was listed as one of the top five most eligible bachelors in the high society yet trashy *Bent Gent* magazine. After the article's release, he was deluged with offers from women around the world, chasing the chance to be the wife of a U.S. Congressman and bask in the high society life that accompanies such a blissful marital role.

Best of all, the women did not have to be in love with him. They simply needed to be in love with the title of "a congressman's wife." A marriage of this type was a fulfillment of both parties, husband and wife, to provide services that each could agree upon by saying "I do." Sonny looked for a spouse that could bring him credibility, campaign contributions, and hopefully some decent sex with her, or great sex without her. Sonny spent hours reviewing the resumes of potential email order brides. He dated several, often consummating the date, but not the relationship. Then came Ashley.

Ashley Woodall was an attractive North Carolina native whose family ran a successful chain of all-you-can-eat ribs restaurants called Swine Dine. Ashley was encouraged to follow in the family footsteps by working in the family business after graduating from one of North Carolina's finer universities with a degree in restaurant management and hospitality. Yet, her soul was not in food. She yearned to leverage her knowledge of hospitality but was more interested in catering to her own needs instead of those restaurant patrons who would eat their ribs from a trough and squeal with overweight delight at the cheap price and unlimited high fat portions. She spent over seven years acquiring her 4-year degree, researching restaurants from around the world between semesters. She convinced her dad that this research would only benefit her business savvy in years to come. Snow skiing in Colorado, Hawaiian surfing, attending bull fights in Madrid and Mexico City, and sampling beer in Munich's Oktoberfest were part of her research. She worked in the family business for several years after that, until she discovered Sonny's availability.

Their lust for something other than love made for a perfect match. Best of all, Ashley's dad, Buford, felt that his connections with a congressman could help his business and reputation as well. Thus far, his highly successful business of all-you-can-eat ribs was based on the notion that you were actually eating pork ribs, especially since the establishment's name was Swine Dine. Yet, nowhere on the menu did the words "pork," "pig," or "swine" actually appear. All a customer read was "$9.99 all-you-can-eat ribs." To be fair, the rib sauce was quite good. It had to be, to cover up the taste of whatever animal-de-jour was used for the cheap, never ending portions. Without anyone's attention and shortly after Buford opened several Swine Dines, the North Carolina Game and Wildlife Federation, and the North Carolina Humane Society both documented sharp declines of a variety of wild and tame (pet) animals. They surmised that global warming was making a significant impact on the reproduction and longevity of animals.

Buford's generous campaign donations, coupled with giving away the bride, resulted in not losing a daughter, but increasing restaurants on tax-free land typically geared for toxic waste dumps. If you build it, and the food's cheap, and you don't glow in the dark afterwards, they will come. And they did, providing a unique way to consummate a marriage without sex. Sonny was married to the Pearl of the South, although Ashley was affectionately known outside proper high society circles as the log hog. To circumvent her lack of funding to quench her thirst for traveling elegance and extravagance, her romances were frequent, easily extending vacations by latching on to the inside of a man's pants (or women's skirt when required with the assistance of plastic, battery operated log simulators). This skill, if known to Sonny, may have come in handy during his congressional campaign, but only a few hundred men and women knew of this open-vault secret.

Even without the use of Ashley's hidden talents, Sonny won the election. Interestingly enough, several of his major campaign platforms were to increase spending to research the impact of global warming and to provide funding to animal rights groups to research the sudden reduction of North Carolina wildlife to the point of threatened or endangered species. One of his most famous and election-tipping speeches harkened the state voters to such concerns while television crews captured his honoraria dining at a new, all-you-can-eat-something Swine Dine.

The following morning, waking rituals were taking place as usual. Helmsford and Sasha took care of the packing for Jeff and Ginger, making them available for makeovers by the hotel staff. Longshot was going to hook up with them in Florida after his next radio broadcast. Since this radio show was going to launch the polygraph campaign, he wanted to have the support of his staff – better known as Bob the sound engineer – available. Longshot knew that this next broadcast was going to add another batch of plutonium to this explosive election spectacle. Jade had already arranged to have his future shows aired at radio stations across the county, thus adding more publicity to the real-time project.

The foursome met for breakfast to discuss last minute plans. Johnson entered the room and mentioned that the hotel offered him a chance to join them on their honeymoon vacation. He said he'd accept the assignment if they agreed. Without any hesitation, all four said, "Absolutely." Not only did he offer a feeling of security and direction, but he also provided a fatherly figure to a team that shared the commonality of minimal parental guidance.

As they convened at the breakfast table, Bob called Longshot and told him that a priority package had just arrived from Omaha. Longshot asked him to bring it up to the suite ASAP. When he hung up, Ellen Spackler called and joined the team via speaker phone to discuss the endorsements. Her professional, legal-sounding voice said. "Jade, I've emailed you the new business opportunities, and it's all good news. All totaled, the endorsements exceed two million dollars, and more are streaming in, including some from some large Fortune 500 companies. Keep on doing whatever it is you're doing." The group didn't even touch their breakfast, as they were busy spending their minds on spending their cash. They decided to wait until they were settled in Florida to make any further commitments.

Jade unveiled a new business challenge while Ellen was still on the phone. "Ellen, I had a hard time finding your email this morning, because it was mixed in with about 3,000 other emails, mostly from people who are simply eager to have contact with Jeff and Ginger. Some of the emails are quite perverse, but I won't go into details. In addition, the hotel manager called me this morning indicating that we have boxes of mail waiting for us in the hotel mailroom. I don't have time go through all this mail. What really worries me is that we might miss good endorsement opportunities. I wondered if I can hire some of my college friends to filter the good opportunities and forward them to me and you. I also thought that they could respond to the sincere emails offering thanks for their encouragement and well wishes."

Ellen responded, "I have a vacant desk in my office, and one student can be hired for starters. Her salary will be claimed against our business activities. If there's too much mail, we'll hire more. Have one of your interested friends call me to get things going."

Jade made a note to make some calls later that day.

Helmsford announced Bob, and Sasha already had a chair and place setting arranged at the table. Bob sat down while everyone got up and rushed to the TV to watch the DVD. Jeff sensed an onslaught of embarrassment flow into Ginger and said, "Sorry folks, but only me and Ginger will watch the DVD for the time being. I'll see about letting you guys watch it later."

Both Longshot and Jade felt as though they were holding a winning lottery ticket, only to have the lottery commission wait a week before they could redeem their winnings. They did understand, and with sadness and crushed anticipation, went back to the breakfast table instead to watch Bob gobble up just about everything in sight. It was nauseating.

Jeff went into the bedroom, and Ginger followed, closing the door behind her. Jeff loaded the DVD into the player, clicked play, and sat in focused silence. Ginger moved to a corner of the room, not really eager to view the replay of a bad dream. She was not really noticeable in the movie. You couldn't even really see what she was wearing, although there was ample supply of PG-13 skin and leather. Blabs and Sonny, on the other hand, were clearly visible and audible. The DVD played all three camera clips in sequence. Each clip caught Sonny and Blabs' romantic encounter from a different gross angle, including the audio of bird and congressman singing "You can't always get what you want."

Jeff forwarded through the other two clips, turned the TV off, and removed the DVD. Although Ginger had made a cameo appearance, her identity was not revealed. She did, however, divulge a glimpse of her former occupation to her new husband, including her lip kiss to Sonny, which was difficult for Jeff to watch.

Before her swelling eyes released a tear, Jeff got up from his seat, walked over to Ginger, wrapped his arms around her, and said, "Man, that Sonny dude sure has a terrible voice, but Blabs sounded pretty good." He felt Ginger's body vibrate in laughter, and he started laughing next. "This video is no big deal. Heck, you're not even noticeable, but I'll destroy this video if you want me to. I don't care about your past. Besides, we're sitting on a pretty nice nest egg with these endorsements."

He released Ginger and continued. "And do you know what these endorsements bought us? A fat, juicy mulligan."

"A what?" she asked.

"A mulligan. In golf, when you're playing for fun with your friends, and you hit a really bad shot, you can call a mulligan, and take the shot over. These endorsements are giving us a mulligan with our lives. A do-over. We're starting from scratch with a load of cash. Let's forget the things we want to forget in our past, take the mulligan, and hit a new shot."

Ginger quietly thanked God for hooking her up with this decent golf nut. She looked at Jeff, smiled, and said, "How many mulligans can I take in this game?"

He smiled back and said, "Well, usually you set the rules before you play, but amateur golfers often take a mulligan on each side. You know, one mulligan on the front nine and one on the back. This means we have one more."

She sat down on the freshly made bed and said, "Let's hold on to the DVD as we might need it in the future. Let's have Jade lock it up someplace safe, along with our mulligan."

Jeff was elated and said, "My wife is using golf metaphors, and we've only been married a couple of days. This is almost as good as the money…almost." Ginger never thought she could please a man simply by using golf innuendos, and chuckled thinking how easy it was to make Jeff happy.

They came out of the room, and by the looks on their faces, Longshot, Jade and Bob thought that they consummated their marriage during the video. Now they really wanted to see it. Jeff pitched the DVD to Jade, and said, "This DVD contains explicit material and graphic images not suitable for younger audiences. Viewer discretion is advised. I know you guys are dying to watch this. Blabs could win an academy award, but Sonny?… well … he ruined the film."

The new wave of critics flew into the room and started the video. Bob came in carrying a third helping of food in fear that the breakfast buffet would disappear during his departure. Jade only lasted ten minutes into the video. She could not stomach the huge hairy stomach of Sonny in a sex video. Besides, the main member of Sonny's club needed some special effects or digital enhancements to warrant some excitability. She came out and approached Ginger saying, "You're right. Blabs is the only pretty thing in that video."

Longshot lasted another five minutes, developing the same conclusion. Bob, on the other hand, thought this was some of the best video he had seen in years, laughing hysterically throughout the raunchy bird feeding display. He kept yelling, "Peck the pecker, peck the pecker. Come on, little birdie, you can do it." His voice easily carried over into the next room, where the foursome was grossed out but with a hint of smile. They all secretly thought that if Blabs were replaced in the scene by a stunt double, they would be cheering as loud as Bob.

While Bob continued his love affair with the parrot porn, Ginger jumped online to access her hosting account and deleted the "SonnyBlabs" video file.

Jade desperately needed to erase Sonny's image from her mind, so when Ginger had finished deleting her file, she asked Ginger if she could check the traffic to their web site. "Oh my God. Our web site is getting over 50,000 hits a day. Everyone wants to find out more about our Vegas heart throb couple."

With that comment, Ginger blushed, Jeff simply shook his head, and Longshot smiled, as he could smell dollars and opportunity. Meanwhile, a huge crowd had gathered in the hotel lobby hoping to catch a glimpse of the new Charles and Di. Jade had contacted several key news groups, leaking that Jeff and Ginger were going to be in the hotel lobby around 10 to wish their Las Vegas friends farewell until their return. Last minute items were completed, as bags were packed and whisked downstairs to waiting limos. Uncommon thank you's, good-bye's, and hugs were transferred between guests and servants. Longshot asked Bob to take the DVD back to the studio and store it in the vault for safe keeping, and told him he'd see him down there in an hour to prepare for his next broadcast. Everyone said good-bye to their Las Vegas Suite at the Hard Rock, ready to begin the Florida tour.

With Johnson's security team in place, and camera lights eager to illuminate, Jeff and Ginger emerged from the middle elevator. They looked stunning. The crowd roared. Chants of "Jeff for President" and "Ginger, come fly with me" echoed around the casino. They stepped up to the podium with an array of mics set up by the hotel manager and news agencies. Jeff delivered a brief speech that he had rehearsed with Jade over breakfast. He did not need any assistance from Ginger, although she was ready to grab something just in case, following Jade and Longshot's suggestion.

"Good morning, friends. Ginger and I would like to thank you all for your warm reception and well wishes. As you know, we're headed off to Florida on our honeymoon. We're looking forward to our trip but would again like to thank you for getting our marriage started with such a bang. We'll see you when we get back. Good-bye for now." They stood on the podium for a few moments waving. The cameras focused on the couple, but they tended to keep Ginger a bit more centered and focused.

As they departed, the crowd again cheered. Johnson then put the security team in motion to safely remove the couple. They hopped into a waiting limo that quickly transported them to the county courthouse so they could register to vote, followed by a quick trip to the nearby airport. Within minutes, they boarded a Best Bet private jet and prepared for take off.

As they were entering the plane, Ginger heard some magic words, "Oh baby, that feels so good." There was Blabs, ready to fly, but without the use of her wings. Ginger turned around to Jade and said, "Thank you."

Jade just smiled and said, "We're all here. Let's go."

Seconds later, the door was shut, and they were schmoozed away in casual elegance to South Florida.

Two hours earlier, Scratch Delacantos angrily sat in row 14, seat A, a window seat on a commercial jet, preparing to take off from Las Vegas to Ft. Lauderdale. There were no first class seats available, and he was unaccustomed to narrow seats and the rubbing of shoulders with commoners. Although in a fowl mood, he could smell a pot of gold at the end of the hooker's rainbow, believing that Ginger was involved with Jeff Taylor for other motives or influences. He believed that uncovering and acquiring Ginger's place in this scheme of things would ultimately be worth a huge amount of money to somebody, possibly Sonny, a competitive politician running for office, a business entity, or Ginger herself.

Little did he know that sitting in seats B and C of row 14 were two FBI agents. They had been anonymously tipped off that a high-powered government official had ordered an assignation plot toward Jeff Taylor, and that a person by the name of Scratch Delacantos may be the mastermind of the potential assignation attempt. The two agents were dressed in Hawaiian shirts and golf pants, obviously disguised to do the tourist thing in Florida.

The four martinis Scratch slurped down prior to boarding put him to sleep before the plane taxied to the runway, omitting him from his traveling companion's enthusiastic discussion of golf and topless women on South Beach. Was this FBI conversation a decoy, or were they just being themselves? Only a person with top security clearance at the FBI knew for sure.

With their jet cruising comfortably at 34,000 feet, Jeff and Ginger relaxed in their flying golf cart, which also doubled as a country club. The flight attendants, Gloria and Lourdes, who were probably hand-picked Vegas show girls, were initially busy catering to their flying needs. The pilots, Woody and Walter, were professional flyers who enjoyed flying anywhere fast.

Jade and Johnson enjoyed the quiet time as well. Jade was busy playing with her new laptop, setting up calendars, schedules, and itineraries with the direction of Johnson. With the help of a satellite-based Internet connection, he downloaded maps of their hotels, along with planned golf outings and anticipated tourist trap visits. He was also on the phone with his Florida-based security team, making last minute preparations for their arrival.

Gloria and Lourdes had served many VIPs before, ranging from rock stars to high-rolling business executives. But Jeff and Ginger were the "newest" celebrities on the planet, and these barely twenty-one flight attendants were tingling, knowing they were some of the first to engage them on a quiet and personal basis. They did their best to be professional and not exploit the "private zone," but one small question led to another. Within an hour into the trip, they were having Bloody Marys with Jeff and Ginger. Their questions were not of *60 Minutes* or *Meet the Press* caliber but were more along the lines of tabloids. "How did you guys meet?" "Was it love at first sight?" "How's it feel to be married?" "Has Jeff got any single, unattached brothers or relatives?"

Over the past few days, Jeff and Ginger had been in the limelight, but they had had no real or personal time with anyone outside their own foursome. They actually enjoyed their conversations with the attendants. Jeff was especially glad to hear that both girls promised to vote for him. This was when the topics became more political. Gloria said, "These old guys that get elected don't have a clue what's going on in the real world. They're millionaires and blind to the real problems of the people. I know I'm only twenty-one (give or take a year), but based on what I see on the news, most people are making less money now that they did ten years ago. If I don't marry someone rich, where will I be in ten years?"

Gloria's comment hit Ginger quite hard. Ginger had been in a similar situation when she was twenty-one and hoped Gloria would not follow in her misguided footsteps.

Lourdes echoed the same concern, "My dad and my brother in Miami have great computer skills, but they both lost their jobs to a tech support group somewhere overseas. They're both working now, but for half their salary. My Dad hoped to retire in a few years, but now he can't afford it. Something has to change. Can you help?"

Jeff simply said, "I'll do my best," but his mind focused on her question; could he help? Jeff dazed off into deep thought. *I simply have no clue what to do to improve the country. Do these guys that get elected really know how to turn things around? What, if by some miracle or mistake, I get elected? I'm a golfer, not a politician. I've never even read the Constitution of the United States. I don't know the difference between Congressmen and Senators. I didn't even vote in the last two presidential elections, let alone local elections, as I didn't know what voting district I was in. How could I ever have let Longshot talk me into this ridiculous situation?* He secretly decided to play some free golf for a few weeks, bank any endorsement money he earned, and announce that he "REALLY" won't run for presidency, or won't accept it if he did win. He also decided to wait a few weeks before he telling Ginger or Longshot.

Ginger asked him if he was okay based on his quiet disposition. Jeff responded that the drinks had kicked in, and he was ready for an in-flight nap. Gloria and Lourdes spun into action. They helped him recline his chair, placed the fresh pillows in the optimum sleeping position, and covered him with a neatly pressed blanket. Ginger accompanied him on his sleep quest, and snuggled within the confines of the blanket. Jade fell asleep with the warmth of her laptop on her lap. Last of all, unusual sounds did not cause any panic regarding engine trouble. It was just the grumbling noise of Johnson snoring high in the sky.

Hole Number 6
Par 3

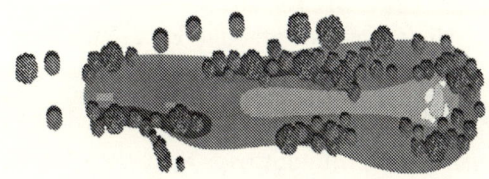

(**Coarse Notes:** Moon over Miami.
Don't get Hot, Hot, Hot or testy when you take the test of truth, unless you can't Beat it, Beat it. No one wants to be defeated, especially by a machine.)

The jet landed flawlessly into some gentle ocean breezes at a small executive airport in Miami. As soon as the door opened, a rush of humidity filled the cabin indicating a change from the desert to the tropics. Woody and Walter came out from the cockpit and welcomed them to South Florida, reminding them that they were at their flying disposal. Gloria and Lourdes assisted them with their carry-on items, including Blabs. Two large, secret service-looking SUVs zoomed up to the staircase, awaiting the party's jet departure and limo entry. When Blabs' cage was carried out and Blabs saw the SUVs, she started screaming, "Cheese it, the cops," and then "Officer, this guy's my cousin from Toledo." Ginger looked somewhat embarrassed. Woody and Walter were biting their tongues to not laugh. Gloria and Lourdes simply made a fuss over Blabs' talking ability. The new security team was stone faced but individually decided to laugh about the comments off-duty. Jeff simply instructed the personnel to put the bird in the car. To cover up Blabs ill-timed verbal humor, Jeff invited the flight crew to join them for dinner, which they graciously accepted.

The Hard Rock Hotel, located on the western edge of Ft. Lauderdale, was completely booked. They were hosting a new televised event called *Rock Wars*. New, up and coming bands competed for a chance to land a contract with a major record label and be the opening act for the RGoodBandMan international tour. Since all rooms were booked, the manager of the Hard Rock arranged for them to stay at The Beach House, a small and exclusive hotel on Miami's famous South Beach. Jose Rodriguez, the Beach House manager, personally escorted them to their suites. Their lavish rooms rivaled their Vegas counterpart. Their balcony had a private hot tub that overlooked the Atlantic Ocean. Ginger fell in love with the ambience of the tropics. The Spanish décor and water view screamed "chill out." She thought, *"Even Bob Marley could have become mellower here."*

Juan Cantour greeted them while they soaked in the salt breeze on the patio. His mission was to make their every dream come true while they were hotel guests. Ginger said, "Juan, we need some new South Beach casual attire, but we're tired from our trip. Where's a place close by to do some quick shopping?"

Juan smiled and said, "Senorita, shopping is what I live for. Best of all, my boyfriend, Palo, owns a cute casual clothing store just one block away. I'll call him to let him know you're coming."

Jade joined them on the patio and reminded them that the flight crew was joining them for dinner. Ginger said, "Jade, tell the flight crew to meet us in the lobby. We're all going shopping. It's warm and beautiful and laid back, and we don't want to ruin this atmosphere with formal clothes. Tonight, let's just chill out on South Beach." Everyone, except Jeff and Johnson, went to Palo's boutique. Johnson stayed at the hotel with Jeff, as he also felt that shopping was as much fun as passing a kidney stone.

While the others shopped, Jeff called his golfing buddy to confirm their next golf outing. Don Mastroe, an old friend of Jeff's, was quite successful offering personal golf lessons at exclusive country clubs in Miami. He arranged for Jeff to play at the famed Blue Monster at Doral. In exchange, Jeff invited him and his girlfriend over for dinner that evening.

The shopping team returned to the hotel with a strong second wind, feeling splashy in their new Brazil inspired duds. Ginger handed Jeff and Johnson their new clothes and made them change immediately. Johnson came out moments later with an unusual smile. He looked at Ginger and said, "I actually like this," as he strutted around like a dashing caballero. Jeff emerged in a lost sort of way. His body was not accustomed to anything far beyond a golf shirt and slacks. Yet everyone applauded his outfit that seemed to merge Argentinean cowboy with Mexican bull fighter. Jeff thought it was weird but wore it anyway and said, "Ginger, olé olé, mucho sexy. Now let's eat."

Don Mastroe and his girlfriend arrived along with the succulent order of stone crabs. After dinner, Gloria and Lourdes changed into their new bathing suits and entered the hot tub, which was cooler than normal to accommodate any hot guests. Music filled the patio from the South Beach street below. Latin, disco, Salsa, and progressive rock were heard from different angles of the wind. Gloria climbed out of the tub to dance solo. Everyone discovered that her suit was made of a remarkable material that became invisible when wet. Woody and

Walter instantly joined her on the dance floor, followed by Lourdes. Lourdes' suit did not disappear, but her natural beauty almost overshadowed Gloria's bare existence. For the first time of their professional careers, Woody and Walter were considering their divorce options if they veered off of the flight plan and engaged in marriage-ending spontaneity. Everyone else simply accepted the moment and enjoyed the tropical evening.

Blabs enjoyed being around a noisy crowd in the tropics, allowing her to talk, sing, and screech with cheers from the intoxicated audience. Her rendition of "I am 16 going on 17" from *The Sound of Music* drew great reviews, and requests started flowing from the easily amused group. Juan was truly impressed by the bird's vocal abilities and attempted to teach her Cu-curru-cucu Paloma, a beautiful Spanish ballad about a parrot, but Blabs seemed to favor classic movie soundtracks and early 80s rock and roll. Miami's Parrot Jungle Park would pay top dollar for a guest appearance if they only knew.

At around 10:30, when yawns started to exceed laughter, Johnson assumed the fatherly role and said it was time to call it a night. He personally escorted everyone to their next destination. He did his best to protect the pilots' wedding vows and the flight attendants' flare for adventure, but once he directed them into their rooms, ground control could not see them on radar, so they had to rely on their own instrumentation. Jeff's golf buddy, Don, and his girlfriend accepted a limo ride back to their apartment in Coral Gables to avoid illegal driving confrontation.

Juan Cantour moved like a soothing ocean breeze in his efforts to tidy up the room and prepare his guests for slumber. He took extreme pride in his position, making his guests feel like royalty, while protecting their privacy. His sense of pride empowered him to never be bribed or disclose any guest information to anyone, except maybe Palo. The *National Enquisitive* weekly tabloid offered him thousands of dollars over the years for any pathetic gossip about his newsworthy guests, but he always refused.

However, several of his staff members, eager to seize monetary gains, had just received advance payment for daily updates regarding the honeymoon couple. Scratch paid them in cash and simply expected timely phone calls with any pertinent and hopefully meaningful information. The FBI agents had taken digital pictures of the transaction. Jack Sciani had a room at the Beach House, and Tyron Hills had a room adjoining Scratch's at the Miami Beach Trade

Winds Hotel located next door. Several surveillance cameras, room mics, and phone taps were set up in Scratch's room. Scratch was typically used to doing the wire tapping and was usually very cognizant of such activities. But, since he was acting on his own with no connections to anyone regarding his quest for information, he let his guard down considerably. Maybe the inappropriate mini umbrellas in his four poolside Bahama Mamas that afternoon minimized his attention to detail.

After everyone left the party, Scratch's undercover consulting staff called him. Except for a detailed description of Gloria's birthday suit convergence on the hot tub, the remainder of the phone call was of little use. The complete conversation was recorded by the FBI.

At 10:55 that night, Jade called Jeff's room to remind him that Longshot was going to announce the polygraph test on his show that night. They invited Jade to come in and listen.

Earlier that day, Longshot was busy preparing for his radio broadcast. Prior to Jade's departure, they had outlined his speech and issued a press release to the news media that this show would have strong implications regarding Jeff Taylor's official decision to not run for office and might therefore be of interest to an audience beyond his typical gamers. Longshot's weekly sponsors were foaming at the mouth at the thought of an audience that could exceed five million, and it wouldn't cost them an extra cent.

Longshot called the Hard Rock Casino manager to find out how his bet was going and found out that just over 4,000 bets had been made for a total of $380,000, with a slight majority voting for Jeff to win. Longshot figured that Jeff's comment regarding his decision not to run may have started to swing the scales. His next broadcast should really get bets flowing once again.

At exactly 8 P.M. that evening (Pacific listening time), Kenny Rodgers' song, "The Gambler" began to play as usual. At 10 seconds after 8, "Welcome to Up Your Odds" was announced by Longshot, who used his professional radio voice. Unknown to his listeners, Longshot was broadcasting in his white boxer underwear for good luck. He was still wearing his cowboy boots and hat, along with his designer frame sunglasses. On cue, Bob started playing "When Johnny Comes Marching Home Again," offering a patriotic theme to add inspiration to Longshot's broadcast.

"We, the gamers and citizens of these United States, have built our proud country based on solid principles. Our magnificent Constitution is a perfectly drafted document that our forefathers created based on honesty, integrity, and high moral standards for our young nation. I would, however, bet the farm, that none of those who signed that document just over two hundred years ago could ever imagine the amount of unpatriotic disloyalty that has seeped into our country. Politics masks dishonesty. Government embraces inefficiency. Influential leaders are shadowed by greed and deception. Money is the driving force behind our politicians, not We the People. Our country is great, but just think where it would be if We the People were honestly placed first before the egos and bank accounts of our leaders. As many of you know, I challenged you with a bet to give you back the White House. I challenged you to Vote for Honesty. I bet that Jeff Taylor would win our next presidential election, and I made this bet to wake up our lethargic voters and proclaim that honesty and politics should be inseparable, unbreakable, and unstoppable. We have become so accustomed to deception in politics, we all consider it the norm. That is wrong, and it's time to right this wrong." Bob raised the volume of the music for several seconds as Longshot wiped the sweat from his brow.

Longshot continued as the music partially faded, embellishing his first conversation with Jeff at the bar. "It's time for us to bring the Constitution back into the center of politics. It's time to replace our current methods of politics with trust. But how can this be done? When I first met Jeff Taylor, we were watching a news broadcast regarding our current selection of presidential candidates. I asked him who he would vote for, and he said none of them. He said, 'I don't trust any of them, and if I can't trust 'em, I can't vote for 'em.' Jeff then went on to say, 'I wish they'd at least hook them up to a polygraph to determine if they can be trusted. They aren't saints. We know this. But, they should at least admit it when they mess up and not cover it up. I may not agree 100% with their past or current actions, but if they at least attempt to be honest, well, that's the guy I'd vote for. If they are hiding their past, just think what they'll hide when the get into office.'

"These inspiring words of Jeff Taylor ignited me to place my bet to Americans, with the hope of waking us up and taking a chance to make our country as great as it should be, for us, and to the eyes of all nations. With this in mind, I challenge all presidential candidates to a polygraph test within the next ninety days. Jeff Taylor has agreed to take the test. As you know, he's not 'officially' running for office, but he would accept the position if you write him on the ballot. Now, what other candidates are willing to participate in this polygraph test? To all you presidential hopefuls, are you willing to tee it up? Are you ready to accept the Honest Scorecard?"

Longshot paused for a moment and said, "To our American listeners, we'd like to have you participate in this unprecedented campaign to elect our next president. What questions would you like to have honestly answered by our candidates? We'll discuss how you can submit questions for the polygraph after this quick break." Bob immediately started playing, "I'm proud to be an American…" bringing a country yet patriotic theme into the break.

When Longshot went off the air, he quickly reached over for a Jack and water. Bob noticed that his hands were trembling, and asked if he was okay. Longshot replied, "I think something is going to explode, but I don't know what." He slammed down his drink and said, "I'm ready to go."

After a short commercial, Bob continued with the music and slowly faded into a soft orchestral version of "I'm a Yankee Doodle Dandy," and Longshot, with an excited nervousness, went back on the air. "We're back, and the discussion of 'What questions would I ask a future president' is our next topic. If you had to ask any presidential candidate a question regarding their honesty, their background, their ability to run the country, and you wanted an honest answer, what would you ask? We're giving you that chance. On Jeff Taylor's Vote for Honesty web site, click on the Honest Scorecard link. Here, you can submit your questions, but there's a catch. It will cost you $5 to submit each question. Ten charities have elected to participate in this event. After you pay to submit your presidential candidate question, you can choose which charity is to receive your donation. That's right, 100% of your donations will go to the charity of your choice. You can help your country in two ways: by submitting your questions and by donating to your favorite charity.

"Our goal here is to generate quality questions that will be used for the polygraph test. What would you like to know about Jeff Taylor and the other candidates? I challenge all patriots to go to the Honest Scorecard and submit your questions. After the next break, we'll open the phone lines to answer any of your questions. So stay tuned."

Bob brought back "I'm Proud to Be an American" and cranked the volume dial. Longshot took a deep breath and his cell phone vibrated. He recognized the number and said, "Hi, Jade. How'd it sound?"

"Well." she said, "Jeff and Ginger are having triple everything in the bar, no ice."

"Perfect. That means it sounded great. Have you designed possible media questions and answers for Ginger regarding her prior work experience?"

"Yes, but I haven't covered them with her yet, and now's not the time. Let's give them a day or two here to mellow out, unless the press starts going nuts. I don't think anything major will happen for a few days."

Meanwhile, the telephone switchboard was lit up like the Vegas Strip at night. Longshot spent the next forty minutes of radio airtime on the phone with callers. What was surprising was that he didn't get many questions about the Honest Scorecard. His calls consisted mostly of people who loved the idea of asking political questions to candidates, and, with the aid of the polygraph, improved the chance to receive an honest answer in return.

When the show concluded and Longshot signed off, he melted back into his chair while Bob said, "Dude, get ready for World War 5."

(**Course Notes:** Unfortunately, most Americans are apathetic when it comes to politics, yet, they are quick to complain about "those" politicians that "other" people vote into office. Giving these lethargic voters the opportunity to ask specific and personal questions online let them think they were proactive in the election process. Even if their question was not used in the polygraph test, and whether or not they voted, they could pat themselves on the back for engaging in some aspect of the election process. It only cost five bucks to submit a question, they could do it at home or on company time, it took just a few minutes, the money went to charity, and the question they submitted, no matter how good or ridiculous it was, allowed them to release some pent up frustration, because subconsciously, they knew they were lousy, lazy citizens.

Jeff could be considered the psychiatric savior, helping to release non-voting guilt to those inflicted masses. These masses enjoyed their renewed feeling of patriotism, and like an addictive drug, wanted more. They wanted to meet the next president who wasn't running for office and his first lady.)

The $300 aristocratic pillows and space age mattress, cradled Sonny into a dream state that few common, blue collar voters could only begin to imagine...

I, Summerton James Hoag, solemnly swear that I will faithfully execute the Office of President of the United States, and will to the best of my ability preserve, protect, and grow my personal financial assets while in office and... Ring, ring, *Dag nabit, would someone answer that phone, I'm busy becoming supreme earthly god of the world... ring, ring...*

Sonny Hoag was rudely awakened just after midnight and picked up the phone. "Who the hell is this? I'm in the middle of a perfect dream. This better be a Gag dam emergency. Who is this?"

"Congressman, this is Blake Silver, your campaign manager."

"Well, what the hell do you want? Do you know what time it is?"

Blake said, "Sonny, wake up and listen. Jeff Taylor has just challenged all presidential candidates to a polygraph test. The press is already calling me to see if and when you will participate. The press loves this idea. In fact, some reporters are suggesting that everyone in the government should be tested."

Sonny groggily asked, "A lie detector test? What kind of questions?"

"Taylor set up a web site where voters can submit virtually any question they want regarding anything for each presidential candidate. The questions will be compiled and provided to the news media. The most requested questions will form the basis of the test. They are going to charge $5 for each question, with 100% of the proceeds going to charities."

While Blake was speaking, Sonny was thinking, *That's a great idea. I wish I could pull off something like this...*

"Sonny, we're kind of screwed. If you don't participate, it clearly demonstrates to the public that you have something to hide. If you participate, you may be asked questions that could jeopardize your personal life and professional career. What do you want to do? My phone is ringing off the hook from the press asking for a response to this challenge."

Sonny said, "I don't have an answer right now. For the moment, just tell them you have not yet conferred with me on this matter, and we'll respond soon. In the meantime, I'm going to make some calls and see if we can squash this entire affair. I'll call you tomorrow morning."

Sonny hung up the phone in disgust. His wife was sleeping in her own bedroom and was not therefore disturbed by the call or his situation, at least for the moment. Sonny called a few of his staff members and other political colleagues, but they were of no use, especially since they were afraid of their situation if approached to take the polygraph test. The more he thought about the test, the madder he became. Unless he could beat the test somehow, one or two questions could bury him alive. He decided that a call to Scratch had to be made.

At 8:30 A.M., (5:30 A.M. by previous Las Vegas time) Jeff and Ginger were abruptly awakened, but not by the already accustomed warm sounds of the Vegas suite. It sounded more like the crowd cheering the winning contestant at the weekly hot bod contest at Swashbucklers tropical bar in Ft. Lauderdale. A tapping on the door could barely be heard above the noise, but Ginger covered up and Jeff moaned, "Come in."

Juan peeked in and apologized for his disturbance, but he thought Jeff and Ginger should be aware of the situation. Just then, Jade's head appeared above Juan's, followed by Johnson's head positioning himself on top as the cherry to complete the 3-J dessert.

Jeff said, "What's going on"?

Johnson exclaimed, "I thought your adoring fans in Vegas were bad, but we're hitting new surf here. It looks like the entire city of Miami and much of Ft. Lauderdale and West Palm are anxious to greet the honeymooners, at 8 friggin' 30 in the morning."

Jeff simply nodded and asked them to leave while they dressed.

Juan took the liberty to lay out several outfits for them, prepared in advance with Palo's help. Jeff and Ginger both opted for designer shorts and t-shirts and then gently flirted with the window curtains without major material ruffles to view out to the abyss.

There were as many people out there as there were grains of sand on the beach. It made Woodstock look like a bingo party in a church hall in Bangor, Maine. Thousands of people were on the beach screaming for Jeff and Ginger in a variety of languages. In addition, hundreds of boats were anchored just off shore. Telephoto cameras were focused and ready to snap any picture of Ginger, hopefully doing anything indecent. Because the beach no longer had foot traffic access, thanks to the Miami-Dade Police, well wishers also showed up via water but with less flamboyant yet buoyant means: beach rafts, inner tubes, noodles, canoes, row boats, and virtually anything else that floated.

Jeff and Ginger stepped away from the curtain and took three paces back with the precision of an Olympic ice dancing pair. They looked at each other wanting to comment on the masses, but words wouldn't come out. They sat down on the edge of the bed with a new and improved blank expression beyond the look of death itself. No words.

Gentle door taps broke the loud silence. Jeff arose and opened the door. Their totem-pole heads were still in their hierarchical place. Jeff asked if there was any coffee, and Juan pounced into action, quickly delivering a pre-breakfast assortment of everything. Ginger and Jade looked at each other, hoping someone had a plan, but, as had been the case for the past week, a new sense of shock and awe was discovered. Ginger looked at Jeff and said, "What are we going to do? These people want to see us. Did everyone in the world listen to that radio show last night?"

Johnson handed them the cover of the local newspaper; the headlines read: "The Honest Scorecard challenges candidates to Polygraph." Johnson also said that portions of Longshot's radio show were airing on the national TV and radio.

Ginger turned back to Jade and said, "Should we call Longshot and ask him for advice?"

Johnson was more used to this type of situation than his indirect employers and offered his own advice. "Why don't we sit down and have a nice cup of coffee, some fresh squeezed Florida orange juice and warm Cuban bread, discuss our options, and see where that takes us?"

Everyone agreed, as no one had a better plan. Juan's suggestion of Cuban coffee helped them to wake up in warp speed. Then Jade had an inspirational idea.

"Juan," she said, "Do you know how we can get 10,000 bottles of cold water to the crowd outside immediately?"

"Si, my cousin Julio works for a food distributor who can accommodate your request."

Jade replied, "But 10,000 or more cold bottles of water within a few hours? We'll pay for it."

Juan exclaimed, "Si, of course. No problemo. They are a business, not FEMA."

She said, "Take care of it right now. Also, if they can include any breakfast rolls or donuts, include them. Last of all, if they do it for free, they'll receive special mention when Jeff and Ginger address the crowd at 11 A.M. Plus, your cousin and his company's owner can have dinner with us tonight."

"Si, si, consider it done." Juan jumped on the phone and spoke lightning speed Spanish.

Then Jade turned to Jeff and Ginger. "Guys, I don't know if you ever read the Bible, but do you remember the story about Jesus feeding over 5,000 people with a just a few pieces of fish and bread?" They nodded yes but knew a miracle was involved with that story and wondered where she was going. "These people have come here to see you, and soon, they are going to get thirsty and, even worse, dehydrated. Why don't we get someone to deliver water to your fans? While that's going on, we'll set up a PA system from your balcony here and just have you say thanks for greeting you. Something real simple."

Johnson jumped in, "Maybe we can do it from the roof so they don't know which room they're staying in. That would make me feel more comfortable."

"Good idea. We'll give drinks to the crowd, and we don't need a miracle, just money and the right connections. I'm afraid that if we don't address them, they'll be here forever, or worse, they'll start dropping like flies from the heat. I'll write a quick speech, and then contact the police to try to disassemble the crowd after the speech."

Jeff said, "It's a good idea, let's do it."

Juan hung up the phone and said, "The first truck will be here in fifteen minutes, and more trucks will arrive every fifteen minutes for the next two hours. My cousin Julio, and the owner, Senor Edwardo Urbina and his wife will join us for dinner sometime after 8 P.M. The drinks are complementary. He is a big fan of yours."

"Perfect," said Jade. "Juan, can you arrange to have a sound system set up on the roof so Jeff can say a few words to the crowd?"

"The roof? Sure, why not." Juan again jumped on the phone.

Jade continued. "I'll write a short speech for you. Quick and easy, similar to your words at the hotel lobby yesterday. Okay? Let's get moving."

At that moment, a call came to Juan's personal phone. Juan turned to Jade and said, "Several boxes labeled 'TaylorMade' are being delivered to your room as we speak."

Jade realized that Jeff, based on his endorsement commitment, was required to wear TaylorMade logo golf attire on the golf course, and these must be some shirts for Jeff. Juan opened the door, and the merchandise was delivered by some of his hotel colleagues.

Jeff opened the boxes like a little boy on Christmas morning. He looked up into the sky and quietly said thanks, and then looked at everyone and said, "Who'd like a shirt?" Since TaylorMade was the first contracted sponsor, the moment seemed extra special. Jeff felt like a legitimate golf pro. Everyone, including Juan and the two delivery boys, picked out a shirt. One box was particularly heavy. Jeff opened it last. It was filled with golf balls, golf hats and visors, and other golf related goodies. While Ginger modeled visors, Jeff sat on the floor, amazed that he would be paid to wear such professional, typically non-Jeff clothing.

Jade brought them back to reality with a clap of her hands. "People, people, we must get a move on. Jeff, I need you in the presidential zone now. Please get ready for our chat with Miami. Oh yeah, don't forget that you're playing golf today at two."

The room emptied, including Ginger, who retreated to the bathroom. Jeff wasn't sure if he enjoyed all this action. On one hand, he loved the luxury, the presents, the golf, the money, and even the new found popularity. On the other hand, he wasn't used to being on such a rigid schedule. Just over a week ago, his only schedule was waking up, going to work, and playing golf. He was never quite successful at the wake up and work routine, but he earned an A for making starting times. Now, he had a press secretary arranging his time minute by minute. Funny thing was, he wasn't nervous about talking to his fans. In fact, he actually looked forward to it.

Just then, a familiar setting occurred. He fumbled with the dial of his in-room stereo and discovered some cool South American Jazz playing just loud enough to drown out the crowd but soft enough to hear the gentle sound of water filling a large roman sized tub. He turned around and saw the shadow of Ginger's clothing falling to the floor. He adjusted the dial of the stereo and walked into the bathroom. Ginger's body was already concealed by the bubbles. She saw a horny and devilish look in his eye, and decided to complicate the matter by standing up asking "Would you like to pop my bubbles Mr. President?" A layer of bubbles refused to depart from her body, increasing Jeff's desire to physically remove them. He entered the tub, clothes and all, and began his temporary assignment as bubble removal engineer. The job suited him perfectly.

The first Havana Dreamer company truck amazingly sped into the hotel delivery area within twelve minutes of Juan's phone call. It was filled with over 1,200 cold bottles of water. Right behind that truck was a van filled with seven Havana Dreamer employees and handcarts. They loaded the water down from the truck, sliced their way through a police barricade into the crowd, and started passing out the water, saying, "Compliments of Havana Dreamer and Senor Jeff Taylor." Within forty minutes, five more trucks appeared, along with several more cars of employees. Within the hour, over 11,000 cold bottles of water were dispersed along with a variety of packaged snacks.

During this time, Jade employed the assistance of the hotel's business service center. They created a quick but professional flyer announcing that Jeff and Ginger would make some short comments to the crowd around 11 A.M. and that they should remain calm and follow any advice given by the Miami Police officers. It also requested that these flyers, bottled water, and food packages be placed in trash receptacles when not in use. Jade thought, "I must have had too much Cuban coffee to be so police friendly and environmentally aware." Several hotel copiers spit out several thousand messages, and every available hotel member was commandeered to assist passing them out. She also created a separate flyer that was handed to the police captain, suggesting that he direct his patrols to disperse the crowd after the brief announcement.

The hotel's audio-visual team set up the sound system on the roof. They weren't sure if they had a system loud enough for an outdoor venue of this size, but they did the best they could with what they had. They connected a CD player to test the system, and decided to play some music until the crowned prince and princess arrived. As usual, an argument broke out regarding the choice of music. Again, as usual, the only CD they could unanimously agree on was the Greatest Hits of KC and the Sunshine Band. When they turned on the amps and cranked the volume, the AV team was quite certain that new speakers would have to be purchased to replace the soon-to-be blown out speakers. While the flyers were being passed out, KC emerged from the speakers. As luck would have it, an unfamiliar breeze was blowing in from the Northwest, helping to push the music into the crowd. A cheerful roar emerged as though KC himself entered from stage right to sing "Shake your Booty." This beach crowd was ready to party, and it was only 10:30 in the morning.

Meanwhile, General Jade was directing orders in the middle of battle. Juan was field commissioned as second lieutenant, controlled and ordered by Jade to assist in anything and everything. Johnson was busy positioning hotel security for this fifteen-minute event. Hotel personnel were Jade's foot soldiers, dealing with the overwhelming crowd head on.

With the battle plans in place, and troops strategically positioned and waiting for the attack sign from the general...

...Jeff and Ginger were taking a sultry bubble bath.

It was warm, bubbly, and seductive enough to stay in for the rest of the morning. Of course, the red phone alongside the tub rang like a call from the Pentagon. It was Jade, asking if they were ready to join the morning war. Jeff said "Jade, you'll have to hold down the fort for another forty-five minutes, as we aren't quite ready for battle."

Jade calmly screamed, "It's a zoo out here! Please suit up as quickly as possible. After your meeting with South Beach, we have a news media golf outing to prepare for. I need you guys out of the tub."

Jeff teasingly replied, "All right Jade, chill out, we'll be out as soon as all the bubbles pop," and he hung up the phone.

For the first time in days, Jeff and Ginger took care of themselves. Jeff appreciated the Vegas ghost staff, but he quietly enjoyed his dressing privacy. Ginger was already spoiled. She missed Sasha's dressing assistance, but she had to bite the bullet and take care of own dressing mission. Palo's choice of clothes had them both looking very South Beach in beach colors, flowing lines, and hip sunglasses. Jeff was ready in twenty minutes, giving him some spare time to watch Just Fore Golf and ESPN. During a commercial, he peered out into the crowd and thought, *It was not a miracle that food and water for 12,000 was distributed within a few hours, or that music, flyers and organized control of a potentially frantic situation had occurred. But, Ginger being able to dress and groom herself within forty-five minutes..., now that's a miracle.* Just then, Ginger entered the parlor wearing Palo's morning glory outfit. It was tastefully revealing. Jeff loved it and said "I'm not so sure that's something a First Lady would wear, but then again, maybe that's exactly what a First Lady should wear. I just don't know if I'll be able to keep my hands off of you."

Before they called Jade to announce their availability, he held Ginger's hands and said, "We're going into a big crowd today. How do you feel?"

She looked confused and said, "Fine, why? Are you okay?"

"Yes, but… I'd like you to say a few words today."

"Like what?" she asked in a weird way.

"Well, maybe you can just thank everyone for being so kind and considerate or something like that. I thought, if we do these press conferences together, it would help me out. Plus, most of these people are very interested in hearing from you."

She paused and said, "You might have to grab me between my legs to help me out as a reciprocal action."

Jeff grinned and said, "Why wait till then?" and made a move to practice the reciprocity, when the door flew open and Jade marched in.

"Guys, don't you…" She noticed that she had caught them in some act of marital bonding and said, "Didn't you already take a bath and do your morning honeymoon business?" She was slightly laughing while Jeff and Ginger stood there like a teenage couple getting caught making out in their parent's house. "Come on" Jade said. "You just have to be cute and say hi to a few thousand screaming, nearly naked people. Then we can go play some golf. Here's a quick speech, or use your own words."

Jeff took a quick look at the cue cards and figured he'd just wing it without the notes. What he didn't realize was that this was the first time he was going to speak in front of a group, a huge group, and he didn't need or want a drink. Sure, it was only 11 A.M., but the thought never crossed his mind.

Just then, Johnson showed up and said, "Are we ready"?

Jeff said, "Let's go to the beach bash."

Johnson jumped on his radio. "Get ready, team, the eagle and the birdie are on the move."

Jeff smiled at the golf jargon. Johnson smiled, knowing Jeff enjoyed his humor. The girls were already discussing shopping, and missed the comment like it was an errant tee shot. Juan also joined them in case they needed something last minute.

"That's the way, uh ha, uh ha, I like it uh ha uh ha..." KC was blaring over the mildly distorted speakers as Juan escorted the entourage to the roof. "Holy shit" was sung in unison as they peered over the edge of the building without being noticed by the crowd.

"Man," Jeff uttered, "this is unreal. Don't these people have anything better to do than come out to beach and see some golf dude with his wife?" Everyone started laughing, because Jeff was absolutely correct. "I could take a crap over the side of the building, and probably get a standing ovation. No wonder so many fools make it into office. I haven't done anything to deserve this except be on TV. Truly amazing."

Jade said, "Welcome to celebrity-ism. Are you ready to go?"

Jeff said, "Let's do it." While KC was still shake, shake, shaking, Jeff grabbed Ginger's hand and they sort of danced up to the microphone. The crowd exploded. They continued to shake while one of the AV guys tapped the mic to make sure it was on, and then he dissolved out of the way. As soon as the song ended, Jeff yelled out, "Helloooo Miami! I'm Jeff Taylor."

The crowd screamed. Jeff felt like a rock star and embraced the rock star rush. Jeff and Ginger simply stood there and waved for what seemed like an eternity, yet the crowd roared like Chicago Cubs fans winning the World Series.

"You guys are just great." He paused for a moment, caught his breath and continued. "Ginger and I would like to thank you all for coming out to see us. Did every one get enough to drink?"

An appreciative audio tremor floated up from the half naked voices below. "I'd like to thank Havana Dreamer for making sure you all don't shrivel up on us."

Jade caught Ginger's eye, and they both realized that Jeff's speech was rather lame so far. Ginger nudged Jeff to the side to his surprise, and stood in front the mic. "Hi everyone, I'm Jeff's new bride, Ginger Taylor." A mostly male howl radiated upward. "My new friends Juan and Palo helped me pick out this outfit at Palo's boutique located just down the street. What do you think?" She curtseyed around as the howl turned into a volcanic eruption. Ginger turned around to face Juan, whose eyes were swelling just to be mentioned. She threw him a kiss and turned back to the mic. "I'd like to thank everyone for your warm reception also. You make us feel at home. Unfortunately, we don't have much time here, because poor Jeff has to go play golf." A wave of laughter rippled.

"Before we go, keep in mind that Jeff is not running for president, although he would accept the job if you write his name on the ballot. Just remember, no matter whom you vote for, vote for honesty. Thank you again everyone." She held up her pointer finger and shouted the slang for peace. "ONE!" Jeff followed his bride's example, and soon their following also raised their arms in the air, holding their index fingers toward the sky and cheering.

The AV team took the cue and started playing KC's "Get Down Tonight" which was ideal mood music, even though it was only 11:30 A.M. Jeff and Ginger waved for a few minutes and then departed. The crowd was well behaved, and the police were slowly able to disperse the majority of the people off the beach and streets.

As soon as everyone entered the stairwell, Jeff looked at Ginger and said, "Thanks, I can't do this alone."

Ginger replied, "And you won't while I'm around," and gave him a kiss. The other team members smiled as they headed downstairs, except Juan. He overheard them and started crying like a baby.

The rest of the day and evening were filled with far less intensity. Jeff played golf with the media while Ginger provided fun teasing and seductive support to the golfers. The press asked him about the upcoming session with the lie detector. "It's really no big deal. Whether I answer your specific questions now, or do it hooked up to a machine won't change my answers."

Ginger was very cognizant of the media and could read them better than a pro golfer reading a green on his home course. As soon as a reporter started a conversation down the path of politics, she'd say something during the reporter's backswing and change the focus onto her or golf, thus giving Jeff breathing room.

The golf course was playing nasty to the reporters, but Jeff stroked his new clubs as though he had hit them for years. He quieted the course like a lion tamer, easily beating the combined score of the media. Jeff's golf buddy, Don, joined Jeff throughout the round, fine-tuning his swing. While they walked down the fairway, Don mentioned to Jeff how impressed he was with his game but was more surprised with his poise and confident responses to the media regarding politics.

Jeff replied, "Whether playing golf or running for office, I have nothing to hide and nothing to lose. I just try to be myself. We'll see how this mess turns out. If I get elected, would you like to be special international golf liaison?"

Don laughed and said, "Is there really such a position?"

"There will be if I'm elected. I envision golf being the bridge of peace between countries."

Don smirked at his response, and Jeff himself was just kidding. Yet, Jeff didn't know that the press was acutely aware of his comments to Don, and they ate it up. The six o'clock news rerouted his words, "Jeff Taylor plans to use sports, not war, as his weapon to bridge peace between nations." Most viewers felt war should be used as a last resort to peace. Maybe playing games to resolve conflicts wasn't such a bad idea, and with that, Jeff's popularity grew.

The climatic and exhaustive day ended with Jeff and Ginger retiring to their suite. They briefly discussed the next few days of their trip. Ginger said, "Jeff, we don't have anything planned tomorrow, and according to the local weather, we're getting some rain."

Jeff said, "Okay? Where's this going?"

Ginger, speaking like a shy schoolgirl said, "We haven't really had any time together since we were married. Why don't we sneak out of the hotel, rent a car, and go down to Key West for a few days. We'll wear silly hats and sunglasses, and pretend to be who we really are, nobodies."

Jeff grinned and said, "I love the idea. But, we'd have to tell Jade and Johnson, and they'll probably give us a lot of crap about going without them. But, we're the bosses, so let's do it."

They called Jade and Johnson and told them their plans. Like parents overseeing their kids, they tried to talk them out of it, but Jeff said, "Sorry, guys, we're going."

The door creaked a bit just then, and Johnson raced to the door to find Juan bringing in some nighttime treats. Juan overheard the conversation and said, "Ooh, you should go. Key West is fabulous. But, a special weekend is going on down there, and it will be crowded. I could help you find a room. No problemo." Jade decided to rent a car for them in her name. For the first time during their short marriage and honeymoon, Jeff and Ginger were going to be alone.

After a few minutes on the phone, Juan said, "Mucho good news. I was able to get you a room at Parrotdice, a cute bed and breakfast, just two short walking blocks away from Old Key West. This place is pet friendly, except the only pets they accept are birds. You could take Blabs if you like." Blabs sensed something exciting was about to happen, but she didn't know what was meant by parrot friendly. She was simply ready for something new. Juan continued. "You must take the traditional route to Key West."

Jeff said, "Isn't there only one road down there?"

"Si, but it is warm, and typically, you must stop frequently to quench your thirst. I'll provide you with a list of my favorite stops and mile markers, but be adventurous and find some of your own."

Jeff felt a little confused but took his mental notes and advice. This was to be the first time they were alone since their first honeymoon night, and that night was a blur at best.

Hole Number 7
Par 5

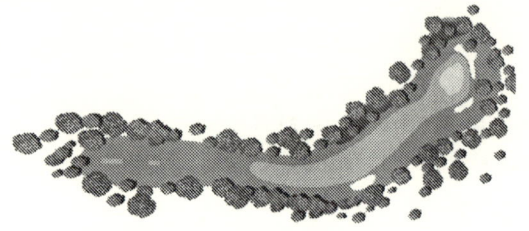

(**Course Notes**: An insane person is considered insane in a sane world. A sane person is considered insane in an insane world. What world do we live in?)

Around 9 A.M. the next morning, Jeff and Ginger attempted to get out of the hotel unnoticed, but Blabs was blabbering quite loudly and ultimately caught the attention of one maid and morning gardener. They were both on Scratch's payroll, and therefore called him immediately to announce their departure. Scratch grabbed his wallet and handgun, jumped into his car, and raced to the exit of the hotel garage.

Jeff had the keys to a rental car that was already parked in the garage behind the hotel. They placed Blabs' cage in the backseat with the overnight bags and eased out of the garage as inconspicuously as possible.

Scratch was already parked outside the garage exit, and used his discreet surveillance skills to stalk Jeff and Ginger. What he didn't know was that there weren't any rooms available in Key West. This weekend was Dress Mess weekend. During this weekend, visitors are urged to only wear what their significant anyone picks out. A wife may select a dress or a thong bottom and tuxedo top for her husband. Wives may be required to wear crotch less underwear all day. Men and women of the same sexual persuasion tended to turn this affair into an extreme sport, pushing clothing absurdity to new limits. Typically, if you knew about this weekend, and you went to Key West, you crossed the boundaries of weird and perverted attire.

Based on Juan's instructions, Jeff pointed their rented rag top south and headed for Key West. After hitting some congested Miami traffic, they finally followed US 1 to the beginning of Key Largo and made their first stop at Alabama Jacks. The air was cool, so they left Blabs in the car, and entered the nostalgic, rustic, weather-worn bar of perfection. It was only a little after 10 in the morning, yet quite a few locals were already on their second drink. The early morning heated conversations were brewing about which bait to use for grouper and the Miami Dolphins draft picks.

Jeff ordered some drinks without attracting any attention. His tourist disguise included sunglasses, a new golf cap, and an unshaven face to look locally off beat. Ginger simply wore jean shorts, an oversized South Beach t-shirt, a Florida Marlins visor to hold her ponytail in place when the car top was down, and fashionable designer shades from Rio courtesy of Palo. They blended in perfectly with people who didn't notice them or care to be noticed.

Halfway through their first Rum Runner, they started to feel the magic of the Keys. A deliciously mild and salty cool Atlantic breeze meandered through the mangroves and occasional palm trees. It was mixed with vast amounts of sun and an occasional puffy cloud that added texture and contrast to the bluest of blue skies. Little waves lapped into the boat dock, creating a hypnotic yet irregular drumbeat that coaxed you to stay forever. Time almost stood still. There was no escaping tranquility, serenity or relaxation. Their brains were washed clean by the beauty and mental aroma of the Keys, erasing anything one once thought important like credit card passwords, electric garage door codes, overdue bills, or the current month or year. The Keys could create this memory lapse without alcohol, but a favorite twenty-one and older beverage helped to speed up the relaxations process.

All in all, the typical Keys meal of the day was fresh fish brain melt. Jeff and Ginger easily and quickly fell under the Keys' spell and were oblivious to anything outside their peaceful state of mind and, therefore, didn't notice that their private honeymoon was not so private. Scratch was sitting at the end of the bar having a beer, hiding behind a group of retired anglers. Just outside the parking lot, FBI agents Jack and Tyron were sitting in their car, enjoying a bowl of conch chowder that they secretly ordered without being seen. Two cars over from them, Johnson was discretely parked in a rented Jeep, drinking bottled water. Jeff and Ginger were like the lost boys in Neverland playing follow the leader, except they didn't know they were leaders, or even playing the game.

Scratch noticed a clothes rack by the entrance of the bar. Realizing he had no clothes to wear, he moved without notice toward the rack. Just then, Jeff and Ginger got up and headed out to the parking lot. Scratch reached over and grabbed a t-shirt and shorts, hoping whatever he grabbed would fit, dropped a fifty on the bar, and dashed to his car in chase.

Juan was right. It seemed as though Jeff's car automatically located a watering hole about every thirty-five miles. They stopped at Kokomo's for their famous Pain-in-the-Ass with a Meyer's floater cocktail and a fresh dolphin sandwich. Their undercover entourage easily remained within viewing distance but often stayed in their vehicles. It took the convoy well over five hours to make the short three-hour trip, but Jeff and Ginger were already under the spell of island time, so time was irrelevant. Their only complaint might be that they wished it took longer. As has been experienced by millions, their drive to Key West on the Overseas Highway was a welcome escape. The series of bridges that connect the island keys created the sensation of driving on water. As they headed further south, the water's color became more turquoise as the Gulf of Mexico and the Atlantic Ocean shook hands. The winds whispered that they should never return to civilization. Many before them had accepted this invitation.

Jeff and Ginger easily found their bed and breakfast. It was on Caroline Street, just a few blocks away from Duval and the famous Old Key West district. The lobby was filled with parrots, all owned by the manager. Ginger carried in Blabs' mobile cage while Jeff carried the luggage. Blabs heard all the screeching and happily started jabbering with her cousins. The manager didn't recognize them, as she was more interested in Blabs.

The newlyweds' elation of checking in and enjoying a few days together made Scratch virtually invisible as he sauntered behind a banyan tree, pretending to look at the birds. Jeff paid for the rooms in advance with cash, so credit card names couldn't be recognized. He was requested to sign the registry, and his mind went blank on choosing a name other than their own. He made eye contact with Ginger and motioned to the book. She took the pen and scribbled "Bonnie and Clyde." The manager looked at the names and smiled with no comment. She knew that Key West was the place to escape, and aliases were simply an important part of the lure. On the way to their room, Ginger said that she was in desperate need of a nap, and Jeff agreed.

Scratch overheard the comment and sighed in relief. The short break in his mobile stake out gave him ample time to check in unnoticed and snatch a few winks himself. In addition to the bar stops along the way, Scratch demolished most of a six pack, which changed his demeanor in an unusual and difficult-to-describe way. He wedged his gun in the front waistline of his pants and draped his shirt over the protrusion. The trigger hammer kept catching belly hairs, causing him to make high-pitched grunt sounds as he walked up the staircase to the outdoor lobby.

After Bonnie and Clyde retired to their bungalow, Scratch approached the manager and slurred out, "Ah need a room." Just at that moment his gun slipped down to his crotch, capturing a few belly hairs along the way. He yelled "Ooooh" and then tried to be discreet and reposition the weapon back to his waistline, but all the manager could see was his disgusting personal foreplay. The manager sensed he was unpredictable and said, "I'm sorry. It's Dress Mess weekend, and we're filled up. But, the Stiff Wind Bed and Breakfast is right across the street, and they had a vacancy. You might try them out."

He pranced to his car, threw the gun on the front seat, and took a sip of his open beer before going next door. Just then, the Conch Train, a sight seeing must-do in Key West, raced by him. Everyone on the train waved, and he waved back, but having a case of beer imbalance, he fell back against his car, and spilled the remainder of his beer all over himself. He climbed into his car to change into the clothes he bought at Alabama Jacks. He didn't notice that the shirt was a small, which would girdle his 172 pound, 5' 8" frame. Worst of all, the shirt was neon pink in color, and it said on the front, "A-Jack's You Off," possibly a famous slogan at the bar. The pants were just the opposite. They were a size 38 irregular black that was probably designed for a rap band and poised to fall down at a moments notice. He had no other choices, though, and put the dry clothes on.

When he entered the Stiff Wind, a friendly person of neutral persuasion greeted him. "Hi, love, can I help you? Ooh, nice shirt!"

Scratch used his beer-induced reasoning to determine that this womanish person was the manager. "Sure can. Ah need a room for a few nights. I'm by myself."

"Wonderful," said the manager. "We typically only allow couples, but I'm currently available, so it should help even things out."

Although she was not quite his taste, he was flattered. Besides, he had been without a companion for some time, and his masculinity was quite backed up. "Most of our guests are having a siesta fiesta in their rooms right now, but we have a fabulous little happy hour kicking off in forty-five minutes. All drinks are on the house. Why don't you join us? I'm sure our guests would make you feel welcome. Besides, they love to drink too much and get crazy, especially during this Dress Mess weekend."

Scratch said, "I need to meet some friends in two hours, so I'll catch some z's by the pool, have a quick drink, and be off after that."

"Perfect, see you poolside." Scratch went to his room, hid his handgun, car keys, cell phone, and wallet, and took the last beer. The pool was deserted. He slugged down his brew and passed out.

A short time later, Scratch was awakened by voices and calypso music. Still feeling the effects of his last beer, he slowly opened his eyes, only to shut them when the falling sun burned directly into his pupils. He sat up rubbing his eyes, when a voice said, "Hi, sleepy head. I'm glad you're up. Can I get you something to drink? I make a killer Rum Punch."

He knew it was the sound of the manager at check in, but his eyes were still nearly blind. "Sure, a Rum Punch sounds great."

"Your wish is my command. Why don't you slide into the pool? That will wake you up. I'll come in with your drink and join you."

Scratch said, "Thanks, I think I will." His eyes focused enough for him to stumble over to the pool. He could tell it was filled with people, and he hoped maybe some single girls were floating around. His combined sleep and beer stupor disturbed his memory, and he plopped in the water, forgetting that his baggy pants were still being worn. When his head bobbed back to the surface, his eyes now burned with over-chlorinated pool water.

While rubbing his eyes to remove the blur, a body rubbed up against him in the pool, and the manager said, "Here's your drink. My name's Toni. Would you like to meet some of the other guests?"

Scratch's eyes finally started to become focused. He looked around, and realized that the pool and patio were filled with men, all naked. Toni had his arm over Scratch's shoulder like they were old war buddies, except Toni was toting a weapon that wasn't issued by the U. S. Army. Scratch jumped out of the pool and grabbed his towel to go back to his room.

Toni yelled, "Sugar, don't go in yet! Take off those silly shorts and stay awhile. It's happy hour."

Scratch mumbled that he had to meet his friends, and he tripped over two chairs and three couples en route to his room. Once he got to his room, he realized that he had locked himself out. If it wasn't for his few personal items, he would have just left.

Scratch sauntered back out to the pool, and everyone yelled, "Welcome back, we knew you'd be back."

Scratch had been in some very unusual situations before, but nothing ever like this. He'd been around thugs, pugs, murderers, killers, thieves, and politicians, but never around a bunch of friendly naked guys. He walked over to Toni and said, "I locked my keys in my room."

Toni got out of the pool, wrapped a towel around himself, and said, "Sugar, I think you're teasing me. You don't need to play this little game. I'd love to come to your room."

When they headed toward the room, everyone cheered and yelled, "Have fun, love birds, don't forget protection."

While Toni opened the room door, Scratch said, "I really have to shower and meet some people."

Toni said, "That's okay, bring your friends back for a night cap. We'll all go into the hot tub later. See you, love."

Scratch just about shit his pants thinking, *Thank God no one saw me. My career dealing with the underworld would be ruined.*

The FBI agents were thinking the same thing as they filmed his romantic encounter from behind the bushes with state-of-the-art digital cameras. The automatic zoom and high frequency microphone on the video camera caught all the action and sound. Tyrone thought, "Now who else would be interested in this video?"

The temporary bandits awoke from a peaceful nap, showered, and prepared to go out and become a pair of faces in the crowd of tourists when there was a knock on the door. Bonnie and Clyde were not thinking and simply opened the door without their official tourist disguises. It was the inn's manager, Mia Stoke, followed by her husband, Dale. He was holding a bird stand. "We thought you guys could use a bird stand for your parrot. We cleaned this one up and put some bird seed and water in the dishes to make his stay more comfortable."

"That was so nice of you, but it's a girl, not a boy. Her name is Blabs."

As Dale brought in the stand, Mia asked if Blabs spoke.

"More than we want sometimes. She loves to sing classic rock songs and show tunes."

Without hesitation, Mia said, "Blabs, what can you sing for me? Come pretty bird, what can you sing?"

It seemed as though Blabs was considering the best song to sing for this audience of two and belted out one of her favorites from Lynard Skynard, "…Fly high, like a free bird, yeahhhhhhhh…"

Mia stepped back and said, "That's fantastic. Can she do this in front of crowds?"

"Sometimes. Why?" Bonnie replied.

Mia said, "Dale and I were going to change into our party clothes and head on over to Mallory Square for Sunset Festival. If you've never been to Key West, you have to go there. It's a sunset party filled with street performers and vendors. You are welcome to join us and bring Blabs along. I have a parrot leash to protect her. Blabs would be a big smash there."

Bonnie and Clyde looked at each other and said, "Sure, why not?"

Mia then looked at their clothes and said, "Is that what you're going to wear?" They both shook their heads yes. "Hmm, that won't do. You do know this is Dress Mess weekend," and she described the attire that was typically required, and how your mate decides what clothes you will wear. "The weirder, the better. Bonnie, why don't you come with me? I have some things you can pick out for Clyde that we use for other crazy events. Dale, can you take Clyde to Sink or Swim and tell Kerri to help him pick something out for Bonnie. But be quick, we haven't much time."

"Sure thing. Come on, Clyde." Bonnie and Clyde were at first confused by their new names. Clyde looked at Bonnie with mass confusion on his face. Bonnie simply looked at Clyde and said, "Clyde, you run off with Dale. I've got to find something for you to wear."

Clyde's lights turned on, and he got up to leave with Dale.

Dale grabbed two beers from his fridge, handed one to Clyde and said, "Sink or Swim is a long walk, so I thought we needed a roader."

Clyde said, "Thanks, I hate shopping, and a beer certainly helps." Dale agreed. During their long two minute stroll, they barely had time to chat, as they pounded down the beer before entering the store.

"Hi Dale. Are you and Mia headed over to Mallory Square? I'm fixin' to close up shop."

"Yep, we'll see you over there, but first, Clyde here needs something for his wife to wear. They're rookies to Dress Mess."

Kerri said, "What size is your wife, and how daring is she?"

Clyde described her, apologizing that he'd never bought her clothes, because they had just met and got married. "She can get daring, especially after a few drinks."

Kerri said, "Okay, let me show you a few things. Dale, the fridge is stocked."

Dale disappeared, returning in seconds with some long neck beers. Clyde raised his eyebrows and said, "This is how shopping should be," caressing his ice cold beer and looking at hot sexy clothes. He picked out one unusual outfit and said, "Gin..., ah er Bonnie will love this, or at least I will seeing her in it."

Dale and Kerri looked at each other, then at Clyde. They didn't say anything, but realized he was somebody, but who? While Clyde was buying the outfit, Kerri instructed Dale to get two more beers for the road, as it was a long walk back to the Parrotdice.

Meanwhile, Mia whipped up a batch of margaritas and poured two huge glasses. "My friend Kerri over at the Sink or Swim is probably getting Dale and Clyde drunk. We might was well join them before we head out."

While she mixed and poured, she took a closer look at Bonnie. She pulled out boxes of costumes, many of which were created by Mia herself that were worn by Dale at the world famous Fantasy Fests in Key West. "Everything is cleaned and washed. Pick out whatever you like. I'm going to get ready." Before she left, she asked, "Bonnie, have we ever met before? You look strangely familiar."

Bonnie replied in a chuckle, "I doubt it," and continued looking at the costumes. She discovered a beautiful Scottish outfit, complete with kilt, cabby hat, and fake bagpipes. "Yes," she thought. She yelled out, "Mia, I picked the Scottish outfit. I'm gonna head back to my room." Mia peeked out and said, "We'll knock on your door when we're ready to go."

Dale and Clyde met Bonnie at the room. Dale said he'd change and come back to pick them up soon. They had had three beers in a matter of twenty minutes, and Clyde fashioned a buzzed based smirk on his face. Ginger was glad to see him so relaxed. He handed the bag to her and said, "It's not a sexy gangster outfit to match your alias, cause they were out of machine guns in violin cases. Anyways, I hope it fits."

She participated in the costume exchange and said, "Here's yours, Mr. Clyde Barrow." Clyde opened his box and put on the clothes. After having three beers and watching the British Open for so many years, wearing the kilt made him feel rather proud (and sexy).

Bonnie headed into the bedroom to try on her outfit. It was the first thing Clyde had bought her since they were married. She was happy to receive the costume but also skeptical. Bonnie came out wearing a body suit that was mostly see through, except for a tasteful array of feathers that covered the important body parts. In addition, a large feather mixture protruded from her butt for increased aerodynamic stability. This costume also included a feathered mask and crown, which Clyde thought might help conceal her identity.

"Oh baby, you look great". Blabs started screeching, probably thinking that the sexy big bird was her new companion.

Bonnie asked, "Can I really wear this in public?"

Clyde said, "I guess so."

"By the way, Mr. Barrow, I hope you're not wearing underwear. A true Scot with golf lineage wouldn't get caught dead wearing anything but the kilt itself." She really didn't know if this was true, but Clyde simply pulled down the boxers from beneath the kilt and flipped them on the bed, thinking she knew more about golf and Scottish tradition than he did. He was adjusting his hat and playing air-bagpipes when a knock from the door was followed by Dale barging in.

"Welcome to your first Key West Dress Mess. Clyde, you look great. Bonnie, WOW. You're the bird lady of Key West!" Mia jabbed him in the ribs, but she had no reason to be jealous. Dale had her wearing satin boxing shorts and matching robe. The boxing shorts were cut high in the butt, and the robe was cut short and had no belt to hold it together. When she moved her petit body, the robe glided around the contours of her partially revealing chest.

Mia had Dale wear a leathery cowboy outfit with chaps, but no pants, displaying most of his butt. Mia was glad to see Clyde wearing her creation and asked him in a poor but understandable Scottish accent, "Aye Laddie, what r' yer weain under da kilt" Clyde replied, "Aye lassie, that's for me and the kilt to know," resulting in laughter.

Mia connected the parrot leash on Blabs with no fuss. Bonnie placed Blabs on her shoulder and secured the leash around her waist. Her white and yellow outfit complemented Blabs yellow head and green body. They were a perfect match. Mia filled up their to-go cups, and they all headed down to Mallory Square.

Johnson was sitting in his parked car when the party of four headed down the street. He couldn't believe his eyes. For the last week, he barely slept trying to maintain the safety and security of Jeff and Ginger. Now, they were running around Key West drunk and half naked with no protection.

Just as he was ready to get out of his car, he noticed a stranger protrude from the bushes wearing a skin-tight pink t-shirt and wet droopy shorts. He seemed to be following the foursome. When he was almost out of view, two other fellows suspiciously came out from behind the building and scooted in the same direction. He wondered. "Who else is going to pop out?" He transparently joined the Jeff and Ginger Key West costume convoy dressed like a casual CIA agent.

When Bonnie and Clyde approached Duval Street with their new friends, they felt they were underdressed. Their clothes could be considered church attire compared to some of the outlandish costumes being modeled in broad dusk light. Blabs blabbered the entire way, enjoying her open air freedom. Many women spoke to Blabs, while their male escorts were being overly friendly with Bonnie. Clyde, after playing golf with the horny news media, was already used to the attention she received. They arrived at Mallory Square, and as usual, it was a laid-back mob scene. But this time, this unique assemblage consisted of irregular souls who were happy to escape reality and use Dress Mess as an excuse to expose their hidden perversions and physical delusions. Mia and Dale knew everyone, and introduced Blabs, Bonnie, and Clyde to all their friends. The locals treated them like family. Blabs kept singing, "Born to be Wild," and anyone within a circumference of five feet would start chiming in.

Just then, two abstract fellows wearing diapers and bonnets came within view. They had a large yellow belt holding them together. No one understood the meaning of their costumes, and no one questioned it. They were drawn to Blabs for no particular reason. Blabs started flapping her wings, and started singing, "Tie a yellow ribbon round the old oak tree." Her timing was impeccable. Bonnie, Clyde and anyone within earshot and eyeshot lost it, including the diaper boys. Laughter was towered by more laughter. Bonnie turned to Clyde and said, "This has got to be one of the funniest days of my life, and we just got here". Clyde shook his head in agreement, unable to speak from laughter.

Scratch, the FBI agents, and Johnson stayed within professional distance of the person or persons they were tailing. Scratch's baggy shorts were still wet from his accidental pool encounter to change sexual preferences. Even though *he* remained straight, his shorts crossed over and experienced bloating and water weight gain from the episode, causing him to have to walk using one hand to hold his water-logged pants up to keep them from falling to his ankles. The awkward walk caused the wet, coarse material to rub against his legs, butt, and groin, thus developing a fire engine red rash. This rash compounded the awkward walk, thus multiplying the pain of the chaffed skin even more. Scratch's cash-only line of work netted a salary that rivaled doctors, lawyers, and most of his political and business employers. Yet, his current down-on-his-luck appearance, and heaped in pain and injury display, stirred the hearts of locals and tourists alike, many of whom offered him charitable contributions of food and money. He refused all generosity as he limped along, yelling at those trying to help, saying, "I'm worth millions and can have any of you killed with just one phone call."

"Poor island soul," they thought. "He's mentally ill as well. Wish we could help."

The FBI agents enjoyed his uneasiness, but they were prepared to barge in if his attitude turned postal. Luckily, the sun melted into the water, allowing darkness to cover Scratch's hideous look and outlook. The crowds headed into town for part two or sixty-seven of whatever Dress Mess chapter they were experiencing.

Mia directed her crew to Captain Tony's Saloon to hear a new band in town. They snaked their way toward the stage as the Polka Pirates band started playing an island version of "Rock and Roll out the Barrel." The band members were wearing German lederhosen and Caribbean pirate shirts. The steel drums and accordion squared off for one-on-one solos that brought the house down. Body parts of every kind flopped up and down the dance floor to the beat of the music. The bartenders developed a Jagermeister pirate punch drink that sounded horrible but tasted great.

After devouring barrels of conch chowder, beer-batter dolphin sandwiches, mountains of "to die for" Key Lime pie, and two rounds of pirate punch, Mia approached the band, and asked if they would accompany a singing parrot for a song. "Aye, mate, absolutely, Polka Pirates love parrots." The lead singer approached the mic and announced, "Ahoy swabbies. As ya may know, a pirate's best friend is his parrot. Tonight, one of our feathered friends will join us in a song."

He looked down at Bonnie who didn't know what he was talking about. Without warning, she was hoisted up on stage with the assistance of Clyde and Dale. Blabs fought for balance on Bonnie's shoulder while she acquired her sea legs. The male crowd howled at Bonnie yelling expected comments of sexual profanity but laden nonetheless with warm Keys humor.

The band captain asked "Ay lass, what'l you two birds be sing'n for us?"

Bonnie said, "Just a moment." She whispered into Blabs ear and placed Blabs by the microphone. The boisterous crowd quieted to a mumble. Blabs looked around, gained her composure, and started to sing, "Wasted away again in Margaretville..." The accordion and guitar harmonized the famous Buffett tune while the drums, bass, and steel drum burned a steady polka island rhythm. For that brief moment, Blabs and the Polka Pirates eclipsed the Beatles as one of the greatest bands in the world. Everyone in the bar joined in the sing-a-long. Blabs just kept repeating the same lyrics, and the band followed along, until Blabs decided to showcase her flying ability. She launched herself into the air, forgetting that she was umbilically attached to Bonnie. Bonnie lunged off the stage to catch and protect Blabs. Their new groupies below the stage cushioned both woman and parrot to safely land, but *Ginger* lost her mask and head piece during the short and ill-timed flight.

Unknown to most biochemists, the ability of the diluted brain sometimes has an adverse increase of mental clarity. When she stood up, the audience, who had drank enough that day to match the doctor recommended yearly alcohol consumption, knew it was Ginger Taylor. Even the band stopped playing in the middle of "Shaker of salt". Then, in fanfare, the entire bar started applauding and screamed, "Where's Jeff?"

Mia and Dale couldn't believe they were partying with TV's newest and hottest stars. Jeff stood up and took off his hat and bagpipes. Everyone cheered and starting yelling, "Vote for Honesty. Jeff for President." Immediately, Johnson appeared, not knowing what the crowd was going to do next. Jeff said, "What are you doing here? We're supposed to be on our own."

Johnson said, "I had a funny feeling Blabs wanted to sing, and I didn't want to miss it." Johnson jumped up on stage and grabbed the mic from the lead pirate. "Hey folks, Jeff and Ginger would love to finish their drinks and have a dance or two. Please provide them that courtesy, and enjoy yourselves. Thank you." Then he turned to the swashbuckling polka singer and said, "What are you guys playing next?" The pirates followed his cue and started playing one of their original songs, "Polish Island of Love."

Johnson's towering physique and dark demeanor could be viewed as ominous to non acquaintances and his presence alongside of Jeff and Ginger provided an invincible shield that everyone respected. They stayed long enough to finish their drinks and thanked Mia and Don for such an unforgettable evening.

Ginger sat down and said, "Well, if it wasn't for Blab's aeronautics, we'd probably stick around for a while. But, I'm sure our father already has an exit plan developed for our departure. I can't thank you enough for letting us join your party."

"Are you kidding?" replied Mia. "Partying with Jeff and Ginger? Famous celebrities? No Dress Mess will compare with this."

Johnson quickly interrupted. "I know I seem like a party crasher, but I'm getting nervous about the crowd attacking, and think we should split now. Mia, can you keep their room number secret?"

"Absolutely. Dale and I escaped to Key West to start a new life away from our past and we're glad to keep their accommodation location in confidence, as long as we get to snap a few pictures of you tomorrow. You know, to hang in our lobby."

"Agreed." Now it looks like a something's brewing outside. Let's duck out the back door."

A small commotion occurred outside when two 300 pound girls started fighting because they wore the same costume. Their billboard sized shirts each advertised the words, "Boobs of Mass Seduction". The back side of their oversized bikini bottoms donned a picture of George Bush sneering on one cheek, and the other cheek displayed the words "Big Ass". The high-tempered girls embraced in summo wrestler like fashion, attempting to deprive her opponent of her costume, thus offering another unique form of Key West entertainment to the tourists. Johnson used this diversion to escort Jeff and Ginger out the back door. Darkness provided cover, and they journeyed the ten-minute walk back to their room unnoticed. Johnson also had secured a room at the Parrotdice B&B without Jeff and Ginger knowing it.

Scratch was outside the bar spectating the girls' battle of the bulge and missed Blabs and Ginger takeoff as well as Johnson's short speech. He and the other sports enthusiasts watched this unique event until the police ended the match, although they were uncertain if summo or Greco-Roman style of wrestling was deployed in this contest. No official winners were declared by the police, therefore, no medals were awarded to the wrestlers from the spectators.

After the match, Scratch surveyed the bar and realized that Jeff and Ginger had escaped, so he decided to call it a night. Before he headed to his room, he dragged his rash remains to a convenience store to purchase some skin ointment. The small three-ounce tubes wouldn't even cover one butt cheek, so his only other choice was to buy a gallon-sized tub of petroleum jelly.

He hoped he could get into his room without being seen or seeing anything. He entered his room from a side entrance of the Stiff Wind. Just as walked up to his room door, the door next to his swung open, and a party of his pool buddies rolled out in quest of more ice. They cordially said good evening, and quickly noticed the enormous container in his hands.

"My oh my, look what our shy boy has here. Say pal, why don't you join us. We're having a little bash next door. You're more than welcome."

Scratch didn't have any hands to locate his room key, which was currently lost in his wet, cavernous pants pocket. One hand held up his pants, and the other hand balanced the seven-pound tub of rash relief. One of the partiers asked, "If you like, I can spend a few minutes finding your keys for you?"

Scratch had never been frightened before, so this new feeling had him bewildered. He dropped the container, dove into his pants and recovered the key, opened the door, kicked the container in, leaped into the room, and closed the door behind him. Outside, he heard disappointing moans and devilish laughter.

His cramped fingers released the pants, which would have fallen on the moon due to excessive weight. He covered all affected areas of his body with the ointment and lay in bed wishing for pain relievers or booze.

The loud party in the room next door continued without him. Incense was burning, which added a unique aroma to the room of close friends. The AM radio in the room picked up a station from Havana, Cuba, and the energetic Latin beat prompted the attendees into dance mode. Two of the dancers were designing new dance moves, and legs tangled during one complicated sequence of steps, causing them to tumble over and knock over the poorly placed burning incense. The cheap carpeting immediately caught on fire. Wine spritzers were poured on the carpet in an attempt to squash the blaze, but the fire spread even more quickly. The two responsible dancers courageously battled the blaze, while the less fire retardant members ran out of the room and into the lobby, where they awoke a sleeping manager to call the fire department.

Scratch had just fallen into a deep sleep, when a vicious banging on his door awoke him to a terrified drowsy and confused state of mind. He jumped out of bed and opened the door. Toni wailed in horror, "Scratch, get out quick. The Inn's on fire."

Scratch rushed outside and stood next to the other hotel guests near the pool, watching several brave guests hold the fire back with a garden hose and fire extinguishers. Seconds later, the sirens increased in volume as fire trucks approached the Inn. The firemen rushed in and quickly put out the fire.

Scratch felt an arm go around him and Toni exclaimed. "I was terrified that you would be burned in the blaze."

Scratch was exhausted from the day, and actually appreciated the concern. Just then, he remembered he was as naked as the proverbial buck. Toni smiled and said, "It was about time you came out to play. Oh my, you're all lathered up and ready for action. I knew you'd come around."

Scratch dashed toward his room, but the firemen blocked him and said, "Sorry, slick, the area isn't secure yet. Get your shiny butt out of here." The lower half of his body glistened in the moon light, generating a chuckle from the firemen.

Toni came up to Scratch and said, "My room wasn't affected by the commotion. You can hang out there until the firemen leave." Scratch had no choice once again and followed Toni to his room. Again a loud cheer erupted from the guests, and again, they yelled out, "Have fun, love birds, and don't forget protection."

Much to Toni's displeasure, Scratch was not interested in changing his love habits. "Can I at least rub some more cream on the affected areas? I see you missed some spots."

Scratch shook his head no. Toni provided him with a pair of pink soffe shorts and a tank top, and told Scratch to keep him in mind if he ever changed his mind.

When the firemen left, Scratch went back to his room trying to forget the last forty-five-minute nightmare. He checked on the few items he had hid, and all were safe, although his cell phone voice mail light was blinking.

New low light-level viewing binoculars and cameras were made available to all FBI agents within the last year due to increased national funding of Homeland Security. (Sonny Hoag spearheaded this funding initiative. His wife, coincidentally, owned thousands of shares of stock in the companies that provided the security equipment to the government.) Tyrone took advantage of the new technology, filming the night version of Scratch's entire petroleum jelly sequence from the same hidden spot in the bushes while Jack sacked out in the car, awaiting his 3 A.M. shift change. Tyrone had been assigned more important details, but at least this one proved humorously entertaining.

Once the firemen left, and a peaceful quiet loomed throughout the Stiff Wind, Tyrone walked over to Scratch's room and placed an inconspicuous motion sensor on the bottom right corner of the door. If the door opened for any reason during the night, Tyrone's receiving transmitter would alert him of the occurrence. He headed back to the car, which was parked just outside the Stiff Wind. Jack was sleeping, although he had been rudely awakened earlier by Key West police indicating he couldn't sleep in a parked car in the street. Jack flashed his FBI badge, mumbled "stake out," and asked them to leave so as not to blow their cover.

Tyrone entered the mobile surveillance motel just loud enough to reawaken Jack. Tyrone said, "Go back to sleep, man. You have another hour of shut eye." Just then, a flashlight flooded their car with light. They both pulled out their revolvers but were unable to see because of the glare. Then they heard a voice. "Steady, boys, steady. You can put the toys away."

Jack quickly opened his door and rolled to the ground, still maintaining his weapon. Again the voice said, "Easy, cowboy. I'm unarmed." Jack aimed his gun over the hood while the stranger backed away from the car. Jack said, "Why don't you put your hands in the air so we can see them?"

Johnson complied with his request. Tyrone jumped out of the car and said, "What do you want?"

Johnson had a feeling that this spying duo was related to some law enforcement group. After he had escorted Jeff and Ginger to their room, he made some quick phone calls, and received confirmation that a team of FBI agents were assigned to the case concerning an assassination attempt on presidential candidate Jeff Taylor. Johnson slowly put his arms down and quietly spoke. "Gentlemen, I don't want to blow your cover. Let's walk into the patio area."

The agents looked at each other, and followed Johnson inside. Johnson continued. "My name is Johnson. I retired from the CIA a few years ago." He showed them his CIA ID card. "I accepted a position with the Hard Rock Hotel chain to beef up various aspects of security. By accident, I was requested to head up security for Jeff and Ginger Taylor during the next few months. I've been watching you tail some dude in a pink shirt and baggy pants who's tailing my clients. I made a call to some buddies, and they said you were assigned to this case for a potential assassination attempt. I just thought we could work together on this, since our goal is now the same."

Jack got on the phone to confirm Johnson's job and story. While he was waiting for confirmation, Tyrone and Johnson chatted about Scratch, Jeff Taylor, and their choice for the best Key Lime pie in Key West. Within a few minutes, Jack got off the phone, and nodded affirmatively to Tyrone, who briefed Johnson on this assignment. "In the eyes of the news media, Jeff Taylor was considered to be running for office, and his current popularity affair with the media was strong enough for the FBI to investigate a lead that came in over the phone. Stewart 'Scratch' Delacantos was mentioned as having a connection with the assassination attempt and was therefore the primary target for the investigation. Scratch's reputation is known to various law enforcement circles, although he has never been convicted for illegal activity; arrested, yes, but never convicted. The fact that Scratch was following Jeff and Ginger in Miami increased the likelihood of some type of illegal activity, strengthening the decision to continue surveillance on him."

Johnson was quick to remember Scratch's name and previous activity with Ginger, but he didn't feel the FBI needed to be informed on her past, primarily to protect Ginger's can of video worms. Johnson switched the conversation back to Jeff. "Knowing that Jeff's life may be in jeopardy is going to change the way I set up my security for him and his wife. For example, I'm going to get them out of Key West first thing tomorrow, as I don't have a team to help me adequately protect them. Let's exchange cell numbers. I'll keep you abreast of their activities and movement. Please reciprocate by informing me if Scratch is anywhere close to them that could create a dangerous situation."

The agents agreed. Jack had the inquisitive eye of an FBI agent and said, "Two questions remain. Who called in the lead, and who wants Jeff dead?"

Johnson and Tyrone had the eyes of dead fish, unable to respond to the perfect questions, while knowing that any countless number of politicians or business leaders would like Jeff out of the presidential way.

The phone message on Scratch's cell phone might have provided a few answers to Jack's question. As a result of the message, Scratch returned the call on a pre-paid cell phone that Sonny purchased for cash that made it nearly impossible for authorities to trace. "It's me. What's up?"

"Where the hell have you been? I've left you several urgent messages. Have you been following the news?"

Scratch replied, "No, man, I've been to busy."

Sonny spoke with an angry yet controlled tone, "Well that son-of-a-bitch Taylor has challenged all presidential candidates to a lie detector test. That Son-bitch. I haven't commented to the press one way or another, but they're hounding the livin' crap out of me for a response. Basically, I'm damned if I do, and damned if I don't. This whole Taylor thing is way out of control. He has thirty percent of the votes right now. Friggin' thirty percent. That butthead only has to fart, and he gets more votes. And he ain't spending one Gad Dang dime on his campaign. In fact, that son-bitch ain't even running, and could win the whole Gad Dang thing. Hell, I'll bet he's worth more than me right now with his Gad Dang sponsorships. So, Mr. fix-all-problems hot shot, what are ya gonna do about it?"

Scratch had had about four hours of sleep in the last twenty-four hours; had been uncharacteristically romanticized by a womanish man; was drunk and hung over; had a painful rash on his butt and legs that burned more than the Florida sun; had been laughed at by castaway firemen; and had been nudily exposed to a motel of horny men on vacation with his legs and butt covered with petroleum jelly. This was the result of his hunch to see what Ginger was doing with Jeff. He had no good reason to be there working pro bono, and several good reasons to bag it and get the hell out of weirdsville. "What the hell you want me to do, Sonny, kill him?"

Sonny felt his anxiety and, like a good politician, decided to raise it up a notch. "If that's your final answer, okay, but how much are we talking here?"

Scratch decided to be political. "Listen shithead, I'm in Key West right now tailing the golfer and hooker as we speak. But I'm being paid by one of your political competitors to develop a situation in their favor. You tell me how much it's worth to work for you instead. Call me when you have a figure that warrants my response, or just kiss your chance for the Oval Office good-bye. By the way, I know how to beat polygraph tests!" and he hung up. Scratch wished he could have slammed the phone down for added accent, but cell phones aren't obviously conducive for slamming.

Sonny attempted to redefine the word rage. His wife came running into the room when she heard things smashing and started screaming when some of her family heirlooms were left for dustpans and brooms. "Have you lost your mind? You're breakin' all my valuable possessions. Stop it."

Sonny wondered if he could add a little on to his bill to Scratch to include his lovely wife in the human disappearance contract. "Ashley, go back to bed. I've got a major problem going on with my campaign, and I don't need your crap right now. If you and your daddy want me in the White House, get the hell out of here."

Ashley was an educated woman and knew a trip to the White House and the chance to snub her North Carolina high society friends was worth far more than the historical artifacts that were handed down to her through generations of her family. She swallowed her pride and ultimate desire to brag, along with the nauseating feeling of throwing up, and lovingly cared for her tortured husband. "Sonny, you seem tense, can I get you something to drink? What can I do to help you relax so you can think?"

Her kind gesture made Sonny feel a little guilty about breaking her heirlooms, as well as his contemplation of her earthly removal. "Well, a glass of wine and a foot massage would be wonderful." He was amazed at her obedience and loyalty as she ran downstairs to retrieve the wine, not knowing that her dinner made an encore performance in the kitchen sink. She poured him a glass of merlot, and, being a refined and delicate woman, chugged the remainder of the wine immediately after puking, and proceeded upstairs to massage his congressional toes. She thought that if sex became part of relaxation process, at least the solids were removed from her stomach to minimize an encore barf performance.

Sonny calmed down during a few wine sips and big toe thumb rubbing, and decided to call Scratch in the morning with a plan and a figure. Ashley avoided another bulimic episode as Sonny passed out before his last little piggy went wee, wee wee, all the home.

At 6 o'clock in the morning in Key West, not many creatures are stirring. The majority of those awake are left over partiers from the night before looking for breakfast, a few joggers, and those who are up but don't want to be. Jeff and Ginger had gone to bed uncustomarily early, waking up even more uncharacteristically at 6 A.M. without headache or hangover. They decided to borrow the complimentary bikes at the B&B and ride to the east side of the island to watch the sunrise. The air was cool but warmed quickly as the sun peeked out over choppy shallow ocean waters. The lapping of the water was soothing, almost mesmerizing. They enjoyed the peaceful quietude, a feeling they had not encountered often since they had married, which seemed like years ago. Jeff noticed the flicker of a light across the street at a breakfast café and retrieved two cups of coffee without fanfare. They felt like escaped prisoners, reveling in the bliss after a successful jail break.

After a few sips of espresso, Jeff turned to Ginger and said, "Ginger, you and I haven't really got to know each other over the past few weeks. This honeymoon is more a dream than a honeymoon. We don't know what's gonna happen in the future. If the money disappears for some reason, I'll end up back at the golf shop in Las Vegas. If and when that happens, life with me won't be that thrilling."

Ginger listened with great anticipation, but she had no clue where Jeff was headed.

Jeff continued, "If at anytime, you decide to back out of this relationship, I'll understand. We got drunk and got married. A very typical Vegas thing to do. Yet, I must admit, even though we don't know each other, I've loved every second we spent together. When I wake in the morning and feel you beside me, my day starts off better than it has in the last forty some years. I just wanted you to know that."

Ginger's eyes became blurry. She heard and absorbed sincere words that were spoken from his heart, elevating a feeling for Jeff that had been slowly growing already. She kissed Jeff and said, "Most people say this after they've dated for a while, and we're already married. But, I...I think I'm falling in love with you."

Jeff gazed into Ginger's poetic blue eyes and replied, "That's what I was trying to say." As they kissed and watched the canvas of colors change while the sun rose in between lazy clouds, they were unaware of several storms that were brewing, one by land and one by sea.

According to typical weather almanacs, they were in the middle of hurricane season. And whether or not global warming was fact or fiction, the increase of hurricane activity over the past few years had risen to new meteorological proportions. The storms simply came sooner, happened later, occurred more frequently, and were quite mean to those in their path. An irregular storm that was not mentioned on any weather newscast formulated rather quickly several hundred miles south east of Cuba. All hurricane models forecasted this squall to simply dissipate, or in a worst case, head in a south-westerly direction toward the northern tip of South America. Mother Nature decided play a trick golf shot and sliced the storm in the direction of Cuba and South Florida. Within a few hours, a little rain storm had grown into a tropical depression. Even as this occurred, no one seemed to take this little storm seriously.

The other brewing storm was Johnson's discovery of the no-where-to-be-found newlyweds. He called his new colleagues in their mobile beds. They were asleep and also unaware of the newlywed's morning bike trek. The door sensor had not been activated during the night, yet they called over to Scratch's room for reassurance. His vocal displeasure, choice of swear words, and groggy demeanor when the agent said "sorry wrong number," indicated strongly that he was alone and unaware of Jeff and Ginger's disappearance. The island was small, so Johnson and Tyrone decided to go search for them while Jack stayed close to Scratch.

Hole Number 8
Par 4

(**Course Notes:** Break the code, and hit the mother lode, but who's watching? You might spill the beans, but don't toss the cookies.)

"Oh Ramone. That feels so good. That's it. That's the spot. Push harder. I love it. You won't hurt me. Oh God, that feels good. We're gonna do this again tomorrow."

"As you wish, Senorita." Jade enjoyed the lapse in her hectic schedule. She caught up on some well-deserved exercise and sleep, and even made time for a massage. She knew Longshot's arrival would increase entries on her to-do list.

Longshot was anxious to rejoin his foursome and took the red-eye into Miami. He met Jade for breakfast to discuss everything. Longshot patiently sat through Jade's summary of the beach bash and Key West trip. When she finished, he finished his coffee and said, "Jade, I'm glad you're sitting down."

Jade looked scared and said, "What's the matter?"

Longshot replied, "Well, it's just that, well, I spoke with Ellen Spackler yesterday morning after my broadcast regarding the polygraph. She...um...she said, well, she said we received quite a few endorsement opportunities." Jade sat in silence with eyes as wide as a fairway. "She's going to send you all the opportunities via email, but she thought I should chat with you before we let Jeff and Ginger know what the balance is thus far."

Jade said, "How many, and how much?"

Longshot answered, "About forty to fifty opportunities. Of course, we wouldn't be interested in all of them."

Jade knew he was hiding something and asked, "How much totaled?" as she began to turn from scared to frenzied.

"Well, all totaled, its come out to about seventy-five big ones."

She laughed. "Damn, Longshot, you got me all worked up for $75 thousand dollars? I can deal with that."

"No Jade," $75 *million*."

"I can't deal with that."

Longshot took a deep gasp of air and said, "There's more. Well, first of all, over $30 million has been donated to a variety of charities on Jeff and Ginger's behalf. Some dot com guy in the bay area donated $5 million alone to some conservation group in Jeff's name, saying he loved the idea of no campaign banners and the saving of trees. Virtually all the charities have sent us emails thanking us for generating dollars for their causes versus campaign advertising."

Jade said, "Is that it?"

"No. About $750,000 has been bet, with 2/3 of it on Jeff. Furthermore, I guess you haven't watched the news lately, but according to the polls, if the election was held today, Jeff has thirty per cent of the country's votes. Sonny Hoag is leading with over forty per cent, but he's quickly losing his share to Jeff. TV news has been trying to find out what politicians are going to take the polygraph challenge, and no one is committing either way. Their aversion to the test is making Jeff's popularity climb. As of right now, he actually has a chance, a good chance, to end up in the White House. And last of all—"

Jade butted in. "I don't know if I can handle anymore."

Longshot nicely butted back. "Too bad. This is important. My friend in the Las Vegas police department found out through the crime vine that someone may try to assassinate Jeff."

"What!" Jade screamed, annoying virtually everyone in the restaurant.

"Keep quiet. That's not all," he said. "Ginger's old colleague, Scratch, seems to be the lead suspect."

Jade sat dumbfound and said, "Who would be behind this?"

Longshot said, "Who wouldn't? Businesses and politicians have been spending billions playing political chess to gain access to the White House. All their money would be wasted if the wrong guy ends up in Washington and doesn't help them with their hidden business and political agendas. The FBI was called in, and there's a good chance they're on Jeff's tail as we speak."

Jade sat quietly for a moment and said, "Do you think, or more importantly, do you think Jeff will think this little political blast is worth his life... or Ginger's, or both? Heck, are we in danger?"

Longshot had no reply. His gut told him that Jeff and Ginger would have to know, meaning they would probably kiss the $75 million good-bye if Jeff decided to abandon this hoax to the presidency.

Jade's cell phone interrupted their disoriented minds. "Hi Jade. It's Captain Woody. I hope I'm not disturbing you."

"No, Captain, what's up?"

"There's an unexpected tropical storm brewing in the Caribbean, and I wanted to alert you, as we may have to move the jet to a safer location."

"Is it coming in the direction of Key West?"

"Well, yes, it is, at least for now. It's only a tropical depression, but conditions are favorable for it to strengthen. Why do you ask?"

"Jeff, Ginger, and Johnson are in Key West right now. The newlyweds decided to take a vacation on their vacation and drove down yesterday. Johnson followed behind in another car. Can they get out in time?"

Woody said, "I expect warnings to go up in the Keys by the end of the day, which will cause a major traffic jam when tourists and residents are asked to head for the mainland. They'll be caught in the traffic. Maybe I should go down and pick them up immediately?"

Jade said, "I'll give them a call and see if they can leave there now before the traffic hits. You may want to head up to the airport and get ready to go."

"Will do. I already alerted the other crew members that we may be altering our flight plan. Key West just wasn't on the list, but it can be added, unless the winds hold us back. I'll wait for your call."

Jade called Johnson, and his voice was uncharacteristically winded. "Is everything okay? You sound like you're out of breadth."

"I've been riding a damn bike all over the island looking for our damn kids. They took off on bikes early this morning with no warning. Worst of all, I have some alarming news. Someone may be out to assassinate Jeff!"

"I know. I just found out from Longshot, who heard it from a Vegas cop friend. How'd you hear about it?"

"I was following Jeff and Ginger and found not one, but two groups tailing them. I made some calls and found out that the FBI received a tip. They assigned two agents to follow Scratch. Ginger's old buddy seems to be the focus of the investigation for the moment. I'm somewhat nervous that they're on their own when some hired nut could be gunning for them."

Jade became distraught over this thought, and Longshot could sense that she was ready to lose self-control. He grabbed the phone from her hand, and spoke with Johnson briefly regarding this situation. He told him about the storm, and that the jet was getting ready to come down and pick them up. Johnson said, "Perfect. Now I just need to find them."

Hurricanes, assassination attempts, corrupt politics, and contract endorsements were of no consequence when you're snorkeling with sharks, parrot fish, turtles, and barracudas. That's exactly what Jeff and Ginger were doing. After their romantic sunrise, they decided to check out the reefs. The water was starting to get choppy from the winds on the front end of the hurricane, but the water was still crystal clear, offering exceptional visibility.

Lack of disguise preparation also provided a clear view of the couple's celebrityism. Halfway out to the reefs, the other passengers easily recognized Jeff and Ginger, sparking autograph signings and countless photo opportunities. Jeff and Ginger embraced their popularity and were courteous to their adventuresome tourist friends who were from virtually every part of the country. Andy and Ruth from Pittsburgh, Santos and Marcia from Rhode Island, Skip, Lu Lu, and Morty from Kansas, and two sisters, Renee and Kristina from Colorado were all snorkeling with a presidential hopeful.

Once they docked at the reef, the boat captain instructed everyone on how to use the snorkeling equipment. He also suggested that if anyone became seasick, to please turn their heads in the direction of the water, not the boat, as the fish enjoyed the pea soup breakfast, and the boat wouldn't have to be cleaned. All nervously smiled, hoping they wouldn't be a victim of the rocking waters.

The boat went to two marvelous reefs that exploded with a variety of colorful coral and active fish species. By the end of the second dive, the chop became choppier. Many of the snorkelers were swallowing too much ocean water while the fish watched them bobbing in the water like odd-shaped buoys. The boat captain blasted a horn requiring the bouncing snorkelers to return to the boat for departure back to the mainland.

Within minutes, the choppy water was cresting small white caps. Alas, one poor soul, Mrs. Nesbaum from Little Rock, decided that her cookies needed to be tossed with little warning. One person's vomit is another fish's breakfast. A multitude of fish surfaced for the free entrée. Although it was quite entertaining to watch normally passive fish act like piranhas, a chain reaction of projectile vomiting that included half of the snorkelers added to the feeding frenzy, as snorkeler after snorkeler relinquished their entire stomach contents for the benefit of fish they'll see again.

Jeff and the other non-sick members of the boat were astonished at the fish's incredible delight with the puke buffet. Jeff thought this should become a major attraction at any marine park but realized it would be very difficult to get so many people sick at the same time on dry land. One stout woman was clearly winning the volume and distance competition, and Jeff was looking for Ginger to point out this women's natural and unknown talent. He noticed Ginger on the back of the boat doing her best to not join in on the fish feeding segment of the tour. Ginger was as green as an iguana but made it back to the mainland without serving the fish dessert. She was amazed at how fast she recovered once her feet hit dry land. After a glass of water and no movement, she was ship shape.

Several of the other fallen victims that recovered from the fiercest of water hazards, invited Jeff and Ginger to go sight-seeing with them. They ended up peddling their bikes over to Fort Zachary Taylor. As they learned about this historic national landmark, Jeff turned into a little boy again, pretending to be in charge of the cannon brigade.

While he played a war scene through his mind and bombed the enemy ships, Johnson interrupted his dream by tapping him on the shoulder. "Jeffrey, don't you know you're supposed to leave your dad a note and tell him where you're going to play?"

Jeff looked a little confused at first, and then realized that Johnson was out looking for them. "Oh man, I'm really so sorry. We got up early to watch the sunrise. Then on the way back to the B&B, we noticed a snorkel boat tour preparing to depart. We bought some bathing suits at the dock in time for the first launch. Man, the sharks were so cool. So were the 'cuda. Then almost everyone fed fish with their own puke. How awesome! But look at these cannons. Wouldn't you like to hear one of these babies blast off?"

Johnson tried to scold the future leader of the free world in a fatherly fashion, but he was doing all these cool things for the first time, and time itself was not on his mind. "All right. Blast your cannon. But be quick. The jet's coming to pick you up. We have a hurricane coming this way."

At 7 A.M., Sonny Hoag called his colleagues (better known as conspirators during Roman times) to discuss what to do with Jeff Taylor and his unplanned impact on the presidential campaign. "Jeff is taking votes away from me and the other candidates at an astounding rate, and he's not even running for office. What should we do?"

They all agreed that taking Jeff out of the picture permanently was just far too risky and probably too expensive. Their best bet was to try to dig up some dirt on him that could damage his image or credibility. But he had neither of those now, especially since he wasn't in business or politics. Therefore, finding anything on Ginger was an even better tactic, especially since her past was quite extreme and potentially filled with incriminating events that U. S. voters would find appalling and not suitable for a First Lady. But they had to plan their attack on her with great care, as she probably crossed paths with their friends, colleagues, and associates, and they certainly didn't want to jeopardize anyone's careers, especially their own. They decided to hire an unknown company that was well known in both political and business circles for their successful, discreet, and typically illegal method of obtaining information. Scratch had worked for this company at one point in time but started his own business and branched off into other types of similarly unethical activities. Besides, Scratch was already following Jeff and Ginger for some other competitor, which could create a conflict of interests.

Scratch fell back asleep after Tyrone's accidentally on-purpose wake up call, only to hear a tapping on the door around 10:30. "Hey Tiger, it's me Toni. I have the lovely breakfast set up. It'll be here until 11. Come out when you're hungry."

Scratch closed his eyes and started falling back asleep only to have his sleep be interrupted by the sounds of construction. He tossed and turned and decided to put the TV on to drown out the hammering and electric saws, only to find out that a hurricane was coming his way. A little tropical storm off the eastern coast of Cuba had become a category one hurricane, and it was headed for Key West. One local station entitled the storm, "Lame Cain Keys Pain." One newscaster said the traffic on US 1 heading out of the Keys was at a standstill, and if you hadn't left Key West by now, don't, as you might get stuck in your car during the storm, which was a terrible option.

During the hurricane news, the TV station switched to more important late breaking news. "Jeff and Ginger are the secret Darlings of the Keys." Scratch couldn't believe it. "Their damn social life is more important than a hurricane that could kill thousands of people." Scratch watched the news, as some local tourists had submitted footage to a news station of Ginger and Blabs on stage, and Jeff and Ginger snorkeling. Scratch thought that the clip showing Ginger in her bikini was the highlight of the newscast. The newscaster said, "Ginger doesn't need to take a polygraph; she has nothing to hide." Scratch figured Jeff and Ginger were stuck on the island as well, so he decided to stay put in his room until the storm passed.

His cell phone rang at that moment. Sonny called Scratch's bluff and said, "Since you're working for someone else, I won't need your assistance with Jeff and Ginger."

Scratch hated bad news in the morning. It tended to give him a bad hair day. He said, "Not so fast. Don't you need some help with the polygraph? I told you I'm an expert in beating it."

Sonny said, "Well, wouldn't your current customer get pissed if you helped me?"

Scratch replied, "No, they decided it was too risky to remove them permanently from the race and backed out of the contract." Sonny half-believed him since that was his group's conclusion. "I'm still in Key West tailing them. We're waiting for the storm to blow over. I can call you later this week."

Sonny responded with apprehension. "Are you certain you can teach me to beat this damn thing? I don't want to go out on the limb with the press and set a date, only to have the scribbling lines knock me right out of the race."

"Sonny, I've never been convicted for a crime. A big part of that was beating the lie detector test. If I can do it, you can do it."

"Okay, call me when you get back to Miami, and we'll set things up."

Scratch took a quick shower and was glad to see that his rash had subsided to the point where he could walk without pain. He went out to get some breakfast and was greeted by Toni and a tremendous gust of wind. "I guess I'm going to have to stay here during the storm. Is that okay?"

Toni smiled. "Of course, sugar. Since I live upstairs, you might be safer in my place. You won't have to worry about those nasty flood waters. Besides, I'm a pro at these things. You'll be safe with me, tiger." Scratch felt like a fish out of water. He knew nothing about hurricanes or what he should do during a storm.

He simply nodded while the trees violently moved in the wind, nervously anticipating the worst of the storm.

After Sonny spoke with Scratch, he called the unknown investigative firm to lay out the plan and goal. Within a few hours, a team of unscrupables called the Internet Thugs, or I-Thugs, delved into Jeff and Ginger's pasts, searching their home, and interviewing their landlords, friends, neighbors, and co-workers for any information. They posed themselves as a secret branch of the secret service, obtaining confidential information for a classified mission that was deemed "off the record" but vital to Jeff's chance of becoming president. They presented official-looking badges, dressed ominously, and spoke like serious law enforcement agents.

Ginger's teenage neighbors provided extreme detail about Ginger's love affair with the Internet, although they never knew her true occupation and thought she was just anxious to become an Internet shopaholic. Jeff's landlord granted them entry to their apartment. Here, they discovered Ginger's laptop, camera equipment, and assortment of seductive costumes. Everything was filmed and categorized with handheld computers. They checked her computer's history of visited and favorite sites, finding out the name of the Internet Service Provider that hosted her web site. Next, they backed up her entire laptop hard drive, so they could embark on a detailed search of her computer at their own convenience. They put everything back in its original place and headed over to the Hard Rock Hotel and Casino.

They were going to break into the room where Jeff and Ginger stayed to look at the computer, but the security personnel prevented them from entering the room inconspicuously or illegally. I-Thug 1 found out that the suite was not occupied that evening and booked the room. The I-Thugs entered the room and were greeted by Helmsford and Sasha, who immediately began showing them around the suite.

The I-Thugs were only concerned with the computer, however, and asked them to arrange dinner in the room, as they did not want to be disturbed. Sasha slowly described the hotels specialties, but I-Thug 2 rudely interrupted. "Listen, lady, I don't care about all that fancy crap. Just send up prime rib and lobster for all of us. Also, send up all the starters; you know, soup, potato skins, whatever. And get crackin', we're hungry."

Sasha replied, "Yes, sir, right away." She looked at Helmsford, who simply rolled his eyes, and escorted Sasha out of the room.

The I-Thugs booted up the computer, checked out the link history, and found that Ginger had contacted her hosting company from the hotel room. The computer saved and automatically displayed her User ID when they went to the hosting login screen. All they needed now was her password. They called the home of the teenage neighbors, but they didn't know her password. I-Thug 3 called an expert code breaker to hack his way into Ginger's account. He asked several questions about Ginger and took it from there.

While they were waiting for the anticipated good news regarding her password, they ravaged and pillaged the bar. Within the hour, dinner was served. Helmsford and Sasha set the dinner table for them, filled up their water glasses, and left without offering any further assistance. Shortly after the I-Thugs devoured their dinner, barely using their dining utensils, a call was made to I-Thug 3 from his web hack expert.

"I'm in. Here's the password: 2hotlovebirds. Some pretty horny video. No wonder you called me."

While still on the phone, I-Thug 3 keyed in the password, spilling beer all over the keyboard in the process, but he couldn't log in to the site. "You're full of shit. I keyed in the password and can't get in."

The web hack responded, "Moron. Let me log off first. Only one person at a time can be logged in."

A few moments later, I-Thug 3 keyed in the password, and presto, a set of files were displayed. They all realized they had hit the "Crush Jeff" jackpot by gaining entry to the site where Ginger stored her videos. I-Thug 2 hooked up the computer to the TV for large screen perversion viewing.

As they started watching the videos, Helmsford and Sasha entered the room, asking if they could be of further service.

I-Thug 2 paused the video and yelled, "Take the night off, coattails, and get the hell out of here."

Helmsford said, "Very well, sir, have a pleasant evening." As they departed from the room, Helmsford caught a glimpse of the adult video and recognized Ginger on TV. He maintained his blank, non-observant expression and assumed the worst.

When Helmsford and Sasha entered the servant's quarters, Helmsford called security and made sure the suite surveillance cameras were activated, which they were. Next, he retrieved Johnson's cell phone number from hotel security and called him immediately. Johnson did not respond, so he left an urgent message explaining what he saw and asked him to return the call. He was not sure what was going on, but he wanted to repay Jeff and Ginger in some way for their respectful and courteous treatment.

The I-Thugs took advantage of the first class accommodations and ate and drank themselves into bachelor party-like oblivion. They watched all the videos, reviewing several two or three times. Some arguments sprouted over which video was the best. Unknown to them was the video they didn't uncover regarding Congressman Hoag, as Ginger had already deleted the "SonnyBlabs" video. They did know that their find was substantial and could be used as excellent blackmail evidence. Since the hotel PC did not have a DVD burner, they downloaded the video files to their own laptop and created eighteen DVD's worth of Ginger erotica. They called their boss and related the good news, who in turn called Sonny. Sonny was so elated that he even took his wife out to dinner and afterwards pretended to enjoy having sex with her. She pretended to enjoy the sexcapade even more than him, knowing his happiness often equated to more shopping without arguments or financial limitations.

Woody and Walter safely bounce-landed the plane through the unpredictable 45 mph winds at the Key West airport. Gloria and Lourdes were flopping around their seats with no one else on board to enjoy the show. Their plane was the last to land at the airport, and the last one going out.

On the way to the airport, a brief stop was made at the Parrotdice bed and breakfast so Jeff and Ginger could retrieve Blabs and their bags, and say thanks to Dale and Mia for a fabulous time. Mia spent part of the morning speaking with Blabs and mentioned that Blabs had a larger vocabulary than her husband. Dale stood there nodding his head in agreement while holding a six pack and said, "It's a good ten minute drive to the airport," so he handed Jeff four beers.

Johnson came out of the car to push them along. Dale said, "So, this is your secret service body guard?"

"Yes," Jeff responded. "He's our conscience. We didn't know that consciences knew the way to Key West, but ours does."

Jeff handed Mia some extra cash to pay for his room while Dale said, "Well, you'll need the rest of the brews then," and handed them to Johnson. Dale continued with a smile, "Jeff, next time you come to Key West, Johnson is more than welcome but have him keep his conscience on the mainland. This is no place for a conscience down here. That's why we left. By the way, if you happen to run into my conscience up there, shoot it. They only get in the way of life."

Everyone simply grinned and agreed. Just then a big gust of wind swirled the banyan trees and shuddered the shutters. Dale said one last good-bye and began battening down the hatches in preparation of the storm. Johnson could see Jack and Tyrone watching them from the car. Johnson nodded to each of them, using telepathy to wish them luck in the storm and their mission.

The threesome quickly departed for the airport, returned the rental cars, boarded the plane, and left paradise. Only three beers were consumed. Dale obviously miscalculated the distance, using bike time instead of car time to determine the estimated time of arrival. Jeff promised to return the beers to Dale one day and made a toast to his new friends as the jet screamed to Miami.

Johnson did not hear his cell phone ringing as the plane thundered during takeoff. Captain Woody had clearance to land at the smaller Opa Locka airport in Miami. Gloria and Lourdes indicated that the storm had stalled over Cuba, but it was still headed in their direction, expecting landfall within forty-eight hours as a category 1 hurricane.

While en route, Co-Captain Walter came out and suggested that they fly to Tampa or Atlanta, as they didn't want to keep the plane grounded in the path of the storm, but Ginger wasn't tolerating the bumpy plane ride very well, surely a leftover result of their morning snorkeling trip. They landed in Miami as planned.

As soon as they got off the plane, the flight crew told them to keep safe, and they took off for safer jet storage. The SUV limo was waiting for them but with bad news. They had just heard on the radio that all the beaches were under mandatory evacuation, and they couldn't get to their hotel room. In addition, all the north-bound roads were jammed with the traffic of people trying to escape the storm. Jeff asked Johnson for his cell phone so he could call his golf buddy, Don, for advice. Johnson saw that he had a message waiting but let Jeff make his priority call first.

Don answered the phone and said, "Come on over to my place. The shutters are up, the bar is stocked, and we can see how far a golf ball travels in 100 mile an hour winds. We'll have a hurricane party. You'll be driving against the traffic, so you should get here in twenty minutes."

After exchanging directions, Jeff gave the phone to Johnson, who was about to retrieve his message when his phone rang. "Johnson, it's Jade. Have you heard? We have to evacuate the hotel immediately. Where are we going to go? Can we take the jet outta here?"

Johnson replied, "No, the jet just took off. But we can stay at Jeff's friend's house. They are well inland and his home is protected." Johnson gave them directions and told them to get over there any way possible. Juan arranged to have his cousin Julio take Jade and Longshot to Don's house. With Juan's assistance, their bags were quickly packed and transferred to the hotel lobby, where Julio was waiting for them.

Meanwhile, Johnson finally retrieved his voice mail. For the first time, he broke his steadfast role and displayed the look of death on his face.

Jeff cringed and asked, "What's wrong?"

Johnson handed him the phone so he could replay the message. Jeff battled Johnson for the best look of death competition.

Ginger said, "What's wrong?"

With a long face, Jeff said, "Helmsford left a message saying that the hotel security surveillance system filmed some suspicious guests who stayed in our suite at the Hard Rock. They were watching one of your videos on the computer. They looked like police types, but they were very rude and offensive."

Johnson said, "They aren't police. The FBI is already involved, and Longshot would know if local cops had any reason to investigate us."

Ginger said, "What is the FBI involved in?"

Johnson took a deep breath and said, "Well... they are following Scratch. He seems to be connected to an assassination attempt on Jeff."

Jeff did a double take and yelled "WHAT? Someone's trying to kill me? That's it. The party's over. I'm bugging out of this race. It's not worth it."

Ginger said, "Relax, Jeff, it's no big deal."

"What do you mean it's no big deal? Someone's trying to kill me, or maybe you, too. That's no big deal?"

Ginger calmly said, "Jeff, listen to me. No one is trying to kill you."

"How do you know?"

Ginger replied, "Several days ago I called an old friend in the FBI. To make a long story short, he owed me a favor. I told him about Scratch and said he needed to be watched. My friend told me the only way to investigate him was to provide some tip or evidence suggesting that a crime might be committed. I told him that it wouldn't surprise me if Sonny Hoag or some other candidate wanted you out of the presidential race, and Scratch might be a suspect to stop your efforts. He said he'd take care of it."

Johnson added, "Scratch was in Miami and Key West following you guys. I met with the FBI agents in Key West."

"Really? Wow," said Ginger. "I guess now we can relax."

Jeff was not ready to relax. "How come all this crap is going on, and I don't know anything about it?"

Johnson used his fatherly voice and said, "Son, you don't need to know everything that's going on. You need to only be concerned with your lovely bride and your quest to not run for president. Let me, Jade, and Longshot worry about everything else. We've got your back covered."

It had been a long time since someone looked out for Jeff. He slumped back into the fine leather upholstery like a little boy and said, "Okay."

Luck prevailed for the southern-most tip of the United States. After the storm left Cuba, it lost some punch, and headed due north, just east of Key West. It regained some of its strength back over the middle Keys, setting its sites on Miami. Since Key West missed the brunt of the storm, Scratch's need of hurricane protection was short lived. Toni hoped a steady supply of gin and hurricane fear would break down Scratch's barrier of affection. But except for several big gusts and pounding surf and rain, the storm was weak by Key West standards, and ruined Toni's chance for romance. It hurt the island economy with lost tourist dollars more than storm damage. Within a few hours of the storms departure north, the power was restored, storm shutters were removed, and Key West reverted back to its eclectic island self.

When the winds died down, Scratch returned to his own room leaving Toni distraught. He was unaware that Jeff and Ginger were in Miami.

Hole Number 9
Par 4

(Course Notes:
Blown away in a hurricane, hitting backward balls in the horizontal rain.)

Don Mastroe welcomed everyone with open arms in the wake of the storm, knowing that this was a very unusual situation for his guests. The original foursome showed up at his house at about the same time. Already, the wind gusts were spiking at 50 miles an hour, bending the large royal palms that governed his house. In his effort to make them feel safe, he discussed a little bit of what would happen during a storm and even showed them how his house was boarded up for protection.

Don said, "As of right now, the storm is going to come up through the middle keys as a category One, turn to the southern end of the tip of Florida, and pass from the south right through the heart of Miami. If it stays on that projected path, we'll be in the eye of the storm. But no worries. We've had some practice with these storms of late, and we're getting pretty good at this. We'll probably lose power, but I've got a backup generator for the fridge. I have enough food and water to last us about five days. Since this is only a cat 1 storm, I would hope that our electricity is back on within the week. It may sound kind of scary for a while, but it's mostly just the noise of the wind. The best thing to do is just to chill out. Enjoy the air conditioning and TV while we have it. This is really an awesome spectacle of Mother Nature as long as you're safe, so let's enjoy it. Now everybody make yourself at home."

While Don attended to last minute hurricane preparations, the presidential crew convened for a short meeting. The major topics of discussion were the conjectured assassination attempt, the invasion of Ginger's videos, and the endorsement opportunities. Jade and Longshot were obviously glad to learn that that no one, as far as they knew, was trying to kill Jeff. That news sort of softened the blow of Ginger's videos getting pirated.

"Whoever is behind this really means business," Johnson said.

Longshot agreed, "You got that right, but we still have the Sonny video, and that is our wildcard."

Johnson countered, "Do you think that DVD is safe in your office? These guys hacked their way into Ginger's files within a few days. I think we need a safer place to store the DVD. We're dealing with pros. I have some friends in D.C. who can hold it for us in a secure area that's typically used for top secret espionage information. All we have to do is get it there."

Jeff said, "Let's do it. Can Bob FedEx the DVD out tonight?"

Upon those words, Longshot called the radio station, but Bob wasn't there. Next, he called Bob's cell phone but received only his voice mail. He left an urgent message for him to call him back ASAP.

Johnson turned to Ginger, and said, "You know what can happen with these videos if they get in the wrong hands? I imagine we'll be contacted by the responsible thieves, asking us to back out of the election campaign. They'll demand ransom money, or who knows what. Do you want to stay in the race?"

Ginger sat there for a minute and said, "I don't know."

Longshot said, "Well, let's add some gas to the fire. As of right now, we have over $75 million worth of endorsement opportunities. Think about that before you make your decision."

Ah, the feeling of total awe and bewilderment rejoined Jeff and Ginger once again. They looked like book ends, matching each other's blank stares. Maybe they needed to relocate to Key West permanently to escape the constant feeling of being stunned. Ginger had a difficult time being able to even fathom that much money but liked the thought of trying and said "SEVENTY-FIVE MILLION DOLLARS. Are you sure? I thought several million was a lot."

Then Jade stepped in. "Yes, I'm sure. Ellen Spackler emailed the list of endorsement opportunities to me, along with her recommendations. Since we'll be hunkered down together for the next few days, I suggest we pick the ripe ones and get moving on these endorsements. By the way, Jeff, your little Keys trip, along with Longshot's radio broadcast regarding the polygraph, has increased your vote count to a third of the country. You've got 70 million people ready to cast their votes for you right now. Do you want to pursue this race? I think at some point you'll have to make an official decision."

Jeff had a minute to ponder the mess of activity that surrounded him like a flash flood. He developed a rare feeling of anger and guilt, thinking that someone could expose his wife to the world, all because of a bet he made with Longshot. However, his anger was not pointed at Longshot or himself but toward the unethical, unscrupulous bastards who would go to any length to get elected. Jeff's expressionless face turned about 180 degrees, adding a rarely seen sense of confidence, leadership, and courage to his demeanor, and he spoke with authority. "You're right. I have made a decision."

Everyone sat on the edge of their seats as though they were ready to watch the climactic ending to a murder mystery movie.

"I can hit a million golf balls at the driving range, practicing shots and refining my swing, but all the practice in the world is wasted if I don't play the game."

Jeff paused for a moment while a wind blast shook the house and continued, "I believe our lives are ruled by destiny. The best golfers in the world can lose a major tournament to an amateur golfer if it's the amateur's destiny to win. I don't know why Ginger and I got married. I don't know how I hooked up with Longshot and let him convince me to participate in this ridiculous bet and campaign." He looked at Jade and Johnson and said, "I don't know how you guys got involved in this mess. But you did. We are all destined to be here right now without any logical explanation. So, let's follow our destiny, and play the game, win or lose. Let's give the other presidential assholes a fight for their money. Just think, we can have a blast pissing off a lot of politicians and business leaders. This would be our way of paying them back for all the lies, bribes and unpresidential behavior we've had to deal with over the years."

Another wind gust interrupted Jeff, but he continued. "But if the attacks on Ginger become too much for her to handle, we'll disqualify ourselves from the game. But for now, we've got a difficult, long par 5 to play that's laden with hazards and strong head winds, and we need a birdie to win. So we're going for the green in two shots. Let's play the game and see what happens."

One of the former presidential ghosts had crept back into Jeff and took over his mind, much to the surprised delight of his campaign crew. Longshot, Jade, and Johnson were inspired by his emotion and attitude and actually applauded. Just then, Blabs started singing, "We Are the Champions," and everyone laughed and wondered how she could know what they were talking about.

Ginger's face glowed from the emotion that Jeff spilled onto her and the group, and she said, "Jeff, I'm ready to play too. If my videos get national exposure, I'll deal with that when it happens. In the meantime, let's get the 'SonnyBlabs' DVD to Johnson's contacts and then take it from there, although I don't want any of us to be in any danger during this game."

Johnson jumped in, "You're right. No amount of money is worth a life. How did we feel when we thought Jeff was a target? You're better off regripping golf clubs on earth than playing golf with the angels. Let's not tell the FBI about the assassination hoax so they can continue to watch our back door. Scratch might be just sniffing around, but having the feds watch him is a good thing. I'll arrange to have the hotel video of the intruders sent to us from the FBI. If we can find out who they are, they might lead us to the person or group who's trying to bring us down. Let's try to stay a step ahead of them, if at all possible. Agreed?"

A chorus of "agreed" sang in unison, including Blabs, who sounded a lot like Johnson.

Just then a huge gust of wind shook the house. Don joined the group and said, "That's the wind I've been waiting for. Jeff, you ever hit a sand wedge into a 50 mile per hour gust of wind? Come on." Don grabbed two high-lofted clubs and a bag of golf balls.

His girlfriend, Carolyn, entertained the houseguests while the boys shagged some balls into the big winds. Blabs squawked during a wind gust and then kicked in her rendition of "Dust in the wind. All we are is dust in the wind."

Carolyn said "How does she know what wind is?" Ginger said "I have no clue, but she sure is good at it."

Apollo was the name of the first hurricane of the season. Apollo stalled over Cuba, but once it left the island, it picked up a huge amount of speed and raced through the middle keys like a wind surfer into the lower tip of South Florida. The wind gusts were like intermittent ocean waves, creating a sense of choppy lull, and then all of a sudden, swoosh, a gusting wave announced that Mother Nature wanted to play. The weakest of branches began to break and flew through the air in an angled proportion based on their size and velocity of the wind gust.

While assessing the wind speed and projected ball placement, Don said, "We're gonna have a nice mess after this. The trees of my southern-faced neighbor end up in my yard, and my tree debris plays tag and ends in my neighbor's yard to the north. The trees receive a natural trimming, and we're all rewarded by cleaning up the mess."

Jeff listened, but he was more focused on the challenge of hitting balls into gusts he couldn't imagine. They were hitting balls into different angles of the wind, while keeping a close eye on the hurricane-created UFOs. Jeff crunched a ball into the teeth of one gust that actually sent his ball flying backwards. Typically, he could knock a strong sand wedge about 130 yards, but his ball got caught up in a powerful wind and sent his ball soaring behind him, much to his delight. He thought of it as boomerang golf in the eye of the storm.

Don and Jeff were like school boys playing stick ball, except they were using golf clubs and hurricane-force winds to play. They started having a closest-to-the-pin contest, deploying the boomerang rules by aiming away from the green and using the wind to grab their well-struck balls and airmail them over their heads to the flag stick behind them. A new version of golf was born; unfortunately, dangerous hurricane-force winds were required to compete.

Ginger came out with a video camera and filmed some of the action. The game was becoming more dangerous as larger tree limbs were starting to detach and race in their direction. Daylight was ending sooner than normal, as the bands of clouds started to combine into one large formation, ultimately taking control of the horizon. Ginger ducked when a house shingle flew over her head.

She said "That's it. Game over boys. It's time to head in before we lose our heads." Don agreed. "You're right. That shingle came too close. Come on Jeff. Time to go in. We can't see what's comin at us."

Jeff said "Go inside. I'll be right behind you. Let me crunch one more with a strong wind at my back, and then I'll head in." Don and Ginger ran back to the house dodging flying debris. Jeff watched the tops of the trees at a distance, timing his swing to connect with the ball at the same time of the gust. *Smack.* Jeff almost fell over from the gust but got the shot off just prior to the gust, balancing himself long enough to watch his ball thunder over a huge set of trees to a house that he thought he could never reach in a million years. It was a thing of beauty (in a golfer's mind) until he heard the sound of glass shattering.

Don and Ginger turned around and saw Jeff walking in the opposite direction and yelled to coax him back to the safety of the house, but with no success.

He walked about 200 yards in the direction of his ball. Through the band of trees, Jeff saw a shattered glass window, along with gray hairs and scared eyes peering through the large broken window. When Jeff approached the home of the old lady, he could see the terror in her eyes, especially since her back patio window was shattered into a million pieces and the storm was approaching. There was tree debris all around the shattered glass window, so Jeff wasn't completely certain if his ball was the culprit. Just then, he started to hear the cracking of an oak tree just above his head.

Ginger still had the video camera on and, like an eye-witness news photographer, pointed the camera in the direction of the cracking tree limb and Jeff.

Without thinking, Jeff acted like a Miami Dolphin middle linebacker. He lunged through the broken window and tackled the older woman for a ten-yard loss into the center of her room. A huge oak branch came crashing down to the very spot where Jeff and the old lady had been standing, demolishing part of the roof and wall. The tree limb was so large, it completely filled up her Florida room with tree branches, twigs, and leaves.

Don pushed his way through the tree limbs and yelled, "Are you okay, are you okay?"

Jeff shouted back over the noisy wind saying, "I'm fine."

The old lady had to catch her breath and hold back some tears of fright as she said, "I'm okay, but I have a tree limb or something pushing into my back."

Don shoved enough of the tree aside so that Jeff could get off the woman. When they pulled her up to her feet, they both saw that a golf ball was the object causing the pain in the lady's back. They both embarrassedly smiled at each other with guilt, but were relieved that the woman was not hurt. Jeff had saved her life, although he might have been the cause of the accident.

Ginger caught the entire sequence of events on film.

The storm was turning very nasty and everyone realized that the old woman could not stay there by herself. Don said, "You're going to stay at my house through the rest of this storm. The eye wall is approaching fast, if it's not already here."

Jeff took the woman by the arm and escorted her to Don's house. As they hurried back, the old lady looked at Jeff and said, "Thank you for saving my life." Then she noticed Jeff and said, "Say, you're Jeff Taylor, aren't you? I recognized you from TV. I think you and your wife are darlings. Can I have your autograph?"

Jeff replied in a subdued yet alarming voice, "Lady, eighty mile an hour winds are throwing roof tiles, branches, and unsecured patio furniture in our direction, and you want my autograph? Let's get inside where it's safe, and I'll give you 100 autographs for you and your friends." She smiled as they played dodge ball with the windy objects flying in their direction.

When they returned to the house, Jade was edgy from the storm and started yelling at them for being outside. Jeff explained the situation, and introductions were exchanged with Stella. Ginger showed everyone the video, and Jade said, "Don, do you have a high speed Internet connection?"

"Sure do, but I don't know how long it will last. Why?"

Jade hooked up the camera to the computer and downloaded the clip of Jeff saving Stella's life. Next, after asking Carolyn the name of local TV stations, she obtained their email addresses from their web sites and sent copies of the clip to them, along with a short note describing how Jeff had saved the woman's life. She didn't go into details regarding the correct golf stance when addressing a ball in 70 mile per hour winds (give or take 10 mph).

Just as the file was sent, they heard the crackling sound of a transformer blowing up, and darkness fell upon them. The storm formally introduced itself to them and the rest of South Florida.

Apollo shook hands with the southern coast of Florida, but a strong jet stream from the northwest persuaded Apollo to head back out to sea. As parting gifts, he left an assorted mess of fallen trees, minor roof damage, downed traffic lights, and blown transformers that resulted in no power. Blabs kept everyone entertained by singing a variety of tunes, including "Hotel California," "Brick House," and "Singing in the Rain." Stella kept requesting classic movie songs from the 1940s, but Blabs hadn't been exposed to music before the 1950s. Meanwhile, the winds subsided, and everyone slowly opted for sleep.

(Course Notes: Crime keeps on slipp'n, gyp'n, dipp'n, into the future. B 4 U Go, I C U.)

At precisely 3 P.M., Summerton "Sonny" Hoag, full of new confidence and grandeur, walked up to the podium with his back facing the Wright Brothers National Memorial. It offered an ideal backdrop to the delight of the press and, hopefully, a nation of couch potato voters. Cameras focused on the hundreds of "Vote Sonny" signs, held up by loyal campaign contributors who showed up and cheered for Sonny Hoag in exchange for a 20 percent off coupon on any selected food item, at any participating Swine Dine restaurant. The crowd that showed up was small in number, but large in raw weight, thus providing the illusion of a large turnout.

"Good afternoon Ladies and Gentlemen. Thank you for joining me on this picture perfect North Carolina day." Sonny had pre-arranged this media event, keeping an eye on a wave of storms that were befalling the North Carolina coastline. "As many of you know, behind me is the Wright Brothers National Monument, the birthplace of flight in the United States of America. Two men, Orville and Wilbur Wright, filled with inspiration, courage, and determination, fulfilled their dream of successfully dancing with angels here at Kitty Hawk. Yes, this is where air travel was born."

Sonny turned around to face the monument and returned with eyes somewhat blurred for special effect. "Orville and Wilbur had many obstacles before triumph. Plane design, redesign, failures, testing, ...and people. Yes, one of their biggest obstacles was people. They were challenged by many doubters. Many people looked them square in the eye and said, 'You can't fly. If we were meant to fly, God would have given us wings.' Yet, my friends, as you know, they met this challenge head on and conquered the non-believers, agreeing with them that God did not give man wings...but, he did give us intelligence and the desire to achieve. These are the qualities that many great men and women have displayed to make America the great land it is. But, my fellow Americans, there will always be the non-believers...Those who relish failure...Those who are afraid to step up to challenges and try to beat them."

During the pauses of his speech, the news microphones picked up the human sounds of rumbling in the background. It sounded like the crowd was murmuring with patriotic emotion by his speech much to Sonny's delight. The sounds were, in fact, the rumbling stomachs of those who had to wait to the end of his long-winded speech before obtaining their discount coupons and rush to the Swine Dine for their afternoon feeding.

"Ladies and Gentlemen, it's my goal to embrace attitudes like those of the Wright Brothers and lead our nation with confidence, diplomacy, and honesty as president of the United States. These ideals, however, are not able to be tested. You have to judge the integrity of the individual and his ability to lead and achieve for yourselves. For example, my successful track record as Congressman for the Great State of North Carolina is one measurement of what I have done, and what I can do for all Americans. Yet, those doubters, those non-believers who hoped the Wright Brothers would fail, still exist. I have been challenged to take a polygraph test by a so-called candidate who does not have the courage or patriotism to run for office. This test is supposed to demonstrate my integrity. I don't understand it. I'm willing to spend the next four, and even eight years of my life devoted to improving our country. My challenger says he'll simply 'take the job' if elected. My friends, being president is not a job. It is a position of utmost importance that affects nearly 300 million Americans and billions of people around the world." The moans started getting louder, and the sound engineers had to back down the dials, as interfering feedback started to occur.

"A president must be courageous, stare challenges in the face, and overcome such challenges. Therefore my friends, I will accept the Honest Scorecard issued by Mr. Taylor, and will set up a date to take the test. I am saddened by this blatant attempt by anyone to use electronic gizmos to determine their ability to lead, and pray that true Americans understand that the results of the test, given by a machine that has proved to be erroneous and often incorrect, are not the key components necessary to be a successful president. The Wright Brothers tested their abilities with a contraption that flew, using guts and determination. I'll honestly answer the questions given by the media, and use guts and determination to show you, the American public, that I am your choice for the next president of the United States."

Just as Sonny finished his last sentence, a Hoag committee member started handing out the Swine Dine discount coupons, and the gallery started cheering, adding a patriotic effect to the end of Sonny's speech. Before Sonny could answer any questions from the press, his loyal followers revved up their pick-em-up trucks, blared gospel and country music, and sped down the road to take 20 percent off their obsessive compulsive eating disorders at the Swine Dine.

Sonny did not say during his speech when he would take the test, and that was the only question asked by one reporter. "Congressman, on what day will you take the polygraph?"

"My schedule is jam packed for the next few weeks, but I'll make a formal announcement when a date is set." A few dark clouds, one distant lightning bolt, and a muffled roar of thunder provided perfect timing to disperse the media and conclude the event that Sonny perceived as successful. He was rather proud of his speech and felt that he articulated a clear sense of presidential tack in his style and delivery, projecting confidence that should gain some votes back from Jeff Taylor.

That night, when he watched the nightly news to gloat over his speech and stoic appearance, he ended up throwing another of his wife's heirlooms into the TV. The main story detailed Jeff Taylor's heroic efforts to save an elderly woman from certain death. While the video clip displayed Jeff's sports-like maneuver to rescue a women in immediate despair, the news commentator began...

"Jeff Taylor, staying at a friend's house in Miami during Hurricane Apollo, heard the sound of glass breaking during the frisky category one storm and went outside the home to investigate the noise. He noticed a large branch wavering violently by the erratic wind gusts near a neighbor's home. He ran over to the house to warn them that the tree might crash down on them. He observed a window had already broken from wind-thrown storm debris, and noticed an elderly woman peering out from the broken glass.

Meanwhile, his wife Ginger, who coincidentally filmed the wildness of the storm, turned the camera toward Jeff, and saw him leaping at the woman just as the branch came crashing into them. The huge limb completely demolished the home. Ginger accidentally filmed the event, and broke down in tears, as she thought Jeff and the woman had perished. Jeff's friend, Don Mastroe of Miami, ran into the remains of the tree-covered home. There he found Jeff, protecting the woman from the titanic limb. They carried the woman back to their home without need of medical attention and remained there until the eye of the storm safely passed back out to sea. Jeff Taylor is Florida's newest Hurricane Hero."
(Ah, no one can embellish a story as good as the evening news.)

Sonny was beside himself while he thought out loud, "Son bitch. How could he arrange that stunt? The footage was exceptional. How about my gad dang speech?" Toward the end of the news, just after a story about a rare species of male artic monkeys in Alaska that used walrus tusks as sleds to glide down glaciers in a perceived mating ritual, a brief video segment ran showing Sonny at his news conference. None of his breathtaking speech was aired, but the newscaster said, "Switching back to the campaign trail for a late story, Congressman Sonny Hoag announced today that he would take the Honest Scorecard polygraph test issued by Jeff Taylor, but he did not give a day or time to take the test. Hmm, will he take it, or will it be just another unfulfilled campaign promise?" The reporter obviously suggested that he was avoiding the test. On top of it all, Sonny's lunch crowd fans had departed to indulge in their discounted food feast, which made it look as though no one showed up for the speech.

On a positive note, Ashley was asleep in another bedroom while the newscast aired. Otherwise, she might have been one of objects thrown into the TV along with her other family treasures. Sonny used an unorthodox method of Olympic discus throwing to launch a picture of Ashley's mother eating at the Swine Dine towards the TV. The glass from the picture frame tore the picture, removing 20 pounds and ten years off the age of Ashley's mother without the help of digital photography enhancing software. Unfortunately, Ashley's mom would never know how good she looked, as the eventual garbage can would not reveal the discarded contents.

Don was the first to wake up in the morning, eager to assess the damage from the storm. Some fallen tree limbs and several blown out panels from his screened pool enclosure were his only calamities. Don had the gas grill fired up and coffee brewing as the hurricane partiers slowly emerged from their sleep. Carolyn prepared breakfast, and Blabs screeched, clearing her throat as she did every morning. Everyone stood around the grill as Don said, "Coffee will be ready soon. We made out okay, only minor damage. We'll be camping for the next few days, so just make the best of it."

Don turned on his portable TV and set it on the outside table. With sleep in their eyes, everyone huddled to watch and listen to the news. "The storm hit land, but made a quick turn northeast, heading safely out to the ocean. Power is out for most Miami and the lower sections of Ft. Lauderdale, but Boca and West Palm have power, so that's where to go if you need ice, water, and food supplies. Now, we're going to show you a video clip that was taken yesterday just as the storm was approaching. Jeff Taylor, presidential hopeful, was apparently hunkered down in Miami at a friend's house while bracing for the storm when he rescued a woman from a fallen tree. This video has been shown nationally already, but we realize that many of you haven't seen it yet due to power outages." The video of Jeff was shown during the commentary.

Within minutes of the video airing, Don's neighbors joined the breakfast club for a chance to meet Jeff and Ginger. Shortly afterwards, TV news trucks arrived with crews speedily setting up their camera equipment in Don's backyard. Once everything was ready to roll, they announced to Jeff that they were ready. Jeff was very calm and laid back while answering the questions from the news teams. "Jeff, in the middle of a storm, you saved a person's life. How did it happen?"

Jeff replied, "It was no big deal. I was outside during the beginning of the storm hitting a few 9 irons with Don. It was a trip to see what a strong wind could do to a golf ball in flight. I was ready to head in when I heard the glass crashing, and I went over to see what it was. Next thing I know, I was leaping at Stella while a huge tree branch comes crashing down on us. Thankfully, no one was hurt."

Just then Stella ran into picture and hugged Jeff saying, "He's my hero. He saved my life. And his bird has a wonderful voice." Jeff and Ginger started laughing.

Of course, an explanation was required, and the news team was eager for extra entertainment, so Ginger brought Blabs out for the camera. Ginger said, "Blabs, what would you like to sing for us today? Come on birdie, sing me a song."

Blabs flapped her wings, thought about the request, and starting singing, "You can't always get what you want…" The crowd surrounding Jeff, Ginger, and Blabs all joined in.

After a couple of verses, the cameraman positioned the camera back to the news reporter who said, "Well, we obviously have a post hurricane party in the making. The animals are safe but restless after the storm. Back to the studio."

After the interview, Johnson checked his cell phone and was surprised that he had one bar of signal strength. He called his FBI buddies. "Hey Tyrone, how'd you make out in the storm?"

"Just wind and rain, and a dormant Scratch. How bout you?"

"Well, we fared okay from this storm, but another storm hit in Vegas. The security cameras in the Vegas Hard Rock suite where Jeff and Ginger stayed caught some goons hacking on the PC. I think they might be trying to dig up some dirt on Ginger. She had some files stored on an Internet hosting service that she would prefer to not share with anyone."

Tyrone said, "I'll arrange to have some of our agents retrieve the hotel security video and also arrange to have the hotel suite and Jeff's apartment dusted for fingerprints. If Ginger's laptop is still in the apartment, they'd review the history of visited Internet links. I'll ask them to be discreet with their findings, but they might need to disclose the files as evidence if it comes to that. Worst of all, I think, at least at this point, it would be nearly impossible to find the paying mastermind responsible for the attacks on Jeff and Ginger, especially if it's a high ranking political figure with clout. But, we'll continue with the investigation and see where it leads us."

Johnson said "10-4. Give me a shout when you and Scratch get back into Miami."

Later that day in his campaign headquarters, Sonny fumed as he watched Jeff's post hurricane interview and Blabs sing-along, but confusion started to overshadow his anger. The sound and image of Blabs singing on the news cast gave him an overwhelming feeling of Déjà vu thinking, *Boy, that bird sounded familiar.* He actually felt good humming a few bars of the song, but he didn't know why. His musical thought process opened his mental eyes and he realized that Blabs was another piece of the Jeff's successful publicity campaign. *That damn bird is making more news than my entire campaign. It's sucking in all the pet owner's votes. I think I need to get the bird out of the picture, and let Jeff and Ginger know who owns this campaign. Bye Bye Birdie.*

Scratch also watched the news segments regarding Jeff's heroics and couldn't believe they were in Miami. While he gathered his few belongings and proceeded to the Stiff Wind office to check out, Scratch sourly thought, *How could they have got out during the storm?* Toni was sad to see him go and didn't say anything while Scratch paid his bill and left.

As Scratch came out of the Stiff Wind, Tyrone and Jack were slouching down in their car and unseen by Scratch. Jack had the video camera on and was ready to turn it off when Toni came flying out, screaming, "Wait!"

Scratch turned around, and before he could do anything, Toni wrapped his arms around him in a boa constrictor like manner and nearly sucked his face off with a passionate kiss that made Scratch dizzy. Toni released him and said, "I wanted to let you know that you'll always have a place in my heart."

Scratch was speechless, embarrassed, and bewildered. He stumbled into his car and drove off with Toni standing in the street waving goodbye. Jack and Tyrone, most likely needing reconstructive plastic surgery to remove the extreme smiles from their faces, almost blew their cover from excessively loud laughter. They had never compromised themselves as FBI agents before, but this scene was far too humorous for them to handle. Toni tearfully went back inside, and the FBI agents regained their composure and followed Scratch back to Miami.

The last I-Thug passed out by midnight, only to be awoken at 9:30 with the aid of perseverant ringing, courtesy of the front desk manager. A grumbling I-Thug finally answered the head pounding phone. The manager requested them to leave because the room was booked for the next night and needed to be serviced. Typically, suite guests are awakened with more pleasant sounds, and they are offered a late afternoon check out when possible, but the call was placed, compliments of Helmsford's desire to rid the suite of the inhospitable guests.

At 10:30, several hotel security personnel confidently knocked on the solid wood door, cordially requested entrance to the suite, and offered removal assistance to the I-Thugs to speed along their prompted departure. They departed without incident but left the suite a mess, littered with lobster claws, dirty dishes, beer cans, and peanut shells. The only clean item they left behind was the digital images of their faces and escapades, filmed entirely on hotel security cameras. Their room bill, which amounted to over $8,000, was a worthwhile business expense. Even with extreme hangovers, they conjured up a logical lie regarding the expense and called their boss to discuss reimbursement, hiding some details of the charge and embellishing others. Their boss didn't care, as he tacked the expense onto the final bill plus 15 percent, which Sonny would gladly pay based on the successful repercussions of the find.

Once the hangovers dissipated, the I-Thugs downloaded the stolen data from Ginger's laptop to the computer in their office. I-Thug 1 browsed through files and realized they hadn't looked at any of her emails. They logged on to her Internet email service and found the notes regarding Ginger's request to have a copy of video the file called "Sonnyblabs" FedEx'ed to a radio station in Las Vegas. Another email provided the tracking number and delivery date of the sent package, along with the name of the person who signed for the package, Bob Allen. I-Thug 1 made a quick call to his boss describing the emails, and the boss said, "Do whatever it takes to get that DVD!"

The I-Thugs jumped at the command of the boss like Pavlovian attack dogs and raced over to the radio station to have a chat with Bob. They brought their guns as conversation pieces. The boss decided to withhold this current information from Sonny until he received payment of current services rendered. He knew he wouldn't get a dime until the DVD was recovered.

Meanwhile, FBI agents swarmed Jeff's apartment and the Hard Rock Hotel, dusting for fingerprints and looking for any other evidence that the I-Thugs may have left behind. Rap Trap, and new multimillion dollar rapper, was outraged when his suite at the Hard Rock was not ready for his highness' arrival because the FBI was still canvassing the suite. To offset his well-publicized rage, the hotel manager decided to throw a party for the new king of rap in the grand ballroom, showering him with free everything to console his pungent smell of rap crap ego until the FBI concluded their investigation. A new PC replaced the computer that was confiscated by the FBI, and fingerprints were lifted from the room. When they completed their thorough investigation, the suite was quickly cleaned and ready for occupancy and probable demolition by the new guest.

Interviews and statements were taken from Helmsford and Sasha. Afterwards, hotel security gave the agents a copy of the video that captured the I-Thugs faces and stay at the hotel. The digital video and fingerprints could be easily downloaded into their national crime database to quickly determine if any of the Thugs could be identified or had any other prior arrests. A separate team of agents were at Jeff's apartment undergoing a similar routine. The landlord and neighbors were questioned and released. The neighbor girls who helped Ginger with her Internet education were in tears as they divulged everything to the I-Thugs thinking they worked for the government. Even the landlord felt ashamed. Ginger's laptop was found and taken by the agents. They returned to their office and started reviewing the contents of the computer and visited historic Internet links. Meanwhile, the hotel security video was being analyzed, and Ginger's user ID and password were revealed which allowed them access to Ginger's emails. They also discovered the emails of the "Sonnyblabs" video and package delivery to the radio station. The agents jumped into their gray government issued vehicles and sped off to question Bob at the radio station.

Hole Number 10
Par 4

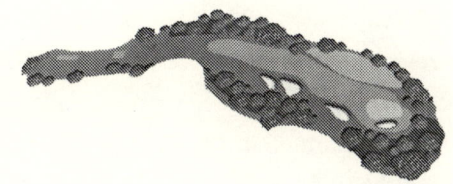

(**Course Notes**: Our environment was never meant, to be controlled, by our government. Corporations and politicians have devised our demise, yet when our world shrivels up, they'll be quite surprised as one might surmise.)

Jeff and Ginger's popularity gained worldwide exposure. The media exploited Ginger's looks, the Honest Scorecard, the unofficial quest for the presidency, and Jeff's heroics. It made them a current reality show with everyone waiting to see what would happen next. Thousands of people camped out in front of Don's house, as the news trucks revealed their hideout.

Power swiftly came back later that day, allowing Jade to check her emails and monitor web site traffic. Fifteen million dollars had been generated by the Honest Scorecard, much to the delight of the receiving charities. In addition, Ellen Spackler and her new young team filtered the business related emails and forwarded them to Jade.

The main foursome was now five, as Jeff asked Johnson to participate in all business meetings. They retreated inside Don's house after the interview so Jade could provide an overview of Ellen's recommendations to the team members. "Ellen suggests that we execute a first wave of endorsements that total $40 million. These opportunities can be legally concluded quickly, and they are with reputable companies. There's also a brief explanation of what's required from Jeff and Ginger. Basically, TV and radio commercials, wearing sponsors' clothing at specific events, and so on."

Jeff, Ginger, and Longshot looked at the list without saying a word. They recognized half of the Fortune 500 names, but the others were obscure. After a ten-minute pause in discussion, all eyes turned to Jeff for guidance. "Well, I guess we'll follow Ellen's lead, except I don't want to do any actual endorsements until after our honeymoon. Let's agree to their terms, as long as we get 10% up front, no matter if I stay in the election race or lose the election. We'll get the remainder after we return to Vegas from our honeymoon. How's that sound?" The heads in the room nodded with approval.

Jade continued with her next agenda item. "The news media is anxious to start reviewing the Honest Scorecard questions. Ellen suggests that we open the flood gates and grant the news media access to the questions."

Johnson chimed in, "I think we should arrange to have each news agency be confirmed and provide them with a user ID and password to the web site. I also think we should have Ellen's team categorize the questions, and have the most frequently asked questions posed to the candidates, in fairness to the people who submitted them." Everyone agreed.

With that, Jade called Ellen and relayed Jeff's contract requests and Johnson's comments. She also asked Ellen to have the companies send them a schedule of planned events that she would schedule after their return to Las Vegas.

Ellen made notes to follow through with the requests and contract terms. She didn't expect any major objections from the legal departments of the proposing companies. She also made notes to contact the voteforhonesty.org webmaster and set up a sign-in option screen and arrange the questions in order for the media.

While Jade was on the phone with Ellen, Longshot's phone started ringing. He recognized the number from the radio station. "Longshot, I've been trying to call you all night, but figured you lost your cell phone signal in the storm. What's up?"

"Bob, is the 'SonnyBlabs' DVD in the vault?"

"Yep."

"Good, write down this address." Longshot detailed the address provided to him from Johnson. "Get the video, back it up on one of the computers at work, make sure the file is saved, and send the original overnight to the contact on the address. Do it right now!"

Bob said, "I knew you wanted to have a copy for yourself."

"No, man, I just want a backup. This video is critical leverage for us. Now go do it, and call me after you hand it to the FedEx agent."

After they hung up, Bob went to the vault and took out the DVD. Since the station was small and only employed a few people, Bob happened to be the only one in the building at the time. He headed over to his computer to start copying the file when several eerie looking men came lurking in. "Can I help you guys?"

"Yeah, we want to speak with Bob Allen about some advertising spots."

"Well, I'm Bob, but I'm not the guy you want to speak to. Diane Lopotamis handles all of our advertising, and she's not in at the moment. Want me to have her call you back?"

I-Thug 1 said, "That's okay. We really just wanted to speak with you."

Bob became nervous. He thought that maybe Longshot made some bet he couldn't pay back, and someone sent these thugs to collect their winnings, but why did they want him? "Well, guys, I was just on my way out. Can you call me back tomorrow?"

Bob tried to make an inconspicuous attempt to leave through the back door exit, but I-Thug 2 jumped in front of him and said, "Hey, Bob, what's your hurry. We just want to chat. I understand you have a DVD that belongs to our boss, and he wants it back. Where is it?"

"Dude, I don't know what you're talking about. Ugghg." From out of nowhere, a fist slammed into his gut. Bob bent over in pain, and heard the cocking of a gun. He looked up to see the barrel of a revolver pointed toward his sweating face.

"Bob, buddy. It's almost dinnertime. We're hungry. Give us the DVD so we can get going."

I-Thug 3 snuck up from behind and bashed Bob's back with a double-fisted punch. Bob fell to the floor. "Listen Bob, we don't like to hurt our hands before dinner. Tell us where the DVD is, or we'll start shooting holes in your arms and legs. And Bob, it'll hurt like a son-of-a-bitch."

Bob, already in pain, knew for certain that these guys would enjoy putting holes in him. "All right, let me get it." He went over to the PC and pulled out the blank DVD and handed it to I-Thug 1.

"Bob, why don't we check this DVD before we leave to make sure it's the right one? For your sake, I hope it is."

Bob knew he was a dead man either way at this point, but he hoped for the best and said, "Wait, I pulled out the wrong DVD. I was going to make a copy." He pushed the button on the drive door, and out popped the drive with the DVD labeled "SonnyBlabs."

I-Thug 1 took no chances and pushed the drive door back in and started playing the original DVD to see what was on it. He looked confused at the sight and sound of Blabs singing with Sonny, and then started laughing. "Do you believe this shit?" he said, turning to the other I-Thugs. "We're getting paid to watch this bird crap. Oh well, a buck's a buck. Thanks Bob."

He pointed the gun at Bob, but Bob said, "Don't you want the copy?"

He threw the disc copy in face of the gun-pointing I-Thug and jumped out the front door. I-Thugs 2 and 3 took several shots and chased after him. As soon as they got to the door, they saw two gray sedans pull up in front of the radio station with guys in suits jumping out of the cars holding guns.

I-Thug 2 yelled, "We've got company. Quick! Out the back door."

Two FBI agents charged into the station blasting away like the gunfight at the OK Corral. I-thugs 2 and 3 were hit and fell down in pain, but I-Thug 1 escaped out into the cover of the setting sun shadows and disappeared into the streets of old buildings several blocks off the Las Vegas Strip. Bob was more scared than hurt and thankful to a higher authority for being alive. The FBI searched the area, and even called the local police for assistance in tracking him down, but for the moment, I-thug 1 was gone, along with the "Sonny Blabs" DVD.

(Course Notes: Most politicians are for the birds, except when it comes to the environment, conservation, ecology, or biology.)

Russell Goldblatz, an attorney who spent more time offering free legal counsel to charitable organizations than practicing his own practice for money, was on the roof of the Homestead Emergency Clinic helping roofers seal up gaping holes that were a result of Hurricane Apollo. The severe water damage claimed the lives of much of the medical equipment, furniture, and supplies in this precious facility. Located in the heart of South Florida farmland on the edge of the Everglades, this tiny clinic was the primary source of medical treatment for migrant farm workers until Apollo decided to concussion the roof. The closest medical facility was only ten miles away, but it was still too far for anyone without a car. Russell was on the Homestead board of commissioners and did everything he could to try to come up with some emergency funds to get the clinic operational, but the disaster dollars were already spent to help the small town recover from the storm.

Russell lived in a modest home with his wife and two kids on a road that was traveled by tourists going to the Everglades National Forest. But due to Apollo, his home was now being used as a command post to the local community to help anyone with anything, food, water, flashlights, toilet paper—any post hurricane supplies that churches or charitable organizations could donate. Most of the donations came from those groups in thanks for the free legal advice Russell provided to them over the years.

Russell received his law degree from a prominent university in Washington, D.C., and was immediately hired by a prestigious firm that happened to represent one of the Florida Big Sugar corporations. A large rally to save the Everglades took place outside the Capitol building one summer evening, and his firm suggested that he attend the rally to become educated on his potential adversaries, as Big Sugar was one the leaders in the demise of the Everglades.

There he met his wife Ashanti. If opposites attract, then their relationship started off like two supersonic trains colliding at record-breaking speeds. Ashanti grew up in Haiti, the child of a Rastafarian father with African roots and a Catholic Cuban mother. When she was a young girl, her family moved and settled in South Florida. Her parents instilled in her a rare and unusual love of the land, teaching her the value of land conservation and preservation. They both landed jobs at the Everglades National Park. Here, they honed their appreciation for nature and hatred of the encroaching civilization, evangelized as "progress" by the average politician and land developer. This compelling attitude was instilled in Ashanti. She never attended college but was astute of the law as it pertained to the environment, ultimately becoming a spokesperson as protector of the Everglades for a variety of organizations.

Russell came from the other side of the world by comparison. His father was a Jewish physician with roots in Germany, and his mother was raised as a Baptist from Mississippi but converted to Presbyterian when she moved to Chicago after graduating with a business degree from Auburn. She worked as a sales rep for a pharmaceutical company, which led her to Russell's dad. Russell grew up participating in both religions, celebrating all holidays as required.

During the rally, Russell stood in the crowd, snickering and making dumb remarks about one of the guest speakers, as his knowledge of Florida conservation had eluded him without his knowledge. Ashanti was standing in front of him and lashed out at Russell for his rude and obvious unintelligent remarks. Her knowledge and passion for the environment was foreign to him. He realized he knew nothing of "the real world," just the purse strings of his affluent client.

He apologized to Ashanti and tagged along with her for the remainder of the rally, for some completely unknown reason. A strong connection was made, just like an amateur golfer who hits a perfect shot with a perfect swing, reveling over the gorgeous feeling that is normally absent. The power of hatred somehow transformed and cultivated into the emotion of love. And love they did. Several days later, the two of them were driving down to Florida together, and shortly thereafter, he started his own crusade helping those less fortunate than him, while assisting Ashanti from a legal standpoint with her conservation endeavors.

They were both warm and kind-hearted, and had virtually no vices to speak of... except... Ashanti liked to gamble occasionally at the Indian reservation casinos. In fact, she was a regular listener to "Up Your Odds," not knowing at the moment that she was about to meet Longshot himself. Russell, on the other hand, was also one of those pathetic individuals with no bad habits except, well, his love of and inability to play golf. The stench of his game equaled the three pack a day smoker who drinks a six pack of cheap beer by 9 A.M., and whose breath is so bad, it can only be concealed by a body odor that's worse.

He became friends to many of the local golf pros by offering them free legal advice in exchange for lessons and invitations to play golf at their prominent country clubs. He received numerous lessons, but it was like teaching a bulldozer to compete in a NASCAR race. No matter what the driver did, the bulldozer just couldn't compete. Even still, he pitched his legal advice to a variety of golf pros, which was how he became friends with Don Mastroe.

When he saw Don on TV with Jeff and Ginger, he quickly surmised that his friendship might warrant a meeting with TV's hottest stars and possibly put in a plug for donations for the clinic, so he placed the call. "Don, it's Russell. How'd you make out in the storm, and how's it feel to be living with a celebrity?"

"The storm didn't cause much damage, but my grass is dying from all the foot traffic. People are trouncing all over my place with cameras trying to snap pictures of anything that moves. What a pain in the ass. But, otherwise, it's quite exciting. How are you?"

"Well, okay, but I'm really calling for a favor. The medical clinic down here took a beating. There's not much left to it, and no money in the coffer's to fix it. Any chance you could ask your buddy Jeff to give us a little plug the next time he goes on the air? I'll treat you to a round of golf, free legal advice for a year, paint your grass, you name it!"

Don said, "Hold on a sec..." After a few minutes, he said, "I spoke with Jeff, and he'd love to see the Everglades National Forest. He said we can swing by tomorrow and pick you up to go sightseeing in the Everglades, and afterwards, hold a brief press conference in front of the clinic. The way he draws attention, it'll probably generate enough funds to build a new hospital. I'll call you later with details."

"Will do, and thanks a million," Russell said in appreciation and awe.

Early the next day, Best Bet Transport sent two large SUVs over to Don's house for a shuttle to the Everglades. The vehicles had to weave through the onlookers, but safely boarded their human cargo and whisked them away for a day in the fragile swamp. Russell, Ashanti, and their two children were picked up to join the adventure. Introductions were made along the way. The kids felt like they were with movie stars, giggling when Ginger made a fuss over them. Ashanti, on the other hand, had already pulled out a deck of cards and was picking Longshot's brain for tips on winning in Black Jack. Jeff was telling Russell about their Key West trip, focusing on the upchuck feeding frenzy that occurred during their snorkeling adventure.

Within a few minutes, they arrived at the park, only to find out that it was closed due to the storm. Ashanti exited the car, and spoke with one of the park rangers for a few minutes. An excited expression came over the ranger's face, and they both walked to the SUV. Jeff and Ginger got out while Ashanti said, "This is Ranger Willis. I explained to him that you wanted to review the damage of the Glades after the storm, since improving national parks by adding funding would be one of your main agenda items if you were elected. Isn't that right, Jeff?" Ashanti did this for the benefit of her own personal quest, as well as white lie her way past the gate for her entourage.

Jeff said, "I don't know if I'll get voted in, but if I do, I'll see what I can do." He shook the ranger's hand and also signed a few autographs with other rangers who swarmed in like bird-sized mosquitoes on fresh road kill.

The gate was lifted and the convoy proceeded in, with Ranger Willis and Ashanti providing commentary along the way. Wildlife was abundant, with gators thrashing around like kids wrestling in a schoolyard. The ranger pointed out with commentary the many species of birds, fish, snakes, and other Everglades wildlife. Jeff and Russell intermittently spoke of topics unrelated to the Glades, such as the storm, the clinic, Jeff's entry into the campaign race, and a detailed discussion of golf. Although they had completely different backgrounds, they connected like long lost brothers.

While in the Everglades, Jade made a few phone calls to the local media regarding Jeff and Ginger's visit to the clinic. The calls were short, as she was more interested in the Everglades than setting up a news conference. The swampy explorers quickly discovered that walking through the outdoors away from the mess of society was refreshing and invigorating. They followed a path that edged an alligator laden lake, but then veered off through an area of short trees and spiky brush, eventually spilling out into a golden meadow, completely free of anything manmade.

Jeff knew that cameras would be thrust in his face at the clinic within a short time. Yet, he was able to put it out of his mind by walking alone through an unprotected and beautiful meadow.

He mentally paddled his canoe back in time over gator laden waters, relishing the smell of the sawgrass and brackish river. He imagined his original Florida Indian brothers preparing fresh fish and deer in the cool hammocks on their once uninhibited swampy playground.

"So, son, where are we now?" as Johnson placed his hand on Jeff's shoulder.

Jeff replied, although he seemed to be talking to the wind. "Can you imagine living out here with no other civilization? Nothing. Just you and the land. No TV, no crime, no pollution, no condos, just peace and life. Then a bunch of European dudes come and bust up the party, permanently. Our ancestors and historic family, of all things. What went wrong?"

Johnson could see that Jeff was having another moment. Maybe this was his method of prayer. His only recourse was to wave the others to move onward without them and let Jeff continue to find his mind.

After ten minutes and several deep sighs, Jeff turned to Johnson and said, "No matter where I am, I'm going to visit this meadow in the Everglades every day for a few minutes." He patted Johnson's shoulder and said, "Let's catch up to the others." In a happy yet sad silence, they traced their steps backwards to leave the serenity of the meadow. Just then, a whisk of wind cooled their cheeks, and a Great Blue Heron flapped her majestic wings as she sailed overhead, bidding them farewell but inviting them to come back soon, either physically or mentally. Jeff and Johnson walked back without words, displaying a hint of smiles as this peaceful memory of the Everglades would always be with them.

On the way back to the clinic, Ginger was being badly beaten in a game of fish with Russell's kids. In order to avoid embarrassment, she ended the game before it ended by asking the driver to stop at Bob Robert's, the only store between civilization and the Everglades in order to order fresh Key Lime smoothies for the young girls. Of course, Ginger joined them. So did everyone else. As usual, live music entertained the steady stream of visitors. This rustic open air store, known for selling fresh fruits and vegetables, somehow seemed to escape progress, and instead, captured a taste of history. Even though the music, parked cars, and cash register were modern, everything transgressed to yesteryear. The cars transposed into Model T Fords. Somehow, the music sounded like Benny Goodman playing sax with his 1940s orchestra. Maybe they put something special in the Key Lime smoothies to turn back the mental hands of time, yet no one complained, except when they had to leave.

The caravan proceeded to the remains of the clinic. TV crews and hordes of people were there waiting for the stars. Jade did not prepare Jeff for this event, but Jeff was at ease and self-assured. He took control of the situation and said, "Okay, everyone, we're going to keep this short and sweet. First, I want Russell to address the media, introduce himself, and describe what the storm did to the clinic." He looked at Russell and said, "I suggest you take Ashanti and your children up to the podium with you during the intro. They'll look great in front of the camera. Next, introduce me and Ginger. Do not call me a presidential candidate. Just call us your new friends." Then he turned to Ginger and said, "Do you mind asking for a donation? I think a charitable plea from you will be more effective." Ginger agreed, yet she didn't know quite what to say.

Jeff continued, "After Ginger says a few inspirational words, she'll pass the baton back to you, Russell. Provide a phone number, address, email, whatever, for donations, and then we're out of here. Got it?" Jeff was concise but concerned. He acted as though he'd done this for twenty years. Ginger, Jade, Longshot, and Johnson were impressed. Jeff was really starting to get the hang of this.

With cameras rolling, Russell hopped into action, holding his kids with Ashanti at his side. He said his pitch regarding the devastation of the clinic and its importance to the migrant community. His opening statement was legal-like, yet warm and sincere. Afterwards, he introduced Jeff and Ginger. The swelling crowd cheered and yelled.

Ginger glanced at Jeff, and then she apprehensively leaned toward the microphones and said, "Hey everyone. Thanks for coming out today. We just had a private tour of the Everglades National Forest. It was beautiful. You are all so lucky to live so close to such a beautiful place." The mostly local crowd cheered for a moment and calmed down. "Through magic, we hooked up with Russell, Ashanti, and their children. They told us about the damage the clinic sustained, and it broke our hearts. Jeff and I ask that you help Russell and the clinic any way possible. Your donations and generosity would really help the local community down here. Thanks again for coming out today. Now here's Russell."

Russell provided contact info and concluded. Immediately afterwards, everyone loaded back into the SUVs and returned to Russell's house. Cuban pizzas, melting an unusual blend of Spanish spices and Italian herbs, were delivered, along with icy cold beer. Russell did not have any time to mingle, as his phone rang off the hook.

While Jade sucked down a beer to wash down hot cheese that tastefully burned the roof of her mouth, she received a call from the manager at the Hard Rock Hotel and Casino in Ft. Lauderdale. "Hello, Ms. Tomsay. I'm Antonio Stempelford, the manager of the Hard Rock Hotel here in Ft. Lauderdale. Stanley Curila from our Las Vegas Hotel gave me your number. The presidential suite is now available, and we'd like to invite you to come stay with us for a few days. In addition, the RGoodBandMan is in concert tomorrow, and we can provide you with backstage passes. Please be our guests?"

Jade asked him to hold, and yelled out to the pizza freaks, "Hey anyone want to go stay at the Hard Rock for a few days and see the RGoodbandMan in concert?"

Ginger yelled back, "Absolutely, I love those guys and always wanted to see them. What seats could we get?"

"Back stage passes!" Russell overheard the question and interrupted his current call, "That band is great. How many tickets can you get? Ashanti and I would love to go if possible."

Jade did a quick head count and returned to the on-hold call. "Antonio, I'd like to take you up on your offer, but, I'd need passes for ten. Is that possible?"

"Done," he replied. "What time can we expect you?"

Jade said, "In a couple of hours. Thank you for your invitation. We'll see you soon."

Russell was back on the phone, but Jade threw him a thumbs-up sign much to his delight. With Russell's ear still glued to his phone, they departed. Ginger gave Ashanti and her kids big hugs, and said, "Well, I guess we'll see you at the concert. Come early if you can, and we can relax in our room prior to the show."

"We'll be there, if Russell ever gets off the phone. We can't thank you enough for all your help. From the looks and sounds of Russell, the clinic might turn into a full hospital at this rate. Many people will benefit from your generosity."

Ginger said, "If being famous means helping people, simply by being on TV, I'll do it all day long. See you tomorrow."

As they headed back to Don's house to pick up their belongings and migrate to their new accommodations, Ginger whispered to Jeff, "Wouldn't Russell make a great running mate?" Jeff slouched into the leather upholstery contemplating Ginger's wise observation.

Bob and the two wounded I-Thugs were taken to the hospital. Bob was evaluated and released with some minor bruises. The I-thugs both required minor surgery from the gunshot wounds, but survived the protective assault by the FBI. Two FBI agents took Bob to their office for questioning. Bob had little choice and divulged the contents of the DVD. He didn't mention Ginger being in the DVD, but he did say that she originally possessed it, which the FBI already knew.

The FBI determined motive and suspected Congressman Hoag behind these illegal activities due to Bob's escape from certain death, the stolen DVD, and the perceived death threat to Jeff. They were quite certain that several layers existed between Sonny and the I-thugs, so they anticipated getting minimal information from the thugs once they questioned them. The FBI was going to have wait several more hours for the I-thugs to become conscious from the anesthesia before they could be questioned and possibly add more light to the cloudy picture.

Jack and Tyrone were still following Scratch. They had just entered the Miami area coming out of the Keys when they received a call from their Vegas counterparts, getting a complete rundown of DVD events. Jack asked the Vegas team to try to trace any calls made and received from Sonny and Scratch. They also suggested that Sonny be "watched" by some agents, but his clout as a congressman made their attempts to survey him more difficult than normal.

The FBI gave Bob a ride back to the radio station to get his car. A few agents were still dusting for fingerprints, but they already identified the two thugs based on the hotel video. Bob hopped in his car and drove home. He slammed down two shots of Tequila and called Longshot with the bad news.

Hole Number 11
Par 5

(**Course Notes:** Washing Tongue vs. Washington — a clean mouth won't get you elected, or will it? "Read my lips, no new taxes". "I'm not a crook." Weapons of mass destruction are in Iraq, but we can't find them. Enron is in good hands. Take this pill and lose weight without dieting and exercise. Hit your ball farther and straighter with this new club using your same old shitty swing, guaranteed!!)

Sonny's formal announcement that he, too, elected to be tested, opened the floodgate of presidential candidates agreeing to take the polygraph test. All major and minor contenders for the presidential throne immediately released some form of press release indicating that they were willing to participate in the Honest Scorecard, but they did so with much apprehension. At this stage of the game, all serious candidates were trained to verbally respond to a multitude of questions by muddying their responses so it always sounded positive and filled with confidence, no matter how much truth was avoided, altered, or down right misrepresented. Convincing a machine to believe them would be much more challenging compared to a human with emotions and far greater—but unused—intelligence. Virtually hundreds of networks worldwide were eager to participate in the challenge. Ellen Spackler's team of interns categorized the questions and then grouped them into the most commonly asked questions in each category. That made it easier for the media to see what questions were of most importance, at least by the reoccurrence of their submissions.

Ellen arranged to have Connelly and Fessler Security, better known as ConFess Security, monitor the selection of questions. They agreed to provide the monitoring service for free, in exchange for placement of their logo on the Honest Scorecard web site. ConFess was to ensure that there was no foul play with the selection of questions, eliminating any backlash comments from the candidates after the test, especially if the test demonstrated a significant amount of non-truth from the participants.

All the questions submitted to the Honest Scorecard were available for viewing on the web site, as well as the categorization of the questions. ConFess set up an online registration form that the news media was required to complete to verify their legitimacy as a news agency. After they registered and received approval by ConFess, the news media were then eligible to submit three questions from the total list of questions. This filter was set up to minimize "off-the-wall or radical" news groups, although they would basically accept questions from just about any media group.

All the details of the submitted questions were monitored to ensure that no preference was given to certain questions or media organizations. In addition, they would summarize all the questions submitted by the media and create a specific list of ten questions for each candidate. The questions eventually asked to the candidates would be revealed on the web site, only after the test was taken. A scheduled time and place to take the test would be arranged with each presidential candidate and a local police agency. The test results would be analyzed by the police agencies that administered the test, along with their score for each question, and given back to ConFess Security. They would then provide the results to the media and post it on the Honest Scorecard web site for all to see. A sizable donation was to be contributed to the participating law enforcement agency from Jeff Taylor's endorsement account. A press release went out to the news media describing how they could participate in the Honest Scorecard, and within no time, hundreds of online registration forms flowed in. ConFess quickly began approving the agencies, retrieved their questions for the candidates, and set up the polygraph tests with the candidates and law enforcement agencies.

Just Fore Golf, an Internet and TV network in Orlando wanted to participate in the Honest Scorecard. They contacted Jade by phone while she was at Don's house packing to move the party to the Hard Rock Hotel. "Hi, Jade, this is Max Snyder. I'm a producer on Just Fore Golf. I'd like to speak with you regarding the Honest Scorecard."

Jade replied, "Hi, Max. I know Jeff watches your show every free second he has. What did you have in mind?"

Max said, "Would Jeff be interested in taking the polygraph in our studio? We'd like to interview him prior to the test. This interview would be golf focused, not political. We'd like to make it fun and enjoyable for Jeff, and give our viewers a chance to meet him up close and discuss a variety of topics, such as favorite tour players, his personal tips for amateur golfers, and funny golf stories he might share. Sometime after the interview, we could arrange to have the polygraph test taken here in our studio. This shouldn't be a problem as the local Chief of Police is an adamant golf nut who plays golf regularly with one of our station managers. Our goal is to give Jeff a comfortable setting to take the test. We're all pulling for him to do well. We'd also like to do another interview after the test, but that would depend on Jeff and the test results. What do you think?"

Jade said, "Let me ask Jeff, but I think he'd be open to it. He wasn't planning on doing any interviews until after his honeymoon, but this is a special situation. I'll give you ring back later today."

Just as she hung up the phone, Longshot's phone rang. "Longshot, it's Bob. I have bad news."

Longshot said, "Bob, did you forget the number to the safe again?"

Bob said "No, that's not it. I got into the safe just fine, took out the DVD and just started to copy it, when three goons came in, tried to kill me, and took the DVD."

"WHAT?" exclaimed Longshot.

"Man, it was real scary. They put a gun to my head after I gave them the DVD. I thought I was a goner. I threw a blank disk at them and ran out the door while they were shooting at me. As soon as I got out, the FBI pulled up and started firing back at them, thank God. I felt like I was in the middle of a Clint Eastwood Dirty Harry movie, except it was real bullets. The FBI hit two of the goons, but no one was killed. The third one escaped with the 'Sonnyblabs' DVD. We're screwed. I just got out of the hospital, but I'm okay. They slugged me around a little, but no major damage. The two other thugs are in recovery now after surgery for the gun shot wounds. The FBI is waiting for them to wake up so they can question them, but I doubt they'll say much. These were the same guys who were in the hotel room checking out Ginger's site. The FBI thinks that Sonny Hoag is somehow behind this, but they believe it will be impossible to link him to the crime, especially since we don't have the DVD as proof anymore. Sorry for the bad news, and tell Jeff and Ginger I'm sorry."

Longshot took a long breath, realizing that the DVD was their ace in the hole, but more than that, he was glad to know Bob was all right. "Bob, I feel bad that you got dragged into this mess. Go do whatever you need to do to relax. I'll be in touch with you regarding my next broadcast."

Bob said, "I already had a few pops, but I may need something stronger. I'm really strung out by this. Oh well, Later."

After he hung up the phone, Longshot called everyone into the living room. They could tell by the look on his face that something was wrong. "Bob just called. Someone stole the DVD, and he was almost killed in the process. If it wasn't for the FBI, he'd be dead right now." Longshot went into the details while everyone sat quietly and listened.

When he finished Johnson said, "You're playing with some pretty powerful people. Ginger's videos are probably already copied and being mailed to the tabloids as we speak. They'll use that as leverage to break Jeff's credibility. No offense, Ginger," as he looked at her with his sympathetic eyes. "Even if they didn't send out your videos as yet, they'll use them when they need to."

They all sat down in painful silence. Ginger's eyes were moist, and Jeff went over and put his arms around her, saying, "I feel terrible that Bob's life was in danger. A few days ago I said I wanted to play the game, as long as no one got hurt. Well, this changes everything. I think we ought to finish the honeymoon, and call it quits. We'll have some dollars in our pockets, and this way, no one will get hurt."

Johnson jumped back in and said, "Jeff, you don't understand the entire picture. Whoever stole the DVD will always have you by the nuts. Even if you get some big endorsements, who's to say that they won't want a huge cut of the action in the future. I hate to say this, but if Ginger announces her past to the media before they air it, it might reduce some of the punch."

Jeff said, "I won't let it get to that."

The quiet in the room was as loud as placing your head in the speaker cabinet of a distorted rap band. To stop the silence, Jade told Jeff about Just Fore Golf's request to do an interview and offer to participate in the polygraph. Jeff said, "Let's agree to the interview for right now. I always wanted to see their studios and meet some of their announcers. We'll let them know about the polygraph within the next day."

Jeff would typically have been very excited about going to the Just Fore Golf studio, but the stolen DVD took the steam out of him and his team. No one had a good sense of direction at this point.

Longshot knew that the tables turned, because in the long run, the house always wins, and now, he was betting against the house. Plus his good buddy was almost killed. Jade was thinking that she might need to start looking for a new job. Johnson had no plan of action, which was new ground for him. Without saying a word, they finished packing up their suitcases.

Ginger went to get Blabs and prepare her for the next leg of their trip, but she was not on her perch. Ginger screamed for Jeff, who came running into the room. "Ginger, what's wrong?"

"Blabs is gone!" They all searched the house, but Blabs had disappeared. The house was empty for almost four hours, and anyone could have come in and taken her. Johnson shook his head and said, "Man, these guys are nasty. They're getting rid of all the evidence." What he didn't say was that Ginger was the last piece of evidence that needed to be removed.

Jade called Antonio at the hotel, and said that Jeff and Ginger needed to access their room inconspicuously. Antonio was used to such requests from celebrity types and gave her directions to where the limo should park once they arrived at the hotel. They entered the hotel without notice, and took a discreet service elevator to their suite. Antonio led the way and was cognizant of the foul mood of his guests, so he was pleasant, professional, and brief with his welcoming gestures.

The past hour stole ten years of age away from Ginger. Her normal radiant glow was now rusted like an old bike in the salty Florida air. As soon as she entered the suite, she immediately rushed into her bedroom suite, closed the door, and leaped into bed crying tears unknown to her since she was a little girl.

Jeff made a dash to follow her, but Jade stopped him. "Jeff, let her cry for thirty minutes, then go in. She needs to release her emotions. You can console her soon, but let her flush out some of her anxiety."

Jeff stood there as though he had awakened from a bad dream but followed her womanly advice. He flipped on the TV and pretended to watch the sports channel. After thirty minutes of agonizing waiting, he rushed into the bedroom and closed the door behind him. They stayed in their room for the remainder of the night.

Scratch was still in a mild case of shock from his close encounter with the gay kind. What really troubled him was that it didn't bother him as much as it should have. He decided to find a woman fast, no matter what the cost or looks, and have a normal, perverted heterosexual relationship in an effort to wipe out the past thirty-six hours of weird feelings. While he was looking up escort services in the personal ads section, his cell phone rang.

"It's me. I have a job for you."

Scratch said, "Are you ready to take your beat-the-polygraph class?"

"Yes" said Sonny, "But I need you for something else first. Listen up. When I was with Ginger in Las Vegas, she videotaped our meeting."

Scratch started laughing. "That's hysterical. I told you not to screw around with the hired help."

"Shut up and listen. I just recovered the only copy of the video on DVD. In the video, there was a parrot. I just acquired ownership of it as well. The bird is in Miami. I'm going to have someone deliver the bird to your hotel room, although you may have to move to a pet friendly motel."

Scratch said, "Hit the road. I ain't babysitting no bird. I'm heading back to DC."

Sonny, with the voice of a stern father commanding his son, said "No, you're not. You're going to baby sit the damn bird. I want to keep it alive until after the election. I'll pay you $1,000 a day just to keep it alive."

Scratch said "$5,000."

"$3,000 and that's it, just for sitting on your ass. Hell, if you listen to the bird, maybe you'd learn something. In addition, you're going to receive the DVD tomorrow, along with some other DVDs we've collected. They're being driven in to you from Las Vegas. We had a situation during the DVD confiscation, and the company I used is being hounded by the FBI. I'll pay you another $2,000 to safe guard the DVDs, so you're up to the $5,000 per day."

"Why don't you just destroy the DVD?"

"I want to view it to see if it belongs in my personal collection."

Scratch rolled his eyes on the phone, but already knew of Sonny's perversions. He also knew that this request had a direct impact on Sonny's future. The election was coming up fast, so he could hang out in Miami for a few months and make a few hundred thousand dollars. "Okay. I'll do it, but you have to rent a house for me. No motel is going to let me keep a screeching parrot in the room."

"Okay, okay. You find a place, and I'll pick up the tab. Just keep the damn bird alive. And one more thing. Buy a camera and a good color printer, and take a few pictures of the bird standing on a newspaper with the current date clearly seen on the paper. Then send the pictures anonymously to Ginger with a note that says if she wants to see her bird alive, Jeff must OFFICIALLY announce that he's withdrawing from his unofficial race for the presidency. Also, if the announcement isn't made, the media gets Ginger's sex videos, and Ginger gets a dead bird, all on the same day. When you take pictures of the bird on the newspaper, put your gun and some knives on the paper to make it look deadly. Now don't screw this up."

Sonny abruptly hung up. Scratch was pissed at his condescending demand, yet he knew he could take off the rest of the year after this gig, and he didn't have to kill anyone or steal anything. All he had to do was feed a parrot some seed and relax in Florida for a few months. This thought really got his manly juices going, and he started looking for phone numbers to hire sex, although he already decided to check out the paid for love partner prior to any physical contact and make sure it didn't have any extra body parts. He was afraid Toni might have a twin something in Miami.

When Johnson returned to his room, his cell phone rang. "Hey, Johnson, it's Tyrone. I heard that a DVD was stolen regarding a congressman doing some weird porn shit, and some dudes doing the stealing were shot in the process. Do you know about it?"

"Yeah. Bob, the radio guy who got banged up in the process, called us. How are you guys treating this case?"

Tyrone said, "Well, the FBI is going to continue investigating the matter, especially since the two suspects who were shot are indirectly linked to some other federal crimes. Our boy Scratch is in his hotel on the beach. Where are you?"

"We're staying at the Hard Rock Hotel. Say, Scratch didn't stop by a house in Miami along the way and steal a parrot?"

Tyrone sounded confused and said, "No, why?"

"Well," Johnson said, "The stolen DVD contains footage of Congressman Sonny Hoag having his pecker nibbled by a parrot. Ginger Taylor's parrot, to be precise. We were sightseeing in the Everglades this morning, and when we returned, the parrot had flown the coop. Someone is trying to get rid of everything related to that DVD. Ginger isn't recognizable on the DVD, but I'm worried that she may become the next target."

Tyrone said, "Nope, not our boy. Scratch came right back to the hotel from the Keys. We did uncover several phone calls on Scratch's cell phone to a prepaid phone number in Hoag's hometown, but the number couldn't be traced to Hoag. But speaking of videos, you should see the clips we have of Scratch at the gay B&B in Key West. It's just about the funniest thing you'll ever see, especially based on Scratch's background and personality." Tyrone briefly described the sequences he and Jack filmed. Johnson listened intently, and nearly fainted when an idea rushed into his head like a .45 caliber bullet. "Tyrone, can you get me a copy of the video?"

At 8 A.M. the next morning, Scratch was sound asleep in his hotel room when a tremendous banging awoke him. Unaware that he was still wearing the pink soffe bottom that Toni had given him, (due to comfort and lack of underwear), he opened the door, and I-Thug 1 pushed his way in. "Special delivery, meathead. Oh my God, look at those pretty pj's."

He threw a black leather case filled with DVDs at Scratch's head. I-thug 1, better known as Fat, worked with Scratch at the Unknown Company before Scratch left to work on his own. Fat looked like your typical gangster. He weighed over 300 pounds, wore a badly fitting suit, had a pock marked face, and smelled like a bad cigar. Scratch sleepily voiced back "So, you're promoted to delivery boy. Hmm, maybe someday you'll work your way out of the mailroom and into a cushy admin position counting paper clips. Oh, I forgot, you don't know how to count."

Fat disregarded the comments and poured himself a half pitcher of vodka, as he was too refined to chug it straight from the bottle. Fat just slammed down the vodka and said, "I wished I killed you when I had the chance four years ago in Little Rock. Putting a bullet to your head would be like finding a cure for cancer, only more personal and self-rewarding."

In the middle of this vocal chess match, another knock came from the door. Fat pulled out his midnight special handgun and slipped into the bathroom. Scratch peeked through the peep hole and opened the door.

"Special delivery, pecker head. Oh my, aren't we pretty." Sticky pushed his way in and dropped a box on the floor.

Blabs started shouting incessantly and Scratch said, "Just great. This is just what I need. A screaming bird."

Fat came out of the bathroom with his gun pointed at Sticky saying, "Oh shit, I wish I killed you when I had the chance in Kansas City."

Sticky gave Fat the finger while Fat peered into the box saying to Scratch, "Oh, what do we have here. A little birdie for a pecker head. I taut I saw a puddy cat… I *did* saw a puddy cat. You call me a dam delivery boy, and you're a dam bird sitter, cleanin' up pet shit for a livin' while wearing homo pj's."

Sticky snickered and said, "Yeah, you are a homo in those pink shorts, playin' wid your wittle birdie." They both started laughing at Scratch, while they stuck out their tongues and pretended to lick him.

Scratch was worried that they found out about his Key West trip, and was thinking about killing both of them right on the spot, as he was too flustered to verbally respond.

Sticky was the direct opposite of Fat. He was tall, lean, muscular, and well poised. He looked like the owner of a health club or a high tech company. He was very articulate and spoke with a verbal dictionary like a Harvard grad. He could have been successful in the legal world but parlayed his glue-like hands talent to acquire rare or expensive items at the paid request of any employer who could afford to hire him. The commonality that he and Fat both shared was a passion of spending money and not working for living, at least not a typical 9 to 5 job.

Scratch composed himself, and sternly said, "Okay, shit heads, you made your drop, now beat it. I'm checking out of here."

Sticky turned to Fat and said, "Fat, let's get out of here. I'm afraid shit for brains will attire himself with sexy garments that would shame Madonna and come out and try to back door us."

Fat headed for the door saying, "Hey pecker head, why don't you just get busted and go to prison. You can get all the ramrod action you want there."

Scratch pulled his gun out and cocked the hammer, waving the gun barrel in the direction of the door saying, "Don't tempt me. Killing you would be worth going to prison. But when I get done with my current gig, I'll be able to the hire the very best to waste you two."

Fat and Sticky slithered out of the room, while Fat added his last two cents. "Oh, I'm afwaid of the da man wid the widdle birdie. I won't sweep at night. Sticky, does the widdle pecker head scare you?"

"Just nightmares of his dog face trying to kiss me. Let's get out of here before he makes a pass at us." Scratch slammed the door behind them, and lunged at the bar for a huge Scotch. Fat and Sticky exited the hotel without killing each other or anyone else along the way.

Tyrone and Jack recorded the entire criminal encounter. They had pictures of Fat from the Vegas hotel's video cameras and identified him as being involved in the DVD theft and FBI crossfire at the radio station. They also figured that the parrot belonged to Ginger. Tyrone called Johnson to relay the good news. "Johnson, I wanted to let you know that the stolen DVD and still-alive parrot are both in Scratch's possession here in Miami. We didn't bust anyone yet. We'd like to see if we can flush out some of the bigger fish."

Johnson said, "Thanks for the good news. Hey, when can I get that DVD copy of Scratch in Key West? Wouldn't that video be awfully damaging to Scratch's reputation and career?"

Tyrone was already laughing, as the same bullet ricocheted from Johnson's head into Tyrone's. "What do you have in mind Johnson?"

Johnson used his years of cunning and strategized a plan that was equivalent to dissolving a major terrorist operation. "Hoag is the front runner for the presidency. He also has the most to lose if the DVD is not destroyed. Yet, you and I know that he can also have the FBI stop all investigations on him with his Capital clout. Our only choice right now is to fight fire with fire. I think Scratch ought to see the video of his Key West escapades. Then, unless he wants those thugs and the rest of the underworld to get a copy of his DVD, we arrange for an exchange. Scratch is smart enough to realize that distribution of his DVD will put him out of business or worse, dead."

Tyrone said, "I love it. Maybe we can bring down Hoag along with him. If that guy gets in the White House, we're in for depressions and war while he gets rich."

"Amen to that," Johnson said, "but when can I get a copy of your video tape?"

"I'll get it to you later today, but keep in mind that the FBI cannot officially be part of this scheme. There's a gray area of legality that would be hard for us to explain to the higher ups."

"I understand," said Johnson. "Get me the video, and I'll take it from there. By the way, just to let you know, Jeff and Ginger are decent people. Sure, Ginger has a past, but who doesn't. She's good at heart, just misguided when she was young. Besides, getting Jeff in the White House may not be the worst thing to happen. If you help him with this little problem, he'd probably be open to get more dollars to the FBI. Hell, maybe even get you promoted. Besides, we've had worse knuckleheads running the country. Jeff couldn't be any worse."

Tyrone said, "Hmmm, a promotion. That's the ticket. I'll give you a ring later when I copy the video."

Scratch was still infuriated about the comment by his ruthless colleagues regarding his sexual preference. After he poured the breakfast Scotch down his throat, he mumbled out loud, "I should have videotaped my date with the hooker last night. They'd see how I can pleasure a woman." He didn't realize that if he had videoed his night of romance, it would have lasted only two minutes, and his date didn't even undress. He was so drunk when she arrived, all she did was touch his zipper and he excited himself, followed by passing out. She took her wages and a handsome tip from his wallet and departed, wishing all her romances were that easy and worry free of disease.

Blabs stopped squawking for a few minutes but started up again, trying to relay the message that she was hungry. A few minutes later, Scratch got a call from the front desk. "Sir, this is Nathan, the front desk manager. We've had complaints about a loud squawking noise coming from your room. I'm sure you realize that this is not a pet friendly hotel, and a bird, or any animal for that matter, is not allowed. Do you have a bird in your room?"

Just then, Blabs stuck her head out of the box and started yelling "Pecker head, widdle pecker head." While Scratch folded the box lid over Blab's head, the manager said, "Sir, insults are not required for this conversation. Please make arrangements to check out immediately."

Scratch said, "I'm checking out now, pecker head," and he hung up the phone. He made three quick phone calls and received prices and directions of homes for rent. Next, he grabbed his suitcase, the DVD's and the box with Blabs and started out on his quest for new, temporary accommodations for himself and Blabs. Within a few hours, he signed a month to month lease for a beautiful waterfront pool home in Ft. Lauderdale.

His next destination was a pet store. He brought in Blabs, thought up a quick lie, and asked a sales person for help. "Hey, I got this bird off my dead neighbor. Poor guy croaked yesterday. I thought I'd take care of his bird until a family member takes him. Can you set me up with food and stuff?"

The salesperson went and got a parrot treat and then carefully took Blabs out of the box and said, "What's your name, pretty bird?"

Blabs devoured the treat in seconds and thanked the sales person by speaking. "Blabs is pretty. Blabs is pretty. Lucy in the sky with diamonds..."

The sales person said, "Wow. Well, you must be Blabs. I'm Helen. You have a beautiful voice. Besides, I love the Beatles too." She reluctantly placed Blabs back in the box.

Scratch was not amused and said, "Okay, okay, the bird talks. Now what do I need for it."

The sales person was leery to let her customer leave with Blabs, but she didn't have any reason to stop him. There wasn't a birdcage large enough for Blabs, so the sales person wheeled a large bird stand to the cash register, along with bird feed. While Helen rang up the order, she asked Scratch, "You do know that this bird is an Amazon, and along with the seed, you need to feed her fresh fruits and vegetables every day. Mango, zucchini, corn on the cob, squash, grapes, bananas, and apples. I also included a few toys that she can play with. Give her a new toy every one to two weeks so she doesn't get bored. I also included a bird mister. She should be misted everyday."

Scratch looked at Helen as though she was from Pluto. "Are you kidding? I gotta do all that crap just for the stinking bird?"

Helen looked sternly at her customer and said, "Sir, if you like, I'd be glad to board your neighbor's bird here until arrangements can be made for her new home."

Scratch didn't want to cause a scene with a bird nut and said, "That's okay, I'll buy the veggies."

Helen continued. "Be sure you feed her properly, change her water dish daily, and make sure she plays regularly. She's very intelligent, yet she requires a lot of interaction. She smarter than you think, and probably knows her owner is no longer with us, so be kind to Blabs. She just lost her best friend."

Scratch thought he was going to throw up and thought, *All this sympathy for a damn bird, a bird that will probably be dead in a few weeks, at least if I have my way.* He placed Blabs in the shopping cart along with bird supplies and proceeded out to his car with the sales person following behind with the bird stand. She helped him place the stand in the back seat and said, "Good-bye, Blabs, I hope to see you soon. And sir, if you have any questions or need me to bird sit, just let me know."

Scratch mumbled, "yeah, yeah" and drove back to his rented house. A car with two FBI agents pursued her customer's vehicle, but she didn't notice, as she was too concerned for Blabs' safety.

That morning, the hotel suite still reeked of depression. Johnson called down to the front desk and had them ring Jeff's bedroom. He didn't even want to knock on the door, just in case they needed extra time and space. Jeff answered the phone.

"Jeff, it's Johnson. I have good news for you and Ginger. When can I speak with you?"

"Did you find Blabs?"

"Well, yes and no, but I've got a plan that might help our little situation."

"Where are you?"

"I'm in your suite. I didn't want to knock."

Jeff said, "We'll be right out. Let Longshot and Jade know."

When everyone convened in the suite's living room, Ginger said, "Blabs is alive. Right?"

Johnson said, "Yes. Unfortunately, Scratch is babysitting Blabs, along with your video collection in a rented house not far from here."

Ginger raised her voice and said, "That goon? He'll end up killing poor Blabs."

Johnson said, "Ginger. Remain calm. The FBI has Scratch and Blabs under surveillance. If things get too crazy, they'll do their best to protect your parrot. The FBI is quite certain Sonny Hoag is behind this, but they need something more offensive than a stolen parrot and DVDs to make any arrests. Besides, I have a plan to get Blabs back, along with your videos."

Johnson filled them in on the footage taken of Scratch in Key West. "We're going to use the videos the FBI obtained of Scratch in the gay B&B as the bait, and tell him we're going to distribute it to key members in the underworld unless he exchanges the parrot and DVD's with us. If word of the video gets out insinuating that Scratch is gay, he'll probably end up dead, or at least, unemployed, as mobs just don't go for that kind of stuff. This is our only hope, but I think we have a good shot at pulling it off. Blabs will have to stay with Scratch for a while until the timing is right to launch the plan. The FBI thinks that it would be better to wait until a few days before the election to approach Scratch. He'll probably have his guard down then, and Hoag will be over confident that he's got the election sewn up. The FBI is monitoring Scratch. His house is bugged, and they will do their best to keep Blabs safe, but there are no guarantees."

Ginger said, "I really want to get Blabs back safely, but if we can get her, and nail Sonny and Scratch, I'll do whatever it takes."

"Good girl," said Johnson, "because the ball is already rolling. Tyrone is going to give me a copy of the Scratch video ASAP. I'm going to personally act as an FBI representative and approach Scratch with the proposal. I'm looking forward to it."

This type of activity was common to Johnson, but very uncommon to the rest of the team.

Jeff sat on sofa with a disgruntled look on his face and said, "Now I'm starting to feel like a true politician."

Johnson said, "Not so fast, Jeff. We're not doing anything illegal. In fact, we're trying to thwart an illegal act by attempting to recover a stolen DVD and parrot. No one will get hurt. You are not being deceptive to voters, and you're trying to protect Ginger, who is not guilty of any crime. This is more of a presidential action to an illegal activity that almost killed Bob."

Jeff nodded his head in confused agreement, while Longshot said, "Johnson's absolutely right. We're simply righting a wrong, and we're doing it legally. All we're asking Scratch to do is exchange a stolen DVD and bird that originally belongs to Ginger. The FBI had legal rights to shoot the video of Scratch, thinking your life was in jeopardy. Besides, if Sonny Hoag ends up in the White House, well, that will be the crime of the century and every American citizen will be a victim, especially the fools who were stupid enough to vote for him." His comment rippled a wave-like effect of head bobbing.

Jade jumped in between head bobs and said, "Well, I've got more good news. I just checked my emails, and Ellen is faxing over some contracts for Jeff to sign to the tune of $25 million. They are all with major companies and agreed to all of Jeff's requests. In addition, we should have a few more within the next few days, tacking on another $15 million. Jeff, you better enjoy your honeymoon, 'cause when it's over, you're going to be a very busy millionaire endorsing products."

Jeff looked at Ginger, and her smile grew quite a bit more. The rust was peeling off her face, and she regained a few more years of youth.

Jade continued, "I think it's time to get back into the swing of your honeymoon. Jeff, I'll call Just Fore Golf to set up the interview and the polygraph. You need to take the test someplace anyways, might as well be there. Next, do you feel like playing golf today? Don Mastroe called and said he could arrange a starting time at Biscayne Bay. I thought you could play some golf while Ginger and I do some shopping. We've got some money to spend."

Jeff and Ginger looked at each other like honeymooners, as each of them mentally prepared for their day away from each other. Jeff said, "I'll call Don back myself and confirm the time. Besides, you girls need some new duds for the concert tonight." Although there was much apprehension regarding Johnson's plan, they did see some light at the end of the fairway.

Prior to their shopping excursion, Jade called Max Snyder at Just Fore Golf to set up a date for the interview and polygraph test. She also put him in touch with ConFess Security to discuss the test procedure.

Max called ConFess immediately. "Hi, this is Max Snyder at Just Fore Golf. Jade Tomsay gave me your number to obtain the questions for Jeff Taylor's polygraph test at our studio."

"Hi Max, I'm Elliot Connelly. Jade told me you'd be calling. We won't provide you, or any other candidate with the questions until the day of the test itself. All we can do today is set the date and time. I understand you've made arrangements with the Orlando Police department to hold the test at your studio."

Max replied, "That's right. We're going to interview Jeff the night before the polygraph, primarily discussing golf topics. We typically allow viewers to call in and ask questions, and we don't know what those questions will be, so they might be more political. The next day, we'd like to do the test. After Jeff sees the results, we're giving him an option to have an after-test interview with us, but it's his call."

Elliot said, "That's fine, Max, but we're really only concerned with the integrity of the test. What Jeff does with you before and after is up to him. In addition, you are eligible to submit three questions if you haven't done so already."

Max said, "I'll have three questions submitted to you later today. Keep in mind that our questions will be mostly golf focused."

Elliot stepped out of his security role for a moment and said, "Well, if you look online at the millions of questions submitted to Jeff so far, there isn't much of anything pertaining to politics. Most people want to know more about his relationship with Ginger than his ability to run the country. That is not the case, however, with the other candidates. To be honest, I wouldn't want to be in their shoes and take the test."

Max could hear and feel a sense of delight in Elliot's last comment and echoed his sentiment. "Well, many Americans are fed up with the lack of trust that our government portrays. That's what makes Jeff so unique. When you think about it, a professional golfer on tour has little room to cheat. Galleries and TV cameras capture and analyze every shot they take. Besides, why cheat? Your goal as a golfer is to play your best game and win with your ability and a little luck. The marketing machine behind a presidential campaign disguises candidates' inability, and hope they are lucky to not have their often unscrupulous past discovered by their competitors, voters, or the media. It's a completely different game from golf. Maybe Jeff's honest attitude is bringing that sense of pride back into politics, even if he doesn't make it to the White House. I guess we'll find out soon enough."

Hole Number 12
Par 4

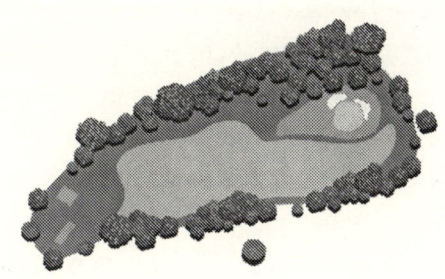

(**Course Notes:** Where's the civil, in our civilization. Ole King George, on the throne, doesn't have a clue what's going on. He doesn't care bout you and me, he's just worried bout his Texas Tea.)

Reggie Goodman of the RGoodBandMan was the perfect, typical left-over U.S. hippie rocker. This flamboyant, energetic singer/songwriter and keyboardist was obviously inspired in his youth by the likes of Elton Jon, Billie Joel, the Allman Brothers, and the Beatles, except his music focused more on the turmoil of the country and bridged generation gaps with the goal of making his music the voice of today's America. And he succeeded.

Antonio, the hotel manager, called Reggie and told him that Jeff and Ginger Taylor were going to be in the audience, and he almost dropped his Marley-like joint in excitement. "Dude. No way. J & G at my show. Very cool beans. Hey, can we hook up with them before the show? We gotta split right afterwards to do Atlanta. I'd love to meet them. Make it happen, Dude!"

Antonio told Reggie to hold and called Jade. Jade and Ginger were at the mall busy enjoying the American dream, that is, spending with reckless abandon. "Jade, what are you doing around five later today? Reggie Goodman and his band want to party with you before the show."

Jade turned to Ginger and said, "The RGoodBandMan wants to party with us before the show tonight. What do you say?"

Ginger screamed, "Hell, yes, let's get down tonight," which happened to be a lyric from one of the band's songs.

Jade got back on the phone, but Antonio already heard Ginger's boisterous response and said, "I'll have them come to your suite at five, and I'll have some food brought in."

Jade replied, "That sounds great. Thanks Antonio."

Johnson and some of the hotel security were with Jade and Ginger, but the longer the girls shopped, the larger the crowd grew. Within a few hours, a thousand people were in the mall following their every move. Before too long, a few camera crews showed up, and one reporter, being held back by security, shouted out "Ginger, how about a quick interview?"

Ginger nodded to Johnson, and the news team was released into the secure shopping area. They quickly set up their equipment and put Ginger in the limelight. "We're at the South Winds Mall with First Lady hopeful Ginger Taylor. Ginger, shopping, without Jeff? What's up, you guys have a fight?"

Ginger seduced the camera with her exotic eyes and responded, "Shopping, yes. Fighting, no. While Jeff is playing golf today, I thought I'd buy a little outfit for his eyes only. It's guaranteed to keep him off the golf course for a few days when he sees it."

The crowd whistled and applauded while Ginger continued. "Giving your husband a little eye candy will keep a marriage going strong for years. Remember that, girls." Again more hoots and hollers.

The reporter asked, "What are your next plans, besides moving to Washington?"

The crowd cheered and started yelling, "Jeff for President, Vote for Honesty."

Ginger waited for the crowd to die down and said, "Well, I'm picking out a hot outfit to wear at the RGoodBandMan concert tonight at the Hard Rock Hotel. In fact, I just found out we're having a little party with the band before the show. Anyone want to join us?"

Johnson's security team almost lost control of the situation, as the crowd tried to burst on to Ginger and accept her offer. Johnson grabbed Ginger by the hand and whisked her into the back room of a small boutique for safety. Jade followed closely behind. He radioed the limo for pickup behind the mall while the security team held back the flood of people like a dam getting ready to burst. The camera team filmed the exit while the reporter said, "She's as much fun to watch running as she is to talk to. Jeff and Ginger, partying with the RGoodBandMan tonight, and we're all invited. See you at the concert. This is Arnold Peyton of WXLX, wishing I was the seat of her limo."

When the shopping excursion departed back to the hotel from the mall, Johnson politely scolded Ginger. "Ginger, you can't rile the crowd like that unless we have proper security. You could get trampled to death. They acted like mad water buffalos on a stampede. Please reserve your comments in public, for my sake."

Ginger put her head down like a little girl and said, "Sorry, Daddy, it won't happen again."

Jade hid a smile while Johnson simply shook his head. Then Ginger grabbed Jade's cell phone and called Jeff. "Honey, guess what, we're going to party with the band tonight before the show. We're going to be groupies, or roadies, or whatever you call them."

Jeff said, "Awesome. We just finished, and I shot a 69. I love these new clubs. I'm going into the bar to speak with some of sales reps whose products I'll be endorsing, then head back home. I'm psyched for the show now. Bye for now, and I love you."

Ginger glowed. That was the first time he said he loved her over the phone.

Shortly after five o'clock, Russell and Ashanti arrived at the suite, dressed not like conservative conservationists but like radical rocker roadies. Russell wore camouflaged combat pants and boots, and a twenty-year-old yet preserved t-shirt that said "The Who- Tommy- Playing for the Queen of England." Ashanti adorned jeans with more holes than material, a tie-dye bandanna, oversized glitter earrings and matching love beads, too much makeup, and a very tight Jimi Hendrix t-shirt and John Lennon-like sunglasses. Jeff and Ginger greeted them as though they'd known them since childhood, but their greeting was quickly interrupted, as the RGoodBandMan members slowly showed up at the presidential suite, moving at the pace of a methodic rhythm and blues song. They were all eating popsicles, which looked very uncharacteristic for a rock band. Yet, they were still "very cool," hiding their enthusiasm to meet the potential presidential couple.

Ginger and Jade were just the opposite. They were jumping up and down like 1960s teenagers at a Beach Boys concert. Jade surprised everyone, except Ginger, by dressing somewhat punkish, certainly unbecoming for a presidential press secretary. Ginger had helped her pick out the unconventional outfit. Reggie Goodman removed the popsicle from his mouth and gave Jeff and Ginger big hugs and cheek kisses. He was wearing a huge red, white, and blue velvet top hat and a patriotic tie-dye shirt. An exotic yet pleasant smoke smell filtered from his being, emitting peace, calmness, and expansion of mind. Reggie bellowed out in a Billie Idol-like voice, "Dudes, I can't believe it's you. Jeff, you got my vote. Can

I play at your inauguration bash? We'd sound so cool in DC, especially with a Pres who believes what we believe in. We aren't well received by those typical Washington demons."

Then Reggie reached around and grabbed Ginger's ass saying, "After you're in office, I can tell everyone I had a piece of the First Lady, and I won't be lying, and it was gooooood."

Ginger reciprocated and ran behind Reggie and grabbed a handful of denim jean butt and said, "Now I can tell everyone I had a piece of the RGoodBandMan, and it was as good as his music."

The other band members, like a high school marching band, paraded into formation, expecting to receive some grab ass as well. Ginger confusedly looked at Jeff. He shook his head up and down saying "They're all yours."

Ginger went down the line grabbing butts, while each member of the newly formed Grab Ass Band each bellowed out a sound reminiscent of their musical instrument. Reggie said, "That's awesome. I ought to write a song about this, maybe the butt grabbin' blues. Hey, Dude, you got a freezer? I brought you some of my home-made popsicles. You gotta try 'em."

Jade grabbed the box and placed them in the freezer behind the bar after taking one out for herself. It had an unusual cherry flavor that seemed to improve as she licked and sucked.

Next, Reggie presented Jeff and Ginger with a bag of band merchandise that included CDs, shirts, posters, and a commemorative band bong. Ginger immediately ran into her room and changed into the RGoodManBand On Tour tank top. When she came out, the percussionist said, "Man, I could play those congas all day."

Jeff didn't hear his comment, as he was too busy admiring the bong rather than his bulging breasted wife and said, "You know, I might need this if I get elected. How else could you go to sleep at night?"

Reggie jumped all over that. "Right on, man. Right on. You know what I always say—say goodnight with a bong, awake with a new song. It works for me. Just think, when you're Pres, you can have a bong blast at bedtime, and wake up with new plans to fix healthcare, solve world peace, improve our economy… Maybe we should test this sucker now?"

Jeff kiddingly said, "Not me, I heard they're doing drug testing before concerts now."

The drummer looked at Reggie and said, "Bummer, dude, I guess we get the night off." Jeff said, "No worries, dudes, I'll sneak us past security. I have some clout with the hotel."

Reggie said, "Awesome, I'd hate to get busted before the show."

Jeff couldn't believe they took him seriously. They must have been smoking some good shit for the last ten years.

Jade put one of the band's CDs into the CD player and cranked it up. While sucking on the popsicle, she started mingling with the band and started swaying to the beat of the music with the drummer.

As drinks and food flowed, Jeff and Ginger took a closer look at the band and were surprised at their age. Jeff quietly said to Ginger, "These guys are one of the hottest bands on tour right now, but they definitely aren't kids, at least physically." Jeff wanted to know more about these "older" rockers and said, "So how long have you guys been jamming together?"

Reggie took the main stage and replied, "Well, we've only been together a few years. We all played music before that, but only part time. I was a history teacher for the past twelve years. Rich, our bass player, was the CFO of a small company. The other guys did whatever to make some bread. One night we were jamming in a club with only six people sitting at the bar, but one of them was the president of UnSung Record Company. We didn't know he was there or who he was, but we played our usual kick-ass progressive rock like we were at Woodstock, and he loved our energy level.

He came up to us and said, 'If you guys are this psyched to play for six people, what kind of show would you do for 20,000?' We didn't know what the hell he was talking about, but we sure found out fast. He loved our music's modern version of the emotional stop-the-war themes of the 1960s and '70s, and he signed us to a record contract. With a little radio airtime, our band just took off, because the music is versatile and edgy enough to attract the college kids, yet it's polished enough for the baby boomers. Score one for music-bridges-age-gap dudes."

The band manager pointed at her watch, signaling show time. Reggie said, "Okay, dudes, let's get ready to rock. Jeff, Ginger, we gotta split, but we'll see you at the show. Thanks for the booze and chow. I really had the munchies."

Just as the band was leaving, Jade blocked the drummer from heading out the door. Then, for no apparent reason, she threw him over backwards and viciously kissed him like a horny nun on vacation. The drummer and the other members of the band didn't think anything of it. Jeff, Ginger, and Longshot, though, stood there wondering if their mouths would ever close again. They'd never seen Jade explode emotionally before and never dreamed of her displaying such a public explosion of lust.

Jade hoisted the dizzy drummer upright and said, "You needed that. Your mouth looked like it needed some hot black mamma lips, and I'm the only hot black mama here." She then put his index finger in her mouth, along with hers, and sucked them.

The drummer was getting very turned on, and wondered if he'd make it to the gig. Jade removed the fingers, and put his fingers on her butt, and put hers on his butt and made sizzling sounds, saying, "Ooh, baby, you're hot. You melted my popsicle. Can I eat your popsicle?

The drummer lunged at Jade like a horny priest on vacation.

Reggie, being very laid back and numb to this common occurrence, said, "Dude, we got a gig. Let's go." He looked at Jeff and said, "I hate to break up their party. They look like they're having fun, but we gotta split."

The other band members just watched and said profound statements like "Cool," "Nice girl," and "Far out," not making any movement to stop the action. Finally, Longshot walked over to the one-on-one floor party and said, "Okay, partners, you guys can continue this rodeo when the music's over." As he pried the drummer off of Jade, she sat up on the floor and said "What'd you do that for? Hey, where's everybody going? I got something for all of you. I need a popsicle, NOW!"

While Longshot corralled the wild ponies and herded them out the door, Reggie said, "Man, these popsicles do it every time."

Russell asked, "What's in 'em?"

Reggie beamed as he responded, "Liquid grass, man. So cool. While flying to a gig in Dallas, I met this chemist dude on the plane and asked him if there was any way to extract the THC from pot so it's odorless, colorless, and can be turned into a liquid. He said he'd look into it if I hooked him up with some concert tickets. He went to our show the next day. A few months later, I received a package in the mail from the dude. There were jars filled with liquid and his note saying, *Liquid THC. Give it a try. Loved the show.* I drank half a glass and ended up on the dark side of the moon. What a trip. I saw everyone along the way, Elvis, Marilyn Monroe, JC, and everyone was cool and happy. I mixed up some of the batch in smaller doses with different types of fruit drinks and froze it. I call them High Pops. Now, I can have High Pops anytime I want, and my throat doesn't get damaged by the smoke. Best of all, you can have them in public and not worry about getting busted. Totally awesome. Make sure you have one before the show tonight. I don't know if Jade needs anymore, at least not till later. I'm afraid she'll cause the band to miss curtain call. See you dudes at the show. It's time to rock." Reggie left chuckling as he helped Longshot tame the broncos out into the hallway.

When Longshot came back into the suite, Jeff was holding on to Jade to keep her from busting out into the hallway with the band. Longshot lassoed Jade, carried her into Jeff's bathroom, launched her into the shower area, and turned the cold water on full blast. She kicked and screamed like a bucking bronco but slowly settled down. After a few minutes, Longshot emerged from the shower with Jade, both of them soaking wet.

Longshot looked across the room and said, "Holy shit, this is all I need." Jeff and Ginger were sharing a High Pop. Longshot instinctively whipped out his cell phone and called Johnson. "Sheriff, you better get a few extra deputies tonight. Something bad might happen," and he relayed the potential for disaster details to Johnson.

Scratch entered his new temporary home with his new fowl friend and his new career. He had a difficult time performing such demeaning tasks such as placing bird seed in the bird bowl, especially since he was used to dealing with influential businessmen and king pins of the free and for-fee worlds. Yet, he knew he had to suck up his ego and try to make the best of this easy money temp job. He made a quick call to Sonny but just left a message saying, "Items delivered and secured. Wire first monthly payment and 3 grand for rent to my account now. I also accept Internet cash."

After making the call, he opened the box to get Blabs out but was stunned when Blabs bit his unsuspecting finger. She flew up and out, exercising her wings until she rested on the second-story staircase railing. Scratch was shocked by the surprise attack and fell over backwards into a short glass-topped bamboo table, smashing it into bits and cutting his leg in the process. "Son of a bitch!"

he shouted. "You just about took off my damn finger." While rubbing his pinched finger and cut leg, he said, "Here's your damn seed and water."

While Blabs comfortably perched herself on the railing, Scratch opened the leather DVD case. The first DVD placed between the clear plastic pockets was labeled "SonnyBlabs." He pulled it out, limped over to the home entertainment center, plopped the DVD in, and turned on the TV. After figuring out how to use the elaborate remote control, he started the video. Blabs watched his every move with great curiosity and intensity. When the video started, Scratch burst out laughing when he saw Sonny getting eaten by the parrot and said to Blabs, "So this is why I'm watching you. I'm sitting on his perverted sin to the presidency. Maybe I can negotiate more money?" Blabs recognized Ginger in the video and started squawking, wishing to be reunited with her owner. "Shut up, bird brain. We're going to be together for a while, so deal with it."

Scratch turned off the DVD player and used the TV remote to switch the channel to a sports station with Blabs watching from above. He turned up the volume and went into the kitchen to wipe the blood off his pants and legs. Immediately, Blabs swooped down to the remote and started pecking it in hopes of bringing Ginger back on the screen. The channels kept changing until one station came on that stopped Blabs' efforts. A young Asian girl was singing, "You light up my life, you give me hope..." She had a beautiful voice, and blended her very strong oriental accent around the English words.

Scratch started screaming from the kitchen, "What the hell is that shit?" He came limping into the room, and Blabs flew back up to her refuge. "Man, I hate that song. Leave the damn remote alone." He flipped the station back to the sports channel and took the remote into the kitchen for safe keeping. Just then, he heard the most horrid sound imaginable. Blabs started singing, "You rite up my rife, you give me ope, to caawee on..." Scratch couldn't believe his ears. "Didn't you hear me? I hate that song. Shut up, or you're a dead bird." But Blabs just kept on singing.

Scratch had no recourse. His only choice was to leave. "I'm going to the damn store to get some damn food for you and booze for me. Now shut up, before the neighbors start calling. They'll think I'm killing someone in here. Shut up." He didn't even notice he was talking to a bird. Just as he was opening the door to leave, Blabs came flying in with the precision of a Blue Angels jet and unloaded a fresh batch of bird shit on Scratch's head. "Son of a bitch. This is the thanks I get for getting your food. When shit head Sonny gets elected, you're a dead bird. One shot, one bullet, and it's bye, bye birdie." Scratch toweled off his head and cautiously went out the door, keeping an eye on his new roommate.

As soon as the door banged shut, Blabs floated down from her perch and munched on the bird seed thinking to herself, *Well, I mastered that black thing, but how do I see Ginger on the shiny round thing?*

(**Course Notes:** It's time to get the fools out, It's time to have a goal, It's time to rock the parties, It's time to rock and roll. Hey, Hey for the monkeys.)

While Longshot and Jade changed into dry clothes, Russell and Ashanti toured the suite, nibbled on lobster fingers, and sipped pinot. Jeff and Ginger sucked on the High Pop, and in no time, started fooling around on the sofa, as they started feeling the effects of this mind-altering dessert snack. Longshot came out and broke up the action before it went further saying, "Come on, guys. Save it for later." Jeff and Ginger untwined.

Jade came out wearing a RGoodBandMan t-shirt and short shorts. Ashanti said, "You look hot, girl. Let's go to the show." Jade replied "I am hot, in more ways than one."

Johnson walked into the room at that moment and said, "Are we ready?"

Jade, Ashanti, and Ginger danced to the CD that was still playing. Jeff thought he was watching a music video with bodies dancing, and sat back sucking on a newly opened High Pop. Ginger kept coming over in between dance moves for cold licks. Ashanti decided to try one out, selecting a purple haze flavor. Russell took a hit off the popsicle, and said "Fairly decent," sharing the frozen drug with his wife. Johnson said to Longshot, "You're right, I don't have a good feeling in my stomach about this," and he called the hotel security to have a few more men placed backstage.

The High Pop presidential entourage managed to use their rubber legs to get to the elevator with assistance from Longshot and Johnson. They plunged down the shaft and poured out when the elevator doors parted. Jeff said "Man, what a rush. Let's take another spin."

But Johnson said, "Sorry sir, only one ride per guest" and moved them along to the band's dressing room. Just as they arrived, the band manager came out and noticed the all too familiar glassy look in their eyes and said, "Hi, guys. High guys?" Johnson rolled his eyes while she chuckled to herself and said, "Go right in. I'm going to let the stage crew know we're ready to rock."

Jeff was phasing in and out of reality but had enough memory to want to know what a band did before a big concert. When they entered the dressing room, he was quite surprised. The drummer was sleeping, much to Jade's disappointment. The bass player was checking stock quotes on the Internet, and the percussionist and guitar player were watching old reruns of *Get Smart* on TV. The only normal artist was Reggie. He was all hyped up, nervous, and unapproachable. After the exchanged greetings, the manager came in and said, "Show time." The guitar player shook the drummer until he awoke. He sleepily joined the other members as they huddled together while Reggie, in a confident quarterback like fashion said, "Let's rock hard, dudes, 'cause it's better than a 9-5 job." They broke the huddle and were escorted out to the stage.

As they left the room, they high-fived the soon to be presidential audience members. When the drummer got to Jade, they pounced on each other. Several security agents, using their hands like crowbars, unwedged them, and dragged the drummer toward the stage. The lights were dim, making it difficult to see and walk, yet the drummer finally perched himself behind the drum set, and the other band members prepared to play.

A minute later, the spotlight slowly started to transmit the image of Reggie on the keyboard. He soloed, "I feel all right, but my soul is naked..." and the band kicked the song into beyond-high gear as the audience felt the rush of musical excitement flow through their veins. Jade fell over from the rush like she was born again, but a security agent caught her behind from behind.

Jeff and Ginger sucked their pineapple flavored High Pop down to the stick by the sixth song. By the end of the concert, they **were** the music, feeling the chords and melodic beats pulse through their body like human metronomes. While waiting for the band to come back for an encore after their last song, Jeff gazed around the stage and noticed some cages hanging in the air, along with some ropes and a trapeze high wire. He turned to a stage crew member and asked, "Why are those cages and wires there?"

"We have a circus coming into town tomorrow, and some of the stage items are preinstalled to save time."

Jeff turned to Ginger and said, "Me Tarzan, you Jane. Follow me." Just then, several concert goers jumped up on stage, and the backstage security agents leaped in to action and threw the over-anxious roadies back into the crowd. That diversion opened a door for Jeff and Ginger. They moved to the back of the stage and found a stagehand who, coincidently, was in desperate need of cash. "Hey, dude, how'd you like to make a quick hundred bucks?"

"Sure, as long as I don't end up in jail. What do I need to do?"

Jeff said, "Do you know how to lower those cages and ropes."

"Yeah. See these switches right here. Just push them up or down. Any moron could do it."

"Awesome, dude. My girl and I are going for a ride. When you see my signal, send us down." Jeff handed the crew member $100, took Ginger by the hand, and climbed up the cat walk to the top of the stage. "Get inside," he said. Ginger climbed into the cage, and Jeff leaned it over the edge of the catwalk. He walked over to the other side of the catwalk and grabbed the rope that the trapeze artists use for twirling stunts, and tied the rope around his waist.

Jade was singing along to the music when the band started playing their encore song, "Raise your glasses high, for those, who do and die, so we can enjoy the day..." She turned to Ginger and said, "I love this song," but Ginger wasn't there. She looked around and turned to Johnson and said, "Where's Jeff and Ginger?"

He looked around and said, "Oh man. Now what?" He asked several agents to check the bathrooms and dressing rooms, figuring they escaped for a concert quickie.

Russell, who was playing grab ass with Ashanti's butt as a partial result of their High Pop appetizer, sidetracked his sexual prowling when he noticed a flailing commotion high above the stage. He refocused and realized Ginger was dangling in the cage in mid-air. "Holy shit, Ashanti, look up there."

Just then, with a thumbs-up signal from Jeff, the cage slowly descended, as well as Jeff's rope. Ginger was dancing in the cage like a Go-Go girl. Two large video screens were set up on both ends of the stage to enlarge the view of the band for the cheap seats. The cameramen saw the descent of the swinging couple, and zoomed in, thinking this was part of the show. Within moments, the large screens clearly divulged the identity of the new presidential circus act. The crowd started cheering when Jeff and Ginger's faces hit the big screens. The band kept playing, not knowing what was going on overhead.

Ginger attempted to do a cool swirl move, but slipped on the bars, and accidentally opened the cage door and partially fell out, holding on to the edge for dear, as well as continuing life. The crew member saw her dangling and stopped the descent, hoping it might minimize her chance of crashing down on the stage. Jeff watched and screamed, "Ginger, hold on." He started swaying the rope in the direction of Ginger's cage, but he couldn't get the momentum of his swing going fast enough to catch her.

Ginger was releasing the last of her grip and screamed, "I can't hold on." Just then, in a superman like action, Russell came swooshing in from another rope, screaming like a gorilla, "Ahh yahaaa, ooga ooga." He snatched Ginger just as her grip expired and said, "Hey, Jane, it's me, Cheeta. Where's that damn Tarzan?"

At that moment, Jeff finally swung into the aerial mix, while Russell said, "It's about time, Tarzan. Cheetah saved Jane's ass. How about rewarding me with a banana flavored High Pop?"

Jeff said, "I'll give you a whole bunch of 'em when we get back to our room. Good boy, Cheetah," and he patted Russell's head. Then Jeff tied part of the hanging rope around Ginger, and motioned to be lowered. The stagehand raised Russell's rope back to the top of the catwalk above the stage, while Jeff and Ginger descended safely on stage next to the guitar player and in front of the drummer. The band was surprised by the unexpected entrance but kept on playing.

The crowd hit new heights of screaming. Just at that part of the song, the drummer, bassist, and percussionist were jamming a cool African tribal beat that mixed perfectly with the Tarzan like entrance. Jeff untied himself and Ginger, and they started dancing to the beat. When the song ended, the crowd would not stop cheering. Reggie walked over to Jeff and Ginger with a big smile on his face, hugged them both, and said, "Hey, you're stealing my show." He grabbed a microphone, and said, "Well, dudes, I guess our next president of the United States and First Lady decided to drop in." So dudes, who you gonna vote for?"

In unison, 21,000 strong screamed, "Vote for Honesty." The crowd's roar was relentless. Several structural engineers in the audience were discussing if the roof could handle the unprecedented sound wave emitting from the audience.

After several minutes of uproar, Reggie handed the mic over to Jeff, who said, "Hi, everyone. Ginger and I were just hanging around, and decided to swing by the show." Jeff's humorous attempt was quite poor, eliciting a groaned laugh by the tantalized audience. "Ginger and I wouldn't miss this concert for the world. Aren't these guys great?" This comment resulted in a Dr. Seuss-like effect, creating more human noise, noise, noise.

(Course Notes: I don't want to work, I just wanna bang on my drums all day.)

While Reggie, Jeff, and Ginger waved to the crowd, Jade snuck up behind the drummer and peeled him off his drummer's throne. She straddled him, ripped his shirt off, and attacked his mouth like Japanese planes at Pearl Harbor. One of the roving cameramen caught the lustful attack, and it was shown on the big concert screens. Like baseball fans pouring out onto a field after a World Series win, the stage was flooded with concert goers, all hoping to get a piece of nostalgia. Within seconds, Jeff and Ginger were on the ground, getting clothes ripped off and hair pulled. The cameras caught as much visible action as possible. Clothes and body parts were flying all over the stage. Hotel security called every available person to the concert venue, declaring an emergency evacuation.

Johnson and Longshot fought through the wave of bodies and forcefully pulled fans off the High Pop couple. Additional security personnel joined in and were able to get Jeff and Ginger off the stage and into the dressing room. Jade and the drummer were nowhere to be found.

Reggie and the band came into the dressing room next with the help of security. Jeff and Ginger looked as though they had been in a cat fight. Their clothes were torn, and they were all scuffed up. Reggie said, "Are you guys okay?"

Jeff looked at him with twisted eyes and said, "Hey, man, let's go out and do the finale. I want to see the end of the show."

Reggie said, "Dude, you were the end of the show. Man, you guys were awesome. You brought the house down. I might need to send you a check for your share of CD sales. This was the best publicity stunt I've ever seen."

Jeff reached into a bucket filled with beer, twisted off the cap, slugged down some brew, and then put the icy bottle on his swollen forehead and said, "Dude, instead, do a free concert for a good charity, and we're even."

Ginger pulled out an icy beer as well and said, "What the hell was I doing in a cage above the stage?" Everyone started laughing, including Johnson, who helped himself to the first of several cold beers.

Hole Number 13
Par 4

(**Course Notes:** Common sense is an oxymoron. What's common to one person may not be common to another, and when it's used in an uncommon way, typically costs more than cents.)

Scratch sat in front of his entertainment center succumbing to the joys of his personal happy hour with vodka and grape juice, trying to enjoy the erotic Ginger videos. But he was uncomfortably numb wearing a pinchy grass hat that was obviously left behind by the landscaper. The hat was his only defense, as Blabs was persistent in her pursuit of bird dropping perfection. She attempted to use her GPS-like instinct to deliver constant messages of roommate disapproval. Making matters worse, the Ginger videos were instigating the Blabs attacks, as she believed her captor was confining her true love in the black box on those shiny frisbees. Blabs was destined to help Ginger escape. Patience and cunning were the best feather in her cap, and she decided to develop an attack plan, once she better understood her enemy.

At 11:10 P.M., Scratch answered his ringing cell phone. "Yeah"?

It was Sonny Hoag, screaming on the other end. "Do you believe that shit? Swinging above the stage, half naked, rescued by her pathetic lover, in front of thousands. I need to hire his dang campaign manager. Every station in the world is playing that damn clip. His ratings are going to jump through the Gad dang roof."

Scratch poured another garbage can-like glass filled with vodka and grape juice while Sonny ranted and raved. Once he chugged the mostly vodka concoction, he said, "What are you talking about?"

Within the blink of an eye, Scratch heard what sounded like a 98 mph fastball made of high quality Korean plastic and mini computer circuitry hitting a high quality, Chinese made 36" flat panel plasma television. What he could not surmise was the winner, but concluded that the smaller Korean device was in cell phone heaven.

Five minutes later, Scratch answered his ringing cell phone. "Yeah?"

Sonny warmly greeted Scratch for a second time. "You worthless son bitch. Don't you watch the Gad dang news? What are you doing, choking your damn chicken watching Ginger videos?"

Scratch thought, *Not yet, but the chicken's ready to roost.* Finally, Scratch said, "I've been busy taking care of your damn package, buying food, cages, and avoiding shit bombs from the sky. What the hell are you talking about?"

Sonny tried to calm down to the force of a Mount Saint Helen explosion and said, "Jeff and Ginger, dangling on ropes during a damn rock concert in damn Ft. Lauderdale. It happened in your Gad dang backyard. Turn off those damn videos and put the damn news on!"

Scratch surfed his TV until he saw the video clip of Jeff and Ginger portraying Tarzan and Jane. He said, "Wow, those guys are great. I wonder how long it took them to practice that stunt?" There was another click on the line, preceded by a sound similar to a high tech, German made football that was fumbled and recovered by three Finland-like helmets made of high tech wireless components. Scratch mused over the sound, thinking, *Cell phone makers should hire Sonny to test out the durability of their products, although they'd have to be made to withstand nuclear blasts.*

A few minutes later, Scratch answered his phone. "Yeah?"

Sonny attempted to regain his composure and asked, "Hey shit-for-brains, are the disks and live contents safe?"

"Yep. And who are you calling shit-for-brains? You don't see me in a video getting a parrot BJ." Just then, a beautiful natural voice beckoned from above, "Shit-for-brains. Shit-for-brains."

Scratch yelled, "Damn pecker head."

Sonny retaliated, "Who you calling a pecker head?"

Scratch responded, "I'm talking to the damn bird. He repeats everything I say. I'm ready to waste him. Anyways, the parrot and DVDs are secure. Tomorrow, I'll take pictures of the contents on a newspaper and mail them out."

Sonny was quiet on the phone and replied, "We got to squash this whole situation, ASAP. I don't even want to see the polls in the morning. In addition, I need your polygraph crash course. I'm scheduled to take the test in four damn weeks. I bought a damn polygraph and everything to start practicing, so sober up by tomorrow." Click. No unusual sound. Scratch was disappointed. He was enjoying his little mind game of "what does a flying and breaking phone sound like?"

Jeff opened his eyes around 11 A.M. the next morning, feeling as though he were in the middle of a thick San Francisco fog. He remembered going to the concert, but the details were sluggishly hidden. Ginger also showed signs of life, moving more like a baseball that was hit into the San Francisco bay courtesy of Barry Bonds... a smash to the head, high flying, then a splash landing with several stitches broken and bobbing in the cold waters. She rolled over and saw Jeff fumbling with TV remote and said, "Did you have the same bad dream as me?"

The corners of Jeff's mouth rose slightly, reducing the newly realized pain of his headache, and he said, "It wasn't a bad dream. It was more like a humorous adventure to the abyss."

Ginger said, "Jeff, you're talking like those damn popsicles are still in you. Come back to earth, honey."

Just then, Jeff turned on the TV, and his High Pop lingering remark was now on reality TV. Ginger sat up to watch the effects of the High Pops at the concert but felt the crash of the High Pop leftovers rush into her head, causing the room to not spin, but swing.

The entire Tarzan sequence was being shown on national news while the announcer provided commentary. "Jeff and Ginger were at it again last night while they attended the RGoodBandMan concert at Hard Rock Hotel in Ft. Lauderdale. No one knows for sure if their flying trapeze stunts were staged or ad-libbed, but either way, the finale was spectacular. Their flare for daring overwhelmed the concert goers, as they flooded the stage afterwards like stampeding elephants, obviously hysterical from their presence and dramatic appearance on stage. A release came from their press secretary this morning that they were not harmed during the riot and were moved to safety immediately afterwards. If they make it to the White House, and run the country like they run their campaign, it sure would be an entertaining term in office. I don't recall ever having swingers in the White House. This reporter can't wait to see what they will do next."

A commercial conveniently followed using smart marketing practices, advertising a new jungle gym for adults. It demonstrated an apparent husband and wife exercising by swinging and swaying, but it subtly suggested that it could be used as a romantic device as well, as new positions could be achieved. Assembly was required.

Just as the commercial ended, the phone rang. Longshot spoke softly. "Are you guys alive?"

"Yeah, we just got up and watched our performance from last night. I wish I wore a loin cloth. I really think it would have added a special touch." Ginger chuckled at the remark.

Longshot said, "Jade hasn't surfaced yet, and neither has the drummer. Reggie called this morning regarding the band's gig in Atlanta tonight. He's nervous that the drummer won't make it. I offered to let him use our jet if the drummer washes up on shore."

Jeff said, "Jade's a big girl with good common sense, but those High Pops, well, they can bend that common sense to uncommon areas. I'm sure she'll turn up, the question is when, and where."

"I copy that, partner. In her absence, I met with the media this morning. The hotel lobby was filled with more news stations you could imagine. I had to tell them something, so I commented that you guys were okay, but your video pretty much said it all. By the way, Johnson is here and has some potentially good news."

Jeff said, "We'll come out in a moment."

Jeff and Ginger came out of their bedroom looking hung over yet devilishly happy. Johnson said, "Good morning Tarzan, Jane. I'm glad to see you survived your night in the jungle."

Ginger said, "Jane needs coffee," and proceeded to the breakfast buffet table that had just arrived.

Johnson continued. "First, I threw out the rest of the High Pops."

Jeff said, "Longshot, I thought you said Johnson had good news."

Johnson replied, "That is good news. It's difficult enough keeping you safe as it is. Those damn things thrust you into a whole new world of unpredictability. I just hope it's not too late for Jade, but I'm sure she's all right. But, more importantly, I just reviewed the FBI copy of Scratch in Key West. You gotta see this. It's hysterical and awfully incriminating for Scratch."

Just as Johnson was getting the DVD ready for viewing, Jade and the drummer came walking into the suite looking like drunken honeymooners. The drummer, being more adept at sluggish High Pop mornings, said, "Hey, dudes.

What a show. You guys are awesome. Oh wow, chow." He raced over to the buffet and used his quick drumming hands to load as much food as possible into his mouth and belly.

Jade was somewhat embarrassed and said, "Somehow, we ended up in the Bahamas. We took the first flight out this morning. Man, no more High Pops for me."

A subtle laughter groaned out in the room while Longshot said, "The Best Bet jet is fueled and ready to take drummer boy here to Atlanta. Partner, did you forget that you're playin' in Atlanta tonight?"

"Dude, I'm on top of it. But I'll gladly take the lift. Reggie's so damn paranoid before gigs. He needs two High Pops just to relax. Let me do some more damage on this buffet table, and then I'll split to Hotlanta."

Johnson turned to Jade and said, "You're just in time. I have the FBI footage of Scratch in Key West." He clicked the play button on the TV remote, and the first scene of Scratch in the pool with the naked men started playing. The drummer started laughing out loud and said, "Those dudes don't have any clothes on. Far out. But that dude with the baggy pants sure looks all fired up. He's runnin' around and fallin' over things like a Three Stooges flick. I gotta show this to Reggie. He loves the Three Stooges." Everyone else in the room watched the DVD with a humorous intensity. The male section mostly groaned, while the girls howled in laughter.

Ginger laughed so hard when Toni viciously kissed Scratch at the end of the clip that she had an unexpected rush caused by the back splash of brain cells that had temporarily disappeared during the High Pop love affair. This resulted in a loss of balance and crash to the floor. No one moved to help her, as the guys were too grossed out from the graphical display of male bonding.

The drummer said, "Dudes, I'll pay you top dollar for that video. We could make millions selling this on the net. I know people. We can call it To Hot to Handle, or maybe, Hanging out in the Keys. Yeah, I like that one. That about sums it up."

Johnson said, "Drummer Boy, you're still floating in High Pop heaven. The video is evidence, so it's a no go. Sorry. Let's get you to your next gig."

Jade called the limo service and went down to the lobby with the drummer to say goodbye. She returned with an envelope that had just arrived at the front desk addressed to Ginger marked "Urgent." Ginger opened the envelope and saw a picture of Blabs eating bird seed while standing on the newspaper. A note was printed below that said, "We have your bird and sex videos. Get out of the election race, or the bird dies and the videos will be delivered to the press."

Johnson took the note from Ginger, who was holding back tears. Jeff said, "Easy baby, everything will be all right." Little did they know that it took Scratch over two hours to take that picture. He chased Blabs all over the house, and in some cases, Blabs chased him. Finally, Scratch put the bird seed on the newspaper and went upstairs. Blabs flew down away from him and started munching on the seed. Scratch zoomed the lens to capture Blabs eating, along with the current date on the newspaper. He downloaded the pictures to a laptop computer, and printed the picture along with the note. As one of the pictures was coming out of the printer, Blabs took flight, and signed the photo with her personal calling card, but the soggy bird stool made his printed note unreadable, so he had to print another copy and protect it from Blabs' poopy signature. He arranged to have a courier deliver it anonymously.

Johnson looked at Ginger's saddened face and said, "We need to improve Blabs' safety, and somehow reply to this note. I think you guys will need to reduce your media attention for the next few weeks. Also, Longshot, I'd suggest that you focus your radio broadcast on gambling techniques. Let Hoag think you're pulling out with minimal exposure and reduce his attention toward us. We'll increase the exposure closer to the election. Ideally, we'll have Blabs and the DVDs in our possession by then." Then he pulled out his cell phone and called Tyrone.

"Hey, Tyrone, it's Johnson. How's our buddy Scratch doing?"

"Well, he just got off the phone with Hoag. He gave him pointers on how to beat the polygraph. He basically told him to answer the questions like he was being interviewed by the press. His confidence, arrogance, and ability to lie with the belief that his remarks are truthful should beat the machine, and, as you know, it probably will. Hoag bought his own polygraph, and he's practicing responding, or should I say, lying to questions while keeping his pulse and heart rate steady. I'm sure he can beat it. He's a politician and a pro at deception."

Johnson said, "We just received a note from Scratch telling Jeff to quit his political run, and he used the bird and DVDs as his weapons. I'd like to start shaking him up and, hopefully, protect the bird. I'm going to start sending him pictures from the video clips of his Key West love affair along with a note to not harm the parrot. He'll know this is coming from Jeff's camp, but he won't know what to do. Every week, I'll send him another clip or picture and include a message saying, 'Wouldn't your colleagues enjoy seeing these clips?' He'll go nuts. As we get closer to the election, we'll arrange the exchange, and maybe, convince him to help us get something on Congressman Hoag as well."

Tyrone said, "Do it. But save his good-bye kiss with the hotel manager for last. That should put him over the edge."

When Johnson hung up the phone, Longshot looked at him and said, "Partner, I'm glad you're on our side. I actually feel sorry for that weasel, but he's got it coming. I just wish we'd get to do the same to Hoag. He's been winning too much, and needs to lose a big bet."

Ginger said, "Don't worry. He will."

Hole Number 14
Par 3

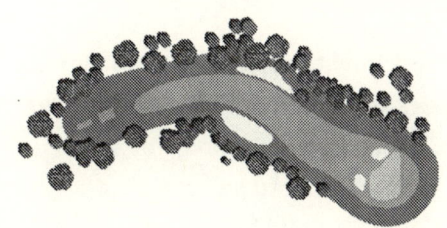

(**Course Notes:** You can marry a hooker, You can marry a saint, You can have fantasies, Make love till you faint. You can live all your dreams, You can live all your lies. You can build strong bonds, Or break all your ties. You can get what you want, It's really quite easy. Just stand for the truth, And don't be so sleazy.)

During the ensuing honeymoon months, the Best Bet Jet was almost overused. Jeff and Ginger flew around the country playing golf and enjoying their extended vacation. The media slowly reduced their coverage of Jeff's race for the presidency, especially when he pushed the polygraph date out to the end of October. Many other candidates followed his lead, hoping to avoid the test completely. He started fulfilling several of his endorsement obligations, which included his appearance in some TV and magazine ads and mingling with sponsors at social events.

Longshot's radio shows were broadcasted live from the hotels and radio stations from around the country, tagging behind Jeff and Ginger. Longshot refocused his show on gambling and screened his callers to answer questions on the gambling topic of the day rather than on the Honest Scorecard or the presidential bet with his listeners. During this time, Jeff kept watching the news with great political interest and saw Sonny reestablish his lead in the election race. With Jeff minimizing his election quest, Sonny had no other true opponents and was poised to become the next president. Yet, Jeff knew in his heart that Sonny was going to continue the downward slide of America, making it more difficult for middle-class citizens to enjoy the standard of living that their parents and grandparents had experienced.

Ginger noticed a change in Jeff over the last few weeks and said, "Jeff, you're playing golf almost everyday at some of the most prestigious country clubs in the country. You're sitting on a mountain of money. What's the matter, don't you like me anymore?"

Jeff bear hugged Ginger and said, "Baby, except for the weird way we met, being married to you and having all this crazy stuff happen to us has been the best time of my life. Yet, when I see Sonny blabbing away on TV, it makes me sick to think that that's our best choice for president. A decent campaign manager and lots of money for marketing are putting a shit head in office, and, it's really starting to piss me off. I actually miss the action of running for office, but I doubt if I could be better than him."

Ginger kissed his neck and said, "Jeff. You're wacky. You're doing it again. Don't sell yourself short. You're one of the most decent men I've ever met. Putting decency in the White House would be a great thing. I don't know if it's been there in awhile. Now, I think you need to take the polygraph test and do the interview at Just Fore Golf. I don't know why, but I think that will be the start of something, hopefully something good."

Jeff said, "Okay, let's take the test."

Thinking he scared him off the campaign trail, Sonny took advantage of the lull in Jeff's publicity activities and beefed up his campaign with more TV and radio ads. He even tried to copy Jeff's successful musical stunt and attempted to hold a free rock concert with Sonny himself being the emcee. He could not find or hire popular bands that would associate themselves with his campaign or participate in this music-for-votes event. A talent agency finally found two members of a one-hit-song band from the early 1970s called Hot Cleevage. They were willing to put on a show in exchange for pardon from their upcoming jail sentence for drug trafficking. The other members of the band were either in drug rehab, nursing homes, or dead. Sonny held the mega election concert event in Dallas, where he desperately needed some votes. He also offered free food from the Swine Dine chain of restaurants as part of the draw. Only a few thousand people showed up for the event, most of whom were hungry, too-young-to-vote kids looking for free food. The band was dreadful, often having to stop in the middle of the song because of missed beats, off-key singing, and general lack of practice or professionalism.

The only news worthy item Sonny received from the event regarded the 600 concert goers who acquired food poising from the free ribs. Sonny turned this potentially bad news around, commending the stellar Dallas health facilities for reacting quickly to the outbreak of food poisoning. He cited faulty plastic containers made in Asia as the culprit, claiming that the snap-on lids did not adequately seal and protect the already but unknown contaminated food. He vowed to bring more jobs like plastic intrusion and manufacturing back to the United States to help the economy and protect the health concerns of the American public. Sonny clearly demonstrated his damage control expertise and actually received favorable press from this otherwise sick-to-your-stomach event.

Scratch and Blabs started living in a peaceful coexistence. Scratch had no one to talk to and started speaking to Blabs out of boredom. Blabs appreciated the attention and reduced her aerial attacks on Scratch as a result. One day, Scratch was attempting to concoct a new alcoholic beverage. He mixed and sampled a variety of ingredients including assorted types of liquor, juices, power drinks, milk, condiments, and even salad dressings. Even though he nearly puked with several specialty drink attempts, he felt like he was a chemist, on the verge of creating a drink that could cure the disease of boredom. Little did he know that this drink had already been invented by millions of others and consumed only by those who created them. The more he sampled his experiments, the more drunk he became, which resulted in even stranger mixing attempts. While mixing a small portion of macaroni and cheese, breakfast cereal, rum, key lime juice, frozen polish perogies, and even some of Blabs' bird seed, a gentle knock came on the door that temporarily saved him from sampling his syrup of ipecac-like concoction. He blurrily signed for his overnight delivered package and went inside while reviewing the abstract sender's address on the outside of the package.

"Who the hell is sending me something from Greenland? I don't know anyone from Greenland. I don't even know where it is. Blabs, where the hell is Greenland?" Blabs didn't know either and squawked a question mark. Johnson had wanted to add some fun and confusion to the delivered pictures of Scratch in Key West, and emailed edited still shots of the video to a CIA buddy stationed in Greenland. There, the pictures were printed and shipped overnight to Scratch. When he opened the envelope, he started to scream, "What the fuc—" but just then the blender started splashing his current experiment all over the kitchen. He raced into the kitchen to abort the current project. When he returned, Blabs was busy chewing on one photograph but jettisoned back to her perch on the railing high above when he rushed back into the room. "Damn bird!" he shouted. Blabs left the semi-chewed photo facing down, and Scratch read the message on the back that said, "The bird has a friend in Greenland. Keep her safe, or the picture becomes your worst nightmare." Scratch was stupefied and grumbled, "Who the hell in Greenland took pictures of me in Key West?"

His bowels were considering an irregular and unsuspecting movement as he glared at the three pictures. The first picture was of him and Toni in the pool, with a backdrop of several naked fellows enjoying the atmosphere. The next picture displayed his urgency to run back to his room in his water logged shorts, knocking over chairs, with a backdrop of naked fellows enjoying his comedic entertainment. The last picture was the icing on the fruitcake, as Toni was naked, escorting Scratch to his locked room to gain entry.

Scratch used his mental and physical abdomen muscles to hold his butt cheeks together, otherwise projectile stomach contents were forthcoming without notice or concern. "Who would take these pictures? And why? How do they know I have the damn bird? How do they know where I live? What's the nightmare? This makes no damn sense." He abandoned the laboratory for the time being, and belted down a few tequilas, attempting to clear his foggy and distressed mind with straight alcohol. Still, no answers came to him, and more questions arose.

(Course Notes: I pledge allegiance, to the golf flags of most any American Golf Association. And to liberal pin placements, in which they stand, One Nation, Under Par, reading invisible breaks, being long off the tee, and just green fees, for all.)

Jeff entered the Just Fore Golf studio on his delayed but newly scheduled time and was greeted with a fanfare greater than the leading money winner on the PGA tour. He had become accustomed to the "Where's Ginger" question whenever she was not around. He spent a few minutes meeting with key studio personnel and exchanged autographs and golf tips. Max Snyder and the rest of the studio crew made Jeff feel like family at Thanksgiving. Max provided Jeff with a sample list of questions that Jeff could review while he was getting prepared in the make-up room. Several questions teetered on the brink of politics, but, for the most part, the questions were golf focused, such as, "Who are your favorite PGA tour players? What are your favorite courses? What's your most memorable golf shot," and so on.

Jeff came out to the set for the live interview and was greeted again by Max. "Jeff, let's have fun here today. This is just the two of us chatting about golf. Just be yourself." Jeff was a little nervous but felt comfortable with the questions he reviewed.

At fifteen minutes before 9 P.M., the stage lights came on high, and production people scrambled into place. One producer came up to Jeff with a phone and said, "Jeff, it's Ginger."

"Hi, we're going on the air now. What's up?"

"Nothing. Just be yourself. Oh, I picked up something special to wear tonight in bed. Hurry home. I love you."

"I love you too. Bye." He handed the phone back to the producer who said, "Jeff, I'd wish you good luck, but I think you already have it."

At precisely 9 P.M., Max smiled for the camera. "Hi, everyone, and welcome to Golf Guests. This week, we're thrilled to have Jeff Taylor, the golfer who is officially not running for president, join us. Hi, Jeff, and welcome to Just Fore Golf."

"Hi Max, I'm glad to be here."

"Jeff, you know my first three questions. One, are you still officially not running for office? And two, where's Ginger? And three, how's the honeymoon going?"

Jeff smiled his million dollar smile, portraying a shy boy with humble personality. "Yes, Max, I'm still, officially, not running for office. Second, Ginger's out doing what Ginger does best. Spending money shopping. And third, as I said previously, I've got the perfect wife. She let me bring my clubs on our honeymoon. How can you beat that?"

Max replied, "You're a lucky man."

In fact, Ginger had been at the Sweet Orange Mall but came home in time to watch the show. She smiled seeing Jeff on TV. Max, keeping true to his word, quickly steered all the questions to golf. Jeff was calm, funny, and enjoyable to listen to.

Toward the end of the interview, Max asked Jeff, "Jeff, would a golfer make a good president?"

Jeff sat for a moment and replied, "Why not? The goal for anyone who plays golf is to play the best you can, and shoot the lowest score possible. When I play golf, my goal is to shoot under par. Par is a great score, but for me, it's not good enough. For the sake of the nation, any president should have the same goal, One Nation Under Par."

The entire production crew started applauding Jeff's response, much to Jeff's surprise. Max, while clapping his hands, stood up and shook Jeff's hand. When the applause subsided, Max sat down and said, "One Nation Under Par. That's a fantastic campaign slogan. Well, Jeff, we have time for one final question. Tomorrow, you're going to take the polygraph test, and, I believe you'll demonstrate that you're an honest person. But, if elected, can you get our nation under par?"

Jeff looked Max in the eye and replied from his heart, "Max, I'm not running for office, but if I was elected president of the United States, I wouldn't leave anything on the course, and with God's help, would simply do my best to shoot the lowest round for the sake of the nation."

Max concluded the interview by saying, "Jeff, I'd like to thank you for being on our show today. And, whether you like it or not, I'm writing your name on the ballot for president this November. Thank you again."

The production crew clapped and applauded while the credits rolled. Everyone came up and congratulated Jeff for a job well done. What Just Fore Golf did not yet know was that this show was one of the most viewed interviews in their short history, and it had the highest rating of non-golfers who tuned in to see Jeff be formally interviewed for the first time. The buzz in the studio was ecstatic, especially since they knew that Jeff was returning in the morning for the unprecedented pre-election polygraph test.

A Best Bet Limo shuttled Jeff from the studio. A well-wishing crowd assembled outside his new temporary hotel accommodations in Orlando. For a change of pace, and against the wishes of Johnson, Jeff entered the hotel through the lobby. Well over a thousand Jeff fans greeted his arrival. They cheered him, shouting "Jeff for President, One Nation Under Par" and "Vote for Honesty." He also heard shouts of "Jeff, great interview. Golf all the way for the USA." With the help of Johnson's security measures, Jeff waved to his flock and gleamed at those wishing him the best as Johnson escorted him to the awaiting elevator. Only he and Johnson entered the elevator. Johnson looked at him and said, "Are you okay?"

Jeff's gleam did not disappear, as he relished his quick trip to celebrityism. While the elevator dinged it's upward climb, Jeff looked and Johnson and said.

"It's weird. Everyone wants me to succeed. They want me to be president. It's just really starting to hit me. But…"

Johnson looked at him as though they were having another father to son chat and asked, "But what?"

Jeff replied, "What if I get elected and fail?"

Johnson could see he needed some fatherly advice and said, "Jeff, the only failure you could have is not trying to succeed. If you do the best you can, in everything you attempt to do, you'll always be successful, because you did your best, no matter what the results are. So…succeed!"

Jeff's gleam turned into a confident glow, and he said, "Thank you, Johnson, for everything. Ginger and I could never have gone this far without you" and he held out his hand to Johnson.

Johnson completed the handshake and replied, "This entire presidential campaign of yours is the most ridiculous pain-in-the-ass experience I've ever had, and I'm having a ball. Thank you for the ride. Now, let's get you ready for that test tomorrow. I want to make sure you pass with flying colors. Besides I know how to beat those lie detectors. It's a snap. Then after the test, we go after Scratch and Hoag. Is it a deal?"

Continuing the handshake, Jeff said, "It's a deal."

When Jeff entered the suite, Ginger floored him while saying, "Darling, you were fabulous on TV, and you didn't need any help from me," hinting at her grab bag assistance in his first press conference at the golf course in Las Vegas. "One Nation Under Par, what a beautiful remark. Let's make it happen."

Jade agreed. "Jeff, that is your new slogan. We'll put it on the website. I'm sure the press is already running with it."

Johnson dismissed Jade and Longshot so he could brief Jeff on the polygraph test and measure his pulse as he asked Jeff very challenging yes and no questions. Johnson said, "Jeff, you're running on a platform of honesty, so your best bet is to answer each question honestly. Let the other knuckleheads worry about their lying responses. Be yourself. If you want to bend a response, believe in your heart that your answer is honest, and the polygraph will believe you. It's that simple."

After thirty minutes of role playing, Jeff said he was tired and wanted to call it an evening. Johnson retired to his room. When Jeff entered his bedroom, Ginger was there with dinner, but, as promised, she wore the teddy of Jeff's dreams, combining leather, lace, silk, a splash of whipped cream and a dash of raspberry vodka, on the side, of course. They completely nourished their sex-starved appetites, and reordered dinner several hours later to nourish their physically starved appetites, as their original dinner was stone cold.

The next morning, "One Nation Under Par" was the top story across all news media, and Jeff quickly regained his news popularity. News personnel camped outside the Just Fore Golf studio, eager to announce the results of Jeff's polygraph test. Jeff's personal entourage joined him at the studio. They were introduced to several members of the Orlando Police Department including the Chief of Police, who wouldn't have passed up a chance to meet some real celebrities besides the usual mice, whales, and assortment of cartoon characters that attracted visitors worldwide to Orlando.

Elliot Connelly of ConFess Security was also present. He asked Jeff, "Are you ready to proceed?"

Jeff said, "Let's tee it up."

Everyone was escorted to a conference room where the polygraph was set up. As they were entering the room, Elliot turned to Jeff and whispered, "Jeff, I reviewed your questions. They are a piece of cake. You'll do fine." Jeff appreciated the inside information, improving his level of confidence.

Officer Tatem connected Jeff to the sensors from the polygraph and explained how it worked. "Mr. Taylor, a polygraph exam is a tool law enforcement agencies use to determine if people are telling the truth. It does this by measuring your heart rate, breathing pattern, and the amount of perspiration that comes off your fingertips. I'll ask you a variety of questions. Please respond by only saying Yes or No. Do not elaborate. We should be done here in no time, and you can be out playing golf by lunch. Any questions?"

Jeff said, "Yes. Do you play golf?"

Officer Tatem said, "As a matter of fact, I do."

Jeff smiled. "Awesome. What's your handicap?"

"Eight."

Jeff said, "Hmm, you play some good golf. Now, if I hook you up to this machine, will you still reply with eight? When we're finished, I may hook you up to this thing to test your answer. Or, we can play a round using your handicap for, let's say $100. Will your eight hold up to the polygraph or a game of golf?"

Officer Tatem pondered the question and said, "Well, if I'm hooked up to the machine, my handicap is 11. If I'm playing you for $100, my handicap is 19."

Jeff responded by saying, "Who needs a polygraph? Let the truth be told on the course." Warm morning laughter mushroomed around the conference table.

Elliot handed Officer Tatum a large manila envelope with the polygraph test questions. Officer Tatum then asked everyone to leave the room. Jeff stood up, and Tatum said, "Sorry Jeff, you're the star. Please be seated."

Tatum opened the envelope and quickly reviewed the questions. He checked the polygraph and tape recorder and said, "Mr. Taylor, we're all set. Are you ready?"

Jeff said, "Fire away."

"Okay. First, I'll ask you two test questions. Again, please reply with yes or no. Is your name Jeff Taylor?"

"Yes."

"Do you hate golf?"

"No!"

"Perfect" replied Officer Tatem. "Your answers indicted true responses and the polygraph is working properly. Let's start with the real test questions. Question one. Do you have the aptitude, courage, and leadership to effectively run the country?"

"Yes."

"Question two. You have no political ties in Washington and no party affiliation. Do you think you can get bills passed without either of these associations?"

"Yes."

"Question three. Did you marry Ginger for publicity sake, to ultimately improve your chance to win the election?"

"No."

"Question four. Have you ever done anything illegal or immoral for personal financial gain?"

Jeff laughed and said, "No," but then added, "Although I've never been in politics or business." Officer Tatum grinned and positively shook his head in agreement.

"Question five. If you were elected president, do you have the courage to command our troops to go to war with another country?"

Jeff squirmed in his seat at this question and responded. "Officer Tatum, that question is too vague. I'd have to have a very good reason to command our troops into battle. I would command our troops to fight if the United States was attacked, either physically or constitutionally. I would not commit the lives of our armed forces for sake of ego, personal or corporate financial gain, or personal supremacy."

Officer Tatum changed the question. "Okay, would you commit U. S. troops into battle to protect our borders and the Constitution of America?"

Jeff replied, "Yes. Absolutely."

"Question six. During your brief campaign, you said that you'd prefer to use other options beside war to solve conflicts. Would you go so far to use competitive events like golf as a means to resolve political issues between countries?"

"Yes. Any alternative to war would be considered."

Officer Tatum firmly stated, "I agree, but please, for this test, simply keep your responses to yes or no.

"Question eight. Do you think any of the current candidates running for the presidential office are better suited to be president than you?"

Jeff thought about this question for a while and said, "This is another vague question. What is meant by 'better suited'? Do you mean wealth, political leverage, governmental experience? Or do you mean having common sense, courage, or integrity? I guess my answer is no!"

"All right, Mr. Taylor. Just two more questions. Question nine. You married Ginger after knowing her for less than ten hours. Do you think this conveys a message of family values and respect for the sanctity of marriage?"

Jeff thought about this and said, "I know people who dated for several years, married, and divorced soon afterwards. I also know people whose courtship was short, married, and remained happily married forever. My parents were a good example of a short courtship. The good Lord brought Ginger and I together for some strange reason. We've only been married for a short time, but thus far, I have no regrets, and look forward to spending the rest of my life with her. Therefore, my response is yes."

Tatum shook his head in approval of Jeff's response, but disapproved of his lengthy answers, and continued with the last question. "By replying with either yes or no, would you like to be the president of the United States?"

Jeff confidently looked Officer Tatum in the eye and said, "Yes."

Officer Tatum said, "That's it, Mr. Taylor. We're done." He turned off the polygraph and the tape recorder and said, "Mr. Taylor, you did great. I have to go over the results with our chief, but in short, the polygraph said you answered everything truthfully."

Jeff shook Officer Tatum's hand and said, "Thank you for the good news."

Scratch burned the pictures he mysteriously received several days earlier, but the mental damage was done. Following the advice of his secret conniver, he took Blabs to a bird vet for a complete physical. She passed with high-flying colors. He also upgraded her cuisine to one that consisted of organically grown fruits, vegetables and nuts, bottled water from France, and "Fit for a Feathered King" gourmet bird seed. He also purchased an elaborate misting system that recreated the humidity and seasonal rainforest showers for birds of Central and South America, but he couldn't figure out how to get Blabs to sit on her perch to enjoy the "Aquatic Spray-sation," as described in the setup literature. Every day, he turned on the high-tech bird bath and left the house, hoping Blabs would indulge in the simulated hometown rain forest showers.

Even after all his attention to bird-tail detail, a horrid knock on the door occurred. "Package, Mr. Scratch." Scratch opened the overnight package sent from Greenland, and nearly fell over when he saw the single photo of himself with his butt glistening like a glazed donut, holding Toni's hand in the middle of the night. The firefighters were not included in this particular photo shoot. He turned the picture over, and his worst nightmare worsened. The inscription on the back of the photo read, "We have complete video, with sound. Protect the Bird!"

"Oh, shit. Why me? I haven't killed anyone in months." Blabs sat high atop her perch, eating a piece of pizza crust that she stole from the nearly empty pizza box left over from Scratch's previous dinner delivery. Splatterings of the crust were falling into Scratch's hair, but he didn't even notice. He realized that these pictures could ruin his career or have him killed. He couldn't tie Ginger in with these photographs. He looked up at Blabs and said "Did some Arab sheik or important client of Ginger's enjoy the same perverted BJ like you gave Hoag, and wants to protect you for future erotic enjoyment?" For the first time in his career and life, he was the prey, not the predator. He was an exposed mouse in an open field, and the hungry hawks were looming.

Jeff joined Ginger in the dressing room while Officer Tatum discussed the results with the chief. Few words were spoken, and the uneasy silence was broken when the Chief entered the room with Officer Tatum, Max, and Johnson. "Jeff, great news, according to the polygraph, you answered all the questions honestly. Congratulations for speaking the truth."

Johnson was smiling, but Jeff looked troubled and asked the chief, "Chief, Mr. Johnson here was a member of several law enforcement agencies, and he said that the results of a polygraph can be misleading or false. Would you agree with that?"

The chief said, "Well, yes. Some people have the ability to lie to the machine, yet the polygraph reports no indication of false responses. Why do you ask? Did you lie on some of the questions?"

Jeff replied, "No, I didn't. I had no reason to. But, I can't expect to continue with the Honest Scorecard. Voters can't rely on an unreliable machine to judge who the best candidate is. They have to go with their gut feeling and a prayer. I know the press is eager to know the results of my test. Please provide them with the results, but after you make your statement, I'm going to cancel the challenge."

The chief said, "As you wish."

Quiet filled the room for a short moment, as no one knew what to do or say next until Johnson spoke. "Jeff, I realize your goal was to flush out honesty in presidential candidates. That was certainly a very refreshing gesture. Knowing that the polygraph is imperfect, and canceling the challenge to other presidential candidates, is, well, a perfect example of being presidential. You're doing what you believe is right and fair regarding the candidates and the election process. I congratulate you for your ethics and integrity." Johnson walked up and shook Jeff's hand, followed by the chief and Max. Ginger was busy gripping Jeff's other hand while holding back tears of admiration.

Jade had a difference of opinion and said, "Jeff, I agree with you that this test is not the best method for choosing an honest president. But, that's not the intention. The goal of the polygraph is not to find truth but to simply encourage our leaders to be truthful—to themselves, to Americans, and to the world. Millions of Americans donated millions of dollars to ask direct questions to candidates. The goal is not to disclose dishonest politicians but to unveil someone worth voting for. I think you can release a statement regarding the inabilities of the polygraph, but let the Honest Scorecard continue. America wants it. They need hope that honesty will prevail in the White House, not bribery, money, or political clout."

Jeff thought about her remarks and said, "You've made a very good argument." He thought about her statement for a moment and replied "Okay. I'll let the polygraph testing continue, but I will make a statement regarding its deficiencies. I realize that my questions and responses, along with those of the other candidates, will be posted on our site. I'd also like to include some links to sites that describe how the polygraph testing works, and clearly show that it's not the perfect answer to the honest answer. Okay?"

Jade smiled. "Perfect. In fact, you're taking honesty to the next level by showing the shortcomings of the machine. That's why you should be president. Others might not be so, well, presidential."

Hands clapped at the conclusion of Jade's remarks. Officer Tatum said, "She right. Mr. Taylor, you have my vote this November."

The Chief said, "And you have mine, as long as we get to play a round of golf together."

Jeff smirked and said, "Well, Officer Tatum and I have a $100 bet going that he's an eight handicapper. Let's play today."

Officer Tatum turned as red as a traffic light and said, "I can't, Mr. Taylor. Betting is illegal."

The room filled with laughter, but Jade interrupted. "The press is probably going to explode out there if we don't clue them in to the results of the test. Let's give them the verbal results, and then you boys can go hit some balls."

The Chief said, "Let's go. I'll reveal the basic results of the test, and then Jeff can provide his comments." They all headed downstairs to the throng of the salivating news media.

"Good afternoon everyone. I'm Chief of Police Murdock. We just tested Mr. Taylor, and according to the polygraph, he answered all the questions truthfully." The Chief quickly read each question and provided Jeff's answers. "The questions and results will be posted on the Vote For Honesty web site. And now, Jeff Taylor would like to comment on the test."

Jeff approached the multitude of microphones alone with a blank expression on his face. The crowd was screaming positive comments in his favor, but he didn't hear them or see them. He turned and looked at Ginger and Johnson. They both displayed faces of encouragement and full support. He turned back to the mics and said, "Good afternoon. I'm Jeff Taylor." The crowd cheered, but he still did not hear them.

"I'd like to speak with you regarding the Honest Scorecard. The lie detector is a machine the police use to determine if crime suspects are telling the truth. But it is not a perfect machine, and people have the ability to lie to questions and have the results show that they answered truthfully. When I first said that we should hook up presidential candidates to polygraphs, I didn't know that it was not 100 percent accurate. What I'm trying to say is that I don't want American voters to place all of their confidence in the results of Honest Scorecard. You need to look at each candidate closely and use your gut feeling to elect someone who will try to make our country a better place for all of us."

Jeff took a deep breath and continued. "Folks, as you all know, a radio personality named Longshot made a bet to his listeners that an unknown person named Jeff Taylor would become our next president. What you don't know is that he also made a side bet with me. He bet me $100 that he'd make me a millionaire. Well, he won that bet. I've signed contracts with several companies to endorse their products, worth well over a million dollars."

He paused for a moment. The reporters and followers quieted down to hear the literal pin drop. "I thought you should know how I unofficially entered this election campaign. It was not from desire to be president. It was based on a bet." He paused again. Jade brought him a glass of water, anticipating nervous dry mouth. She knew he had something more to say but didn't know how to say it.

Jeff continued. "My desire, however, has changed significantly over the past few weeks, primarily due to you, the people of America. Your encouragement and desire to have me run for office has given me a craving for something I never knew I had. Now, I answered all the questions posed to me truthfully, but I might have lied on the first question." A murmur simmered in the crowd.

"I was asked if I had the aptitude and courage to run the country. I responded yes and meant it. But a better question might have been, do I think I have the ability to run our nation. Well, folks, to be honest, I'm not so sure." The murmur grew to a quiet noise. "Think about it. The biggest decisions I've ever had to make in my life are the same as yours. How do I make more money? What kind of car should I buy? Can I afford next month's rent? Until recently, will I ever get married?" A subtle wave of laughter swept through the flock. "I've never been in any type of political office, having to make decisions such as how to improve our educational system or economy; or what should we do about healthcare; or how do we resolve international conflicts. So, when you elect a president, you need to determine if they have the ability to tackle these monumental problems."

Jeff took a sip of his water, made strong eye contact with the media and camera, and confidently continued, "But, also keep in mind that I am coming from a background like most American citizens, and I completely understand what it's like to be like you. I am you." Like an emotional congregation in a quaint Southern Baptist Church, several hoots and hollers resounded, instead of, but similar to, the bursts of Amen. "Do you think our politicians can relate to the challenges of most of us Americans?" A positive roar of agreement quickly multiplied, feeding off Jeff's heartfelt words.

Reverend Jeff could feel the connection between himself and his erupting choir as he sermoned on. "The bottom line is that I had no desire or intention of becoming president. But, over the last few weeks, it's become very clear to me that America needs a new voice...not the voice of a politician, but a voice of the people. You have expressed to me that you want me to succeed. I feel like I'm playing a sport, and you, America, are cheering me on, giving me the confidence of having home court advantage. Your support has dramatically changed my attitude, and driven me to want to become your president. Your encouragement encouraged me to be your voice. I AM YOU. I am your voice. If you elect me as president, I will simply do my best to make our country, and our world, a better place." The now emotional congregation exploded to a near frenzy state. The words of Jeff's sermon seeped into the hearts and souls of all who heard it.

Jeff took one final sip of water and concluded. "I'd like to thank Just Fore Golf and the Orlando Police department for their hospitality and for administering the test. Also, I wish the best of luck to all of the other candidates who'll participate in the Honest Scorecard. Now we have to split. I have a golf match this afternoon with several members of the Orlando Police Department, and I don't want to receive a ticket for a delay of game violation. But, before we leave, I wanted to let all voters know that...that..." Jeff looked at Ginger, and she was nodding her head up and down in approval, "…that I am now, officially, running for president of the United States, and ask you to write in the name Jeff Taylor on the ballot this November. Let's bring honesty back into our White House and our great country. Let's make this country, One Nation Under Par. Thank you."

The crowd screamed "Jeff for President" and "One Nation Under Par" with the emotion of spectators watching the final seconds of a tied NCAA Basketball championship game. The reporters swarmed the podium to ask questions, but Jeff departed quickly. Johnson's team, along with members of Orlando's police department, intervened, and let Jeff escape to the quiet of the first tee.

The day ended on the golf course, with Officer Tatum beating Jeff by one shot with the aid of his 19 handicap. Since betting was illegal, Jeff paid for drinks at the 19th hole, which more than covered the bet.

The impact of his speech compared to a meteor the size of Australia hitting the earth at the equator. Jeff's impromptu remarks and official entry into the election race was spoken from the heart, and everyone who heard it knew it. Sonny was trashing his bedroom, smashing everything with everything. Ashley took the demolition of her bedroom in stride, knowing she'd get the opportunity to purchase new bedroom furniture as a result. After Sonny's rage subsided to the force of a low-grade typhoon, he realized it was time to launch the attack on Ginger and discredit the leading presidential contender.

Johnson also realized that Jeff's unexpected and motivational words would position him as the formidable obstacle in the election race and figured that Sonny would retaliate immediately with a full strike, bordering on nuclear missile deployment. He decided that Scratch would have to join their team sooner than later, or else Jeff would lose the election if Ginger's past was exposed. Johnson briefed his team members of his plan and action.

Next, he called Tyrone to signal the full-scale assault. "Did you happen to catch Jeff's latest speech on TV?"

"Sure did. I imagine that you want to pick up the pace of Scratch's blackmail campaign?"

Johnson replied, "Those are strong words. I don't think of it as blackmail. I think of it more as a friendly act of coercion to manipulate the deranged thinking of an enemy, in order to construct a complementary alliance rather than a competitive obstacle and therefore leverage our advantage."

Tyrone said, "Pretty words, but it's still blackmail."

"Okay, okay, blackmail. No matter how you say it, Sonny's going to want to put Ginger's videos in the hands of the press. I'm flying down to meet Scratch today and see if he'd consider joining our team in the middle of the game. I don't know how he could say no."

Tyrone replied, "Well, we'll keep your back door covered, and turn the tape recorder off and cameras off so no one will know of your meeting."

"Thanks. I'll call you when I land in Ft. Lauderdale."

Hole Number 15
Par 4

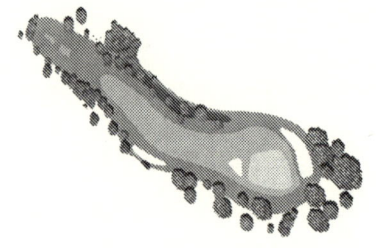

(**Course Notes:** Wet dream extremes, pecker head blasphemes)

    Blabs awoke from her mid-afternoon nap courtesy of the loud, banging door exit of Scratch, who left to pick up groceries and an assortment of medicines at the local liquor store. When his car sped away from the house, Blabs flew down to take advantage of her personal misting system, followed by her scavenger like quest to nibble on Scratch's fallen lunch morsels. Although Scratch increased his conversations with Blabs, she was still lonely, and longed for the company of her true owner. She was reminded of Ginger when Scratch watched some of her seductive videos the night before to once again consummate his love affair with himself.

    Blabs was destined to release Ginger from the disk objects and flew over to the black box were Ginger was being imprisoned. Blabs used the precision of her pointed beak and sure-footed claws to press the buttons on the DVD player until a small trap door opened, pushing the surprised parrot off the entertainment center. Yet, Blabs, forging forward like a mountaineer ascending Mt. Everest in the most adverse conditions, climbed back up to the ledge to combat the slippery technology monster and rescue her beloved Ginger.

    The DVD door remained open, and Blabs was able to push the shiny disk object out with one clawed foot, while grabbing the end of the disk with her beak. With a grip strong enough to easily crack hard nuts, she grabbed the disk in her beak and fluttered down to the floor. Once on solid ground, she began biting the metallic object, hoping Ginger would in some way be resurrected. After several minutes of constant biting and scratching, she decided that Ginger was not in that specific disk object, and waddled over to the smooth leathery case where other disk objects potentially concealed her best friend and owner. Blabs continued her life saving efforts by removing each disk from its protective sleeve, and attempted to bite her way through the polished disks and find her soul mate. In some cases, the disk objects cracked from her super bird biting strength.

Scratch returned several hours later with a car full of groceries. After several trips to the car and undergoing the subservient task of putting everything away, he popped open a cold beer and retired to the living room to watch more Ginger videos and perform his personal job at hand. When he saw the DVDs on the living room carpet all broken and scratched, he immediately pulled out his hand gun, thinking someone broke into his home to retaliate for the stolen bird, but noticed Blabs perched in her usual spot on the staircase above. Scratch looked at Blabs and said, "Who the hell destroyed the DVDs, but left you behind?"

After checking the house for intruders or forced entry, of which there were none, he attempted to play all the DVDs, including the "SonnyBlabs" video, only to have an error light display when the play button was depressed for each video. Scratch could not come up with solid ideas regarding what occurred or by whom. He looked up at Blabs and said "What the hell is going on here?"

Blabs looked down at Scratch and screeched out, "Pecker head, shit for brains."

Scratch was so confused and irritated, he took aim on Blabs. Just as he cocked the trigger of his .38, a loud knock came from the front door. He took a pull on his beer and opened the door slowly while holding his cocked gun behind the door and said, "What the hell do you want?"

Johnson was not surprised by the greeting and remained calm while replying, "A friend from Greenland asked me to pay you a visit. Are you alone, or do you have some of your boyfriends over for a manly love fest?"

Scratch was ready to waste the large black stranger right there on his door step in broad daylight and then use the last bullet on himself, but he took a deep breath of air and angrily said, "I don't know what you're talking about, shit head, so why don't you just turn around and split before I waste you right here."

Just then, Blabs yelled out, "Pecker head, shit for brains."

Johnson muscled every facial muscle into control as though his cheeks were holding a car filled with kids from falling over a cliff. He was remarkably able to not laugh in Scratch's face when he heard Blabs' remarks. Tyrone and Jack, on the other hand, were sitting in their car sweating profusely from the gut wrenching laughter. They had decided to keep the concealed mics on to offer Johnson assistance if needed. They never thought it would be so entertaining.

Johnson simply replied, "Oh, you do have company? Obviously, your guest does not think highly of you. Are you taking care of your guest?"

Scratch was playing a new game with no home course advantage. He quickly assumed that the stranger was responsible for the demolition of the DVDs and decided to use force as his only weapon, similar to a rat or snake that's backed into a corner. He removed his gun holding hand from behind the door and said, "So, asshole, you think that smashing up the Ginger DVDs is going to scare me from killing your parrot? Well, think again."

Johnson showed a truly surprised face, but was trained to respond in a way that produced calm and protection and said, "What DVDs?"

Scratch noticed the surprised look on Johnson's face and said, "You mean you don't know nuthin' about Ginger's scratched up DVDs? Bullshit!"

Johnson, whose face remained like an unchanged brick wall, thought up a quick story and said, "Listen, pal, I'm only here for the safety of the bird. A very high governmental official, a power higher than any congressman, judge, or cabinet member, has very deep feelings for this bird, and suggests that you release the parrot in my custody now. He has connections all over the world, including Greenland. If you don't release her, a video of your sexual activities in Key West will be distributed to all of your past, current, and future employers, colleagues, and competition."

Johnson slowly pulled out a DVD and said, "A special security task force was ordered to provide protective services to the parrot. No reason was given, but national security was assumed. While undergoing our Miami and Key West surveillance operation of a specific couple and the parrot, you were discovered tailing the protected threesome. As a result, you were duly witnessed, observed, and recorded, ultimately uncovering your sexual mating preference. A Toni LeBlac has already confirmed that you spent the night with him on several occasions. Your choice is simple: release the bird, and I'll release the video to you. The preside…er, I mean the task force is ready to use force if you don't comply with my demand."

Scratch stood there dumbfounded, thinking, *That bird must give one hellava blow job. Maybe I should try it out before I give her back?*

Johnson added some fuel to the already hotly burning fire and said, "By the way, unless you really do have shit for brains as the bird seems to think, you probably already know that my boss has more leverage than your boss. You might want to consider working on our team as a third option." He handed Scratch a business card that simply read "Johnson" and his cell phone number.

"We can't pay you, but we would destroy your embarrassing history, which is worth more than money. You would, however, be required to assist us in removing your boss from the election race. You'll basically be doing the same thing you're doing now, only changing teams. Tell you what, keep the bird alive for the time being and think about my offer. I'll contact you for your decision within a few days."

During the conversation, Johnson had the gun pointed at his face, but he knew his delivery shattered the mind of his adversary, and he casually walked away from the front door without any gunshots. After a few steps, he turned around and threw the disc at Scratch who caught it in mid-air and said, "Hey, Hollywood, a word of advice. You look bad on camera. Gay guys would become straight if they saw this. I'd keep it to yourself."

Scratch stood there holding his gun in one hand and his video nightmare in the other hand while Johnson disappeared.

Tyrone erased the entire conversation from their recorder.

While Scratch stood on his front porch in complete disarray, his cell phone started to ring. Scratch knew it was Sonny. He decided to let him go to voicemail, as he needed some time to digest his situation and options.

Once again, Scratch found himself in uncharted waters. He poured himself a large glass of 90 proof something, chugged half the glass, and nervously played the DVD. The high-tech surveillance cameras used by the FBI agents created a sequence of unsurpassed digitally clear video clips. It recreated his hellish nightmare encounter with the other side. His hands started to shake, and his chest pounded as though his heart was going to explode. During the video, he picked up his gun, and started toying with the idea of leaving the world behind. He chugged the remainder of his drink while the end of the video drew near.

Then, during the final clip when Toni sucked his face off, Scratch said, "That's it. I can't go on." He put the gun to the temple of his head and was ready to pull the trigger when SPLAT. Blabs unleashed a direct hit of sticky bird poop on Scratch's head and hand holding the gun while saying, "Pecker head. Shit for brains."

He jumped up and said, "That's it. You're a dead bird," and started blasting away at Blabs. Luckily for Blabs, Scratch was smashed and saw three birds flying in the air.

Tyrone and Jack heard the gunfire, causing Tyrone to break role. He ran to the front door and banged with force. He kept one hand on his gun inside his sport coat.

Scratch regained his composure and opened the door saying, "What the hell do you want?"

Tyrone said, "Hi, I'm John, a neighbor from down the street. I was just taking a walk and heard banging noises coming from your house and wanted to make sure everything was all right." Tyrone looked up and saw Blabs sitting safely on the staircase railing.

Scratch looked like he was fighting death and nastily replied, "Yeah, yeah. I saw a rat and tried to shoot it, but missed it. Now go put your meddling nose on some other neighbor's door." He slammed the door shut, and poured a glass of some other 90 proof something. He took a big gulp, and passed out on the sofa. Blabs embraced the calm and quiet, and also decided to take a cat nap.

Tyrone called Johnson, who was just taking off for the short flight back to Orlando. "Our boy is starting to lose it. He watched the DVD you gave him, and started taking shots at the bird. This might be a good time to get the bird out of there. I broke my cover and don't want to have Jack break his. Any ideas?"

Johnson thought for a moment and said, "We've already taken off so I'm stuck. What's Scratch doing now?"

"We hear him snoring, so he's out for the moment."

"I'll call you right back." Johnson immediately called Russell "Hey Russ, this is Jeff's security manager, Johnson."

Russell said, "Johnson, good to hear from you. Hey, I caught Jeff's speech from Orlando. Wow. He's a politician and doesn't even know it. He was great."

"Yes he was, but his speech started a new tidal wave of events. I need your help. What are you doing now?"

Russell said, "I just pulled up in front of the Sawgrass Mall with the fam. What's up?"

Johnson replied, "Drop off your wife and kids at the mall, and head east on Broward Blvd. Once you're on your way, I'll call you to explain everything. You'll be back at the mall within an hour. Dinner's on me and Jeff if you can help."

Russell said, "I'm on my way. I'll do anything for Jeff and Ginger. We have more money than we know what to do with. We're building a new wing at the clinic, thanks to them. "

Russell dropped off his family, and headed east as directed. Johnson called him and filled him in on the situation with Blabs and Scratch. "Russell, I need you to break into a house and steal Blabs back for Ginger. But you have to be careful; a lunatic with a gun is protecting the parrot."

"What? Breaking and entering, and a good chance of getting shot?"

Johnson said, "Don't worry. The bird thief is passed out from over drinking, and the FBI is there to help you. You're our only choice. I'll call the FBI agents and alert them to your mission. They could probably help you get inside the house."

Russell then asked, "How do I catch a bird?"

Johnson was stumped and said, "Great question. I didn't even think about that. I don't know. Maybe coax her with some bird treats."

"Does she bite?"

Johnson again said, "I don't know."

Within minutes, Russell pulled his car alongside the FBI car. Tyrone rolled down his window and said, "Hi Russell, we were expecting you. We already unlocked the front door. Our bird thief is snoring away. All you have to do is quietly go inside and get the bird. Her name is Blabs. We'll be outside the front door giving you cover. Don't worry."

Russell was worried, but parked his car and went to the front door with the agents. He poked his head in and saw Scratch sleeping on the sofa. The house stunk like raw sewage in a high school gym locker. He saw Blabs sleeping on the staircase railing. He silently crept up the staircase and was ready grab Blabs when she noticed him and took off, landing on Scratch's belly. *Oh shit. Now what?*

As he climbed down the staircase, Blabs was walking around Scratch's belly saying, "Oh baby. You're hot. Oh Baby. You're the best."

Scratch started talking back while in his sleep. "Toni, this isn't right. You got the wrong parts. But you sure feel good."

Russell was confused at the conversation. He looked out the door and saw the FBI agents doing their best to not laugh out loud, but he didn't understand why. Then he noticed a bag of bird treats on the dining room table. He grabbed one and held it in front of Blabs, not really sure how to pick her up. Blabs hungrily looked at the treat and said, "Eat the treat. Eat the treat."

Scratch replied by saying "Yes, eat the treat. It's yours, Toni."

He heard a commotion by the door and saw Jack running back to the car. He couldn't stop the laughter. Tyrone was biting his lip with such a laugh stopping force that he started breaking lip skin with his teeth. Without any warning, Blabs jumped up on Russell's arm, and started eating the treat. Russell slowly moved in the direction of the door while Blabs said, "Hmm, Hmm good."

Scratch responded, "I'm all yours, Toni."

In order to prevent her from flying away outside, Russell put both hands around Blabs, much to her dissatisfaction. She started squawking violently. Russell bolted toward his car and threw Blabs in. He started the car and peeled away from the curb when he heard a crack, then smash. His rear car window was hit by a bullet. It cracked, but didn't break. Two more shots were fired, one hitting his back tail light, but he made his first right and drove out of harm's way. The FBI agents hunkered down in their car, as Scratch was only a few footsteps away from them. They didn't retaliate fire, hoping Russell would escape unharmed, which he did. Blabs was flapping her wings in panic but calmed down when Russell started playing some classical music. Blabs still had her treat and calmly devoured it to the unruffled sounds of Mozart.

Scratch stood in the road for several minutes, his gun still emitting smoke from the hot barrel. He was hunched over and pathetically distraught. His easy and lucrative bird sitting gig immediately ended. The DVDs were ruined. His career and reputation were in jeopardy, and his life was on the line by himself and other killing suitors. In addition, he just couldn't erase the dream he had prior to the bird napping. He actually enjoyed the horrible dream of him and Toni together, which made him think he was losing his mind. He dragged himself back into the house, and his cell phone started ringing. This time he answered.

"Gad blasted son bitch. Where the hell you been? I've been trying to call you. I'm paying you a heap of money to be at my beckon call. It's time to pull the plug on those campaign intruders. I want copies of that whore's DVDs sent to every major network in the country."

Scratch said, "Okay. When?"

Sonny said, "Yesterday, you Gad dang moron."

Scratch responded, "Well, I'll need several hundred copies of the DVDs, and mailing addresses of all the news stations. Can you get one of your college co-op suck-ups to get all the addresses and mailing envelopes sent to me? I'll work on getting the DVDs copied. It will probably take your staff a week to pull this together, three weeks if they're learning to work for the government."

Sonny grumbled, "Dang it. All right. I'll have them shipped to you as soon as they're ready. Now get off your fat ass and start copying those disks. I want this whole Jeff fiasco nipped in the bud pronto."

Scratch sat back in chair and slugged down whatever was left in his thinking glass, grumbling "Ass wipe, Congressman. I think I'd rather work for Jeff and Ginger. Besides, I'm minus the DVDs and bird anyway. I'll stall shit head until he sends me the addresses and force him to pay me the full amount of my service fee before I pretend to mail any DVDs out. Once the cash is in my hand, I'll split. Where to go? Costa Rica. *Hmm...too close. Hmm...New Zealand or Australia. That's it. I'll move all my cash to a bank account there with a new identity. Shit head won't ever find me. That's the plan. That's the plazzz....*" Scratch passed out snoring on the sofa with a new attitude.

While Scratch dreamed more dreams of Toni, Tyrone called Johnson. "The bird is safe. Scratch got a few shots off at Russell's car, but they got away unharmed. Since the DVDs and bird are no longer in the picture, we're going to tell our boss to take us off the case. Scratch is no longer endangering Jeff or his team."

Johnson said, "10-4. Thanks for all your help. I hope I can return the favor some day."

"Well, do you know any good doctors? Jack's going to need surgery to repair his stomach lining from gut wrenching laughter. Hell, I think I popped a hemorrhoid from this comedy mission. Anyways, good luck on the election. We're out."

Johnson immediately called Russell. "You did it. Are you okay?"

"Yes," replied Russell. "I'm just starting to calm down. Mozart helps. The bird is in the back seat eating. My car was shot up pretty bad. I'm not sure what to say to my wife. Oh yeah, what do I do with the bird?"

Johnson said, "First, tell your wife the truth, but you may want to downplay it somewhat. Next, don't worry about the car. Jeff will pay to get it fixed or buy you a new one. Now, when you go back to the mall to meet your family, stop by a pet store and pick up a portable birdcage and bird food. You'll need to hold on to the bird for us for a few days. Again, Jeff will pick up the tab. You're doing Jeff and Ginger a huge favor. Also, I'm sorry about the shooting. I hoped it wouldn't have gone to that level. We'll give you a call later to see how you're doing. Thanks again."

Johnson hooked up with Jeff and Ginger after their round of golf with the police. He had a huge smile on his face. "Guys, I have fantastic news. First, Blabs is now a guest of Russell's and Ashanti's. Russell once again did some heroics and, with the help of the FBI, rescued Blabs from Scratch. But that's not all. It appears that Blabs tried to eat all of the stolen DVDs and scratched them so badly that they can't be viewed. Since the FBI confiscated the PC at the Hard Rock, no other discs can be copied."

With tears in her eyes, Ginger hugged Johnson and immediately called Russell to thank him. "Russell, thank you so much for recovering Blabs for me. Johnson told us what happened. We'll take care of your car damage and parrot expenses."

Russell said, "Ginger. It was my pleasure. Blabs is in good hands. She and my kids are singing songs together. They're spoiling the crap out of her, but she loves the affection. But I have a question. You said you're going back to Vegas. What about your trip to Washington?"

Ginger said, "Well, we haven't done anything stupid lately to attract media attention. Therefore, we're losing our share of the voters. Hoag's spending a fortune on his campaign, and it looks like he'll get presidency."

Russell screamed, "No. Not Hoag! You can't do this. He's promising discount coupons to Swine Dine's if he's elected. The entire country will be dying from obesity and high cholesterol, and the foolish voters are falling for it. Jeff's got to stay in the race."

Ginger said, "Well, you know what he needs. He needs a motivator. A mentor. Somebody who will be his eyes and ears. Someone with political savvy and an understanding of the law. Someone he can trust and rely on to help him succeed. He needs you, Russell."

"What do you mean?"

Jeff was listening to Ginger, and she handed the phone to him. "Russell, it's Jeff. Would you like to be my running mate?"

Russell exclaimed, "Your running mate? Are you kidding?"

"Nope. You're an attorney. You understand law. You're currently an elected official. You're smart. You're down to earth, honest and decent. You know how to accomplish tasks."

Russell's mind whirled like he was on the Galactic Spin ride at a county fair. "Jeff, I'm on a board of commissioners for a little town with a population of 650. That's not a governmental position. It's a boring hobby that no one else wants. I don't know anything about real politics."

Jeff responded, "Listen to me Russell. First, running a little city is like running the country. You simply add a whole bunch more zeros at the end of the budget. Next, I don't want a politician as a running mate. The people who will vote for us don't want politicians. They want someone who will try to improve the country and not line their pockets or the pockets of their campaign contributors with gold while in office. They want real people, like you and me. Dude, we have a chance to make things better. I can't do this alone. I need your help. More importantly, think about this. Will your kids be better off after four years of Sonny Hoag?"

That question hit Russell like a falling rock, bashing him in the center of his forehead. Jeff was right. Sonny was eating up the other presidential competition, and Jeff was the only chance to prevent Hoag from oozing his way into office. Russell said, "Jeff, let me chat with Ashanti, and I'll call you back within a few days."

Jeff said, "Dude, time is of the essence. Ask her now."

Russell turned to Ashanti and said, "Ashant—" Before he could finish, she draped her body around Russell and sucked the breadth out of him with a ferocious kiss. After letting him come up for air, she looked at her adoring husband and said, "You better say yes. This is our chance to make a difference."

Russell took two large gasps of air and went back to the phone. "Jeff, I'm in. What do we do next?"

"Hey, that's why I picked you. You should already be on step three of your action plan. I'm just the front man to this masquerade."

Russell laughed and said, "Great. I feel like I'm back on the board of city commissioners. Why don't we all get together and have a pow wow? We have to get your ratings back up, without the help of High Pops this time."

Jeff said, "Perfect. We're heading up to Hilton Head to play some golf in a few days. Come and join us? You can bring the family and Blabs. I'll have the jet pick you guys up." Jeff heard a thud and crackle sound like a phone dropping.

Afterwards, Russell was back on the line. "Hilton Head? Oh man, I always dreamed about playing there."

"I'll have Jade contact you with the details. Welcome aboard."

A few days later, the Best Bet jet landed at a small airport near Hilton Head. Russell's kids jumped off the plane with Blabs and screamed to Ginger, "We have Blabs. We have Blabs."

Blabs screeched wildly and flapped her wings in excitement as Ginger was finally released from those shiny rounds things. Ginger gave the kids warm hugs and said, "Thank you so much for taking care of my little baby."

Just as Ginger took Blabs out of her cage, Blabs started singing a new song using a weird far eastern accent, "Uoo rite up my rife, Uoo give me oope to car-wee on."

Ginger asked the girls, "Did you teach her that song?"

They replied, "No, she was singing that song after Daddy brought her home."

Ginger thought, *I wonder what else Scratch taught her?*

Later that morning, while Ginger and Blabs fussed over each other to make up for lost personal time together, Jeff and Russell played a round of golf. During the game, they discussed several topics and strategies regarding the campaign. They retired to their rooms for a short afternoon break and then convened with Team Taylor, dubbed TT, to develop a campaign strategy. Jade had already asked each member to attend the meeting with a list of topics and ideas regarding the now official campaign.

Jade kicked off the meeting. "Well, our little group has grown since we first started. Welcome, Russell, to our first official presidential campaign meeting. Just think, all the other candidates held a similar meeting over two to three years ago, and we're doing our first meeting just several weeks prior to the election. Yet, I think we can beat those losers. TT has something the other fools don't. We have a golfer, a newlywed bride, me, a recent college grad, a sports broadcaster, a former CIA agent, and a lawyer. Individually, we wouldn't stand a chance against Sonny and the other wannabees. But, together, we constitute the future of America." The small and attentive group hooted and hollered. "I'd like each member to come up and make a presentation regarding their individual plan to get us into the White House. I'll take notes and use them to build our eventual strategy. Longshot, you're up."

Longshot clomped his boots while he strolled up to the front of the table while holding an icy cold beer. He removed his sunglasses and said in his take command radio voice, "Partners, I'm going to raise the stakes in my bet to my listeners. Right now, I'd break even on my bet. I'm going to jump it up to $10 million. That should get us some pretty hot exposure. In addition, I'm going to use every broadcast from here to the election as a medium proclaiming Jeff as the only choice for the presidency. I won't bash the opponents, although I'd like to. I will, however, use all the contacts I have at race tracks, gambling venues, magazines, radio stations, you name it, asking them to help us in our crusade to put Jeff in the White House. Yea Haaa!"

After a motivational applause, Johnson stepped up to the front of the table. "Folks, until now, I've been here to protect you. Now, I'm going to help promote you. My personal web of contacts in government is deeper than a two pound hemorrhoid suppository pushed deeply into the smelly compartment of a constipated elephant. No shit." The Taylor Team exploded in laughter.

Jade commented, "Now, in the time of seriousness, he cracks one." Johnson never broke a smile but continued as though he was making a professional presentation to the president.

"I'm going to start a secret chain email letter to law enforcement agencies proclaiming Jeff as the only choice for president. Many of my former colleagues already agreed to pass the email forward, including our new buddies in Orlando. Every police and fire rescue affiliation will be commissioned to respond and react to this email, and penetrate the email to every American at will." Jeff started a wave, which flowed around the table for three iterations.

Next, Ginger stood up. "Guys, I really put us into some deep do-do over my DVDs. I need to make a significant contribution. Jeff and I discussed this at great length, and I've decided to do as many magazine and TV interviews as possible. Jade, I'll need your help in creating a press release and setting up interviews. Any interview fees I receive will be donated to children's charities. Hopefully, we'll get some great coverage from this exposure." Ginger sat down with hands clapping loudly.

Jade said, "Ginger, I'll have some of the girls at Ellen's office do some leg work for us. If we play our cards right, I'll bet we can line you up with at least a hundred interviews from now until election day. Okay. Who wants to be next, Jeff or Russell?"

Russell stood up and said, "I'm speaking on behalf of Mr. President. First, I must tell you that I love my wife and kids. They mean the world to me. I joined this crusade, not only to support Jeff, but also to keep knuckleheads like Sonny and the other money monger bastards from running and ruining our country. I want to protect my family from the evils of politics. Now, as you know, my golf game sucks, but I think 'One Nation Under Par' is our platform, our slogan, and our goal. Par is not good enough. We must shoot better than par. We're losing jobs overseas, because other countries are beating us at our own game. We're working longer and harder for less money. We're caught up in wars that don't make sense, and innocent people around the world are dying as a result. With that being said, I want Jeff to continue playing golf with any influential person who'll play with him. I'm going to set up a registration page on the web site to invite mayors, governors, Hollywood celebrities, sports stars, anyone who can help bring his message to the media."

"Next, I spoke with Ellen, and we're going to set up a trust fund and donate 15 percent of Jeff's endorsement fees to a variety of charities, and publicize it. Jeff is going to announce me as his choice for VP. I'm going to hit the campaign trail, and speak at as many local clubs and organizations around the country as I can regarding Jeff's desire to improve our county. I'll focus on leveraging my ties to Jews, Hispanics, Christians, Blacks, conservationists, golfers, and the poor. Jade, you'll need a secretary to support this effort. One of you is not enough. After this, we'll convene once a week to review our progress and make changes as required. Any questions?"

After a short pause of silence, Jeff stood up and said "Guys, this is the real deal. I'm ready to do this. We have to make birdies from here on in to win the tournament. Par is not good enough." He put his hand out, and everyone joined him. Jeff yelled, "One Nation Under Par."

They echoed, "One Nation Under Par," and cheered in excitement. Six nobodies against the world.

Hole Number 16
Par 3

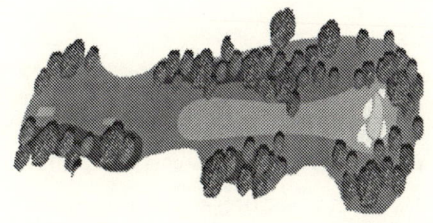

(**Course Notes:** I solemnly swear to tell some truth, part of the truth, or anything but the truth, with help from God. I do. I really do.)

During the next few weeks, many of the lesser known political candidates started participating in the Honest Scorecard. The questions posed to them were far more challenging and personal than Jeff's questions. The difficulty of the questions was in direct relationship to the candidates' political tenure. Obviously, the length of a candidate's political career created more questions regarding their perceived achievements or cover-ups.

Yet, since most politicians were masters on bending, hiding, or embellishing the truth, many of the candidates' responses to questions were inconclusive, according to the print out of the polygraph. It was difficult to determine if they were being honest or just beating the machine, although one candidate who was a land developer from New Jersey, responded with dishonest answers for every question, at least according to the polygraph. Not only did it take him out of the running for president, it also generated an investigation into his business practices and got him indicted for racketeering and embezzlement.

Sonny, on the other hand, honed his craft of lying to the polygraph so well and so confidently, he could say with bold confidence that his father was the Pope, his mother was the Easter Bunny, and he played bridge twice a week with outer space aliens, and the polygraph would indicate his answers as true. In addition to preparing for the Honest Scorecard, he was relentless in maintaining his lead in the polls. He used every means possible to keep him ahead in the presidential race including political clout, the cashing in of favors, the use of strong-arm tactics, and blackmail when required. His campaign spent hundreds of millions of dollars in advertising and candidate bashing. All of his efforts paid off, as he led Jeff and all the other candidates in the polls.

Sonny crisscrossed America in his private jet and delivered speeches to address every facet of society. His speech coach taught him to use dialects specific to every part of the country in order to portray him as a local hometown son, but it was not always a successful tactic. After throwing out a ceremonial pitch at a New York Yankees game, he comically addressed the vivacious crowd and said, "Yous guys are blessed with the most beautifully historic stadium in the world." His comment backfired. The large Manhattan contingent booed his poor English. Also, Sonny's southern ties still didn't sit well with true Yankees, so supporting cheers were overshadowed by more boos.

In Pittsburgh, he fared even worse. Prior to his campaign speech, Sonny rode several roller coasters at the regionally famous Kennywood amusement park. During his speech, he said "Yins have the best roller coasters in the country," which got him going on the right foot. But he blew it when he started talking about the history of the Pittsburgh Steelers football team, as he kept referring to them as the Iron Curtain, instead of the Steel Curtain. Boos and nasty shouts abounded over this, as the coined 1950s Soviet Union Cold War phrase was detested by all true blue and patriotic Steelers fans. After he unknowingly said the incorrect phrase several times in his speech, the crowd almost rioted, and he had to conclude his speech much sooner than he planned and was escorted out of the park with heavy security so as not to feel the wrath of a fan based Steel Curtain.

When campaigning in southern states, he used "Y'all" to death, and even true southerners tired of its overuse.

The polls had Sonny lagging behind Jeff regarding the young voters in the country. Therefore, while campaigning in California, he staged a political stunt and took some surf board lessons from a local LA surfing favorite. He was shown on the nightly news using young, cool words like "awesome," "tubular," and "shut up." What he found out afterwards was that young people could easily tell when hip language is forced out by dinosaurs, and his ratings actually dropped with the youthful segment as a result. Despite all these campaign blunders, he was still the elections front runner according to the polls.

Sonny's staff was so overwhelmed by taking care of the typical high pressure campaign activities that no one took responsibility of his request to obtain the contact information of news media organizations and forward it to Scratch. Sonny himself was up to his neck in frantic campaigning, and he also lost track of his time and his campaign orders.

Scratch, on the other hand, was perfectly opposite to Sonny's stressed out and over worked staff, and was very diligent in not reminding Sonny of his request to send the videos to the media. Instead, he became under stressed and under worked with addictions to sun tanning and eating out. His most productive assertions included the acquisition of a fake passport, and the setting up of bank accounts in Switzerland and Australia. He also lost some weight and started growing a beard and long hair to cover his identity. He still planned to disappear in front of the out back kangaroo country, once he received the last of his fee money from Sonny.

Longshot flew back to Las Vegas to do the rest of his radio shows. Bob was instrumental in adding musical excitement to his broadcasts, and Longshot needed his help to make his shows glitter like the Las Vegas skyline at night. When Longshot opened his broadcast, Bob's selection of music and subtle exploding fireworks rivaled the hottest Vegas nightclub act. Longshot announced on his show that he was so sure Jeff Taylor would win the election, that he raised his bet to ten million dollars. The spark was lit, but more fuel was still to be added to the election fire.

Johnson started his email chain letter a week prior to all branches of the U.S. security and military. Within that short period of time, the Internet acted as though it were infected by a network stopping virus, as millions of chain emails were transmitted. His comrades stepped up to the challenge. They sent the emails to friends and families across the country, saying that Jeff was a strong supporter of the mentioned governmental organizations, and that their vote was required to back their currently silent voice in government.

Jade sent out a press release indicating that Ginger was accepting offers to give interviews immediately. Minutes after it was released, her email in basket almost exploded, as virtually every magazine, radio, and TV station wanted to interview Ginger. Jade hired another one of her classmates to handle Ginger's calendar, with the goal of minimizing travel time for Ginger. In most cases, any interested media related group was more than glad to send someone to Ginger's location to conduct the interview. In some cases, three interviews were scheduled each day.

With Jade's assistance, Russell sent out a press release inviting anyone to "Play some golf with Jeff." The release included a web page to register. In addition, he contacted Hollywood agents and sports columnists, and used their clout and networks to offer celebrities the chance to play some golf with a potential future president. Within a few days, some of the hottest movie and sports stars were lined up to join Jeff in a game of golf. The public was always welcome to attend such events. Within a few weeks, the simple plan of Team Taylor sent the voting polls racing head to head with Sonny, while leading all of the other weak contenders.

Sonny couldn't believe the progress they made in such a short period of time and made repeated calls to Scratch. But he kept getting the same response from his voice mail, "I'm busy. Leave a message." Scratch was wise in prolonging his profitable no-work gig and did return calls to Sonny, but he always returned the call when Sonny was in the middle of an uninterruptible campaign function.

Finally, Scratch decided to let a call come through and answered, "Yeah?"

Sonny, speaking like a parent when their teenager comes home at three in the morning asked, "Where the hell have you been? I'm getting my Gag dag ass ripped out by that damn golfer and whore, and you're nowhere to be found. I need those videos on the air now."

Scratch was very calm and said, "I'm all set to go down here. Where do I send them? Your people never sent me the list."

Sonny's spleen just about exploded, and he grabbed the first campaign victim volunteer who walked by him and said, "Drop whatever you're doing, and email a list of all news media contacts to my associate in Miami. I want it done today." Little did Sonny know that he was just about strangling the college co-ed during his Hitler-like command.

He got back on the phone with Scratch. "All right, you'll have the damn contact list later today via email. I want to see those videos on the air within the next few days."

Scratch said, "No problem. I'll send out the videos as soon as you pay me the rest my fee."

"WHAT? Gag damn, shit for brains. I'll pay you at the end of the job."

Scratch again was very cool and said, "Once the DVDs go out, you'll win the election, and our business is over. The bird is meaningless at that point. You'll have no reason to pay me. I want my payment now. I have all the DVDs copied and packaged in envelopes. I just need addresses. Overnight a bank certified check. When I get the cash, I'll send out the DVDs, and you'll become president. Bye."

Click.

Scratch had hung up on Sonny, but Sonny didn't get mad. He devised a new plan to rid himself of his debt and connection with Scratch, thinking, *I'll have Sticky and Fat retrieve the DVDs and have them arrange to do the mailing, and save myself several hundred thousand dollars. I should have thought of this sooner.* He made the call to Fat.

"Fat, it's me. I have a job for you. Get Sticky, and go to Scratch's house, get the Ginger DVDs you originally delivered, and bring them to me. Also, destroy the DVD of me."

Fat said, "What about the bird?"

"Screw the bird."

Fat said, "Okay, what about Scratch?"

Sonny snickered while he said, "Use whatever means necessary to get the DVDs."

Fat's mouth started salivating as though he were ready to sit down at an all-you-can-eat buffet at the Swine Dine and said, "Scratch may have to be removed, but I won't charge extra for that service. Think of it as a bonus."

Sonny said, "That's why I called you. How soon can you do this? I need it done ASAP."

Fat replied, "I'm finishing a job here in LA, and I believe Sticky is completing a job in Detroit; something about acquiring plans for a car that gets 150 miles to the gallon. Detroit and the oil companies just won't go for that."

Sonny didn't say anything, but he was already on the payroll with the oil companies to curb anything that had to do with the reduction of oil consumption. Sonny said, "I want you guys down there within the week. When you recover the DVDs, hire a company to anonymously mail them to all the news media. I'll provide the addresses. Scratch was supposed to have the DVDs copied and in mailing envelopes, but I doubt it. Get this done within the two weeks, and you'll get a tip the size of a king's ransom."

Fat was dreaming about Scratch's fate and said, "Consider it done."

(**Course Notes:** I mail, you mail, we all scream for E Mail. **Should the words "Made in America" be placed on the endangered species list?**)

Jeff, Ginger, Jade, and Johnson flew to New York to mount their assault on the presidency. Ginger had numerous interviews lined up with TV news and talk shows, as well as magazines. Ginger was a natural on camera, and discovered an ability to get an audience to eat out of her hand.

Jeff had golf outings arranged with the mayors and governors of New York and New Jersey, along with other NY based celebrities. To attract attention, he wagered that he would donate one million dollars to the charity of their choice if anyone could beat him. Longshot publicized the bet, and increased the interest level. Jeff never lost a match but donated at least $10,000 to each of his opponents' charities. Jeff replicated these golf outings to the states of the Union that represented the largest share of electoral votes. Ginger joined him whenever possible, often doing local newspaper and radio interviews at each outing. Their vibrancy and lust for winning was clearly seen and heard in their actions, and, with just a few weeks prior to election day, they had 44 percent of the vote. Sonny had 49 percent, and the other presidential scavengers made up the rest.

Johnson sent out just over 100 emotional email chain letters. In less than two weeks, it was estimated that over nineteen million emails were chained as a result. The email went out as follows:

Subject: Protect America

"Friends and Citizens of America.

Our beautiful nation is on the verge of falling into the hands of a political regime that will speed up the continuing demise of our precious United States. Police officers, fire fighters, school teachers, members of the armed forces, and all public servants are finding it more difficult to enjoy the prosperous life that we once knew. Two incomes cannot pay our bills anymore. Wars are being waged with no clear enemy or goals. Jobs are being lost overseas. Political power, dishonesty, and greed have replaced honor, love of country, and courage. We need to start over. We need to protect our children's legacy. We need to put honesty and integrity back in Washington. We, the People, need to vote for Jeff Taylor.

Please forward this email to as many friends as you can, so we can rebuild our nation, and make it like it was, and what it could be.

Marion Johnson

P.S. A One Nation Under Par screen saver is attached to this email. Place it on your computer desktop, and let's bring America back home, to us.

The email became so popular, that it became a major topic of discussion for all the news media. A small company called Hole-in-One Software, known by all computer golf freaks for the extreme golf games they made, created the screensaver after seeing Jeff on Just Fore Golf, and sent it to Jade as a gift. She thought it was a perfect addition to Johnson's email.

It blended a faint image of the American Flag in the background, with images of famous Washington landmarks on the top of the page. The bottom of the page included scenic holes of famous American golf courses. When the screensaver opened up, a cute animation portrayed George Washington and Abraham Lincoln playing golf together. When George sunk a putt, the words "One Nation Under Par" would display, and Abe would high-five George. When Abe sunk his putt, the words "Vote for Honesty" would illuminate the screen while multi-colored fireworks exploded in the background. The boom sounds could be heard through computer speakers, along with the orchestral version of "God Bless America."

The screen was so emotional that true patriotic golfers flooded the courses to play. Country clubs around the country noticed a 20 percent increase in player attendance. In addition, golf shops sold out of any type of red, white, and blue golf accessories and attire, such as balls, golf shirts, hats, and even the new, high tech action underwear, guaranteed to keep you dry during your sweaty round and take two shots off your final score. When golfers found out that the underwear was made in America, they became the hottest selling garment in the country and impossible to find. Pre-owned and pre-worn versions of the underwear were selling for triple their normal price on eBay.

Hole Number 17
Par 4

(Course Notes: Can you really judge a book by its cover? Seek, and you shall find.)

The back door was open, making it easy for Fat and Sticky to enter Scratch's home. They had their guns out but quickly discovered that Scratch wasn't there. The house stunk like five day old decaying water rats, swimming in a pool of sewage. They thought the bird was dead and expected to find its decaying body, but no bird was found. Just massive amounts of dried up bird shit located all throughout the house. Scratch never cleaned up any of Blabs' air mail packages. While Fat looked for the Ginger DVDs, Sticky kept looking out the front window from behind the Venetian blinds to see if Scratch would appear.

Within just a few minutes, Fat said, "Hey, check this out. Shit for brains left his passport and bank statements on the coffee table. Hey, the passport's a fake. Look at him with the beard. He even changed his name to Leo Scratchmore. He also has some bank accounts set up in Switzerland and Australia. I think our bird is going to fly away." After a few more minutes of searching, Fat said, "Bingo. I found them. Man, shit for brains must have been doing a lot of chicken choking. These things are really scratched." One by one, he placed the DVDs in the player, but they had been so badly scratched by Blabs that nothing played. Sticky noticed a couple of DVDs under the sofa and said, "Fat, check those two out." One of the DVDs was the "Sonnyblabs" video. He put it inside the player, but only an error light displayed. He pulled it out and, using his fat yet forceful hands, bent the disc into two broken pieces. "Okay, Sonny," Fat said, "Your perversion is now protected.

Fat called Sonny, who happened to be available at that moment. Sonny answered and said, "Tell me the good news."

Fat said, "Well, we destroyed your DVD, so you're in the clear. The bad news is that all the Ginger DVDs are so scratched up they don't play. We also found a fake passport and bank statements from accounts that he's opened overseas. Looks like he's gonna skip town."

Sonny said, "Well, I think our boy is up to some espionage. At least that's how I'll present it to my buddies in the CIA. Email the bank account numbers to me. I'm going to have his accounts frozen. But I really need those Ginger DVDs as a backup to secure my election. Can we recover any tracks from the DVD's?"

Fat said, "No way. These things are destroyed. Hey, wait a minute. I have an idea. If you believe in God, start praying."

Sonny said, "What? What is it?"

Fat said, "Maybe we can hack our way back into Ginger's porn website. I still have her user ID and password. If it doesn't work, I'll make a few phone calls for help. Maybe we can still download the videos."

Sonny said, "Do it. Do whatever it takes. I have a press conference planned the day before the election at one P.M. I'll show the videos live if necessary. This will take candidate bashing to an all time high and end up being my best shot for removing Jeff completely out of the race. Fat, you get those videos and you guys will be rich men."

"We're on it. Check your email later today for the account numbers and the links." They both hung up. Fat turned to Sticky and said, "With a little luck, we can retire when we complete this job." Sticky smacked his lips thinking about his future.

Scratch's laptop was on the coffee table. Fat turned it on and accessed the Internet. He keyed in the web address for Ginger's Internet Service Provider, and clicked on the login button. He typed in Ginger's user ID and password, and nearly fell off the sofa yelling, "I don't believe it! We can still get in. She never changed her ID or password, and all of her videos are still there. Man, Sonny is the luckiest son of a bitch. No wonder he'll become president."

Next, Fat went to his own Internet email account and typed a message to Sonny. In the email, he included the link to Ginger's porn, her user ID, password, and Scratch's bank account numbers along with the added message, "We don't need to copy DVDs. Just put the computer on the air, and click on any of the Ginger files. You and all voters will see her at her best." He clicked the Send button, and received the acknowledgment, "Email sent."

Fat said, "Well, that should put Sonny in the White House for sure. Maybe we should get fake passports and split from the U. S. for the next four to eight years. This country will be a mess when asshole gets in. I can't believe the fools that would vote for him. If it wasn't for the money he owes us, I'd vote for Jeff, just to see Ginger on the tube."

Then Sticky said, "Me, too. But a buck's a buck, and Sonny's paying our retirement fund. Hey, what's on this other disc?" Fat placed the DVD in the player and couldn't believe his eyes. Sticky's mouth opened larger than the Grand Canyon. There was Scratch, running out of the pool surrounded by naked men. In unison and without saying a word, they slowly sat down on the sofa with their eyes glued to the screen. After forty minutes, the DVD ended with Toni giving Scratch a huge kiss in front of the Stiff Wind Bed and Breakfast sign.

Fat shook his head and said, "I knew it. He's a frickin' fruitcake. I just knew it. Man, it gives me the jeebees."

Sticky laughed and said, "I knew he was messed up, but this, ... this will get him killed if it gets out." They both looked at each other and burst out laughing.

Fat said, "Showing this to our inner ring of contacts is better then killing him. We'll be heroes, and shit for brains will end up dead. Now that's poetic justice. Let's make copies and get them on the streets."

Sticky said, "We will, but I have a better idea."

After a few phone calls and four hours later, Sticky and Fat were at the front desk at the Stiff Wind in Key West. A friendly person of neutral persuasion entered the lobby when they rang the bell and said, "Hi, I'm Toni. Would you like a room? My, you two make a nice couple."

Fat and Sticky felt uncomfortable, but proceeded with their plan. Sticky said, "No thanks. We're not here for a room, but we did come here to meet you. We're friends of Scratch's."

Toni's eyes and mouth opened in disbelief, and he fell down into a seat behind him while Sticky continued. "Scratch is in some trouble, and we think the only person who can help him is you."

Fat had a difficult time playing out this charade but did his best and said, "I'm Freeman, and this is Sticks. We're old friends of Scratch's. We're straight guys, but we realized over time that women weren't the choice for Scratch. He spoke to us at great length about you, especially how you watched the fire together."

Toni jumped out of his seat and said, "Did he tell you how I saved his life in the fire? My poor love might have suffocated from the smoke if it wasn't for me."

Sticky said, "Yep, he told us all about it. You know, Scratch ended a relationship with a woman about the time he met you. He said he realized that he had feelings that he never knew he had. We tried to have him come back down here to speak with you, but he won't. We thought you might come back with us and speak to him. He's really depressed. Who knows, you might end up with him."

Toni wiped away a tear from his eye said, "Yes, of course I'll come with you. Let me get my buddy to come cover for me." Toni made a few phone calls and packed an overnight bag. He jumped in the car with Fat and Sticky, full of hope and passion.

Sonny was anxious to receive an email from Fat. He hadn't checked his personal email account in over a week. Later that evening, he went to his email basket, and it was loaded with over 300 emails. It was loaded with all this junk mail called "Protect America." Sonny responded out loud to his computer. "Dag nabit. I thought we put a stop to all this junk email. What the hell good is it to pass a law if it's not enforced, or, I don't make money from it." He cleared out all the junk emails until he came to the email from Fat. He smiled the smile of the devil who just captured a new soul for eternity. He opened the email, clicked on the link and was directed to Ginger's Internet account. He keyed in her ID and password, clicked on the first file, and his smile turned even more evil. His face became flushed, as he recovered his ace in the hole for the presidency. "Soon, I'll wear the crown. I'll rule the world." He watched the video, and became extremely horny and confused. He couldn't decide whether to relieve his own lust, or force his wife to join him.

Just then, Ashley walked into the room and said, "I'm ready for bed. Care to join me?"

Sonny perked up and said, "I'll be right there." Sonny made mental love to Ginger, using Ashley's physical presence to complete the act. Unfortunately, Ashley would have preferred if Ginger was really there.

During Sonny's lust release, six more "Protect America" emails cluttered his in basket.

One of Jade's college friends, who was employed to monitor emails from the Vote for Honesty website, observed a huge increase in emails indicating that

Sonny Hoag was the only presidential candidate who didn't take the Honest Scorecard. She contacted Jade, who contacted Longshot at the radio station. Bob answered the phone. "Hi Bob, it's Jade. How ya doin'?"

"I'm fine, but I wish we were doing better in the polls."

"Tell me about it. Is Longshot there?"

"You bet. I'll put you on the speaker phone."

Longshot said, "I'm here. What's up?"

Jade replied, "Longshot, I just got off the phone with my friend who works in Ellen's office. She said that Sonny never took the polygraph."

Longshot said, "Holy shit. You're right. I completely forgot about him, and he was our main target. He dodged the bullet, but I don't blame him. Can you imagine the questions he'd get?"

"Yes," said Jade, "and that's why he needs to take the test."

"Not so fast, missy. He's a pro at lying. I'll bet he can beat the machine. If he's asked tough questions, and it shows that he answered them honestly, he'll win the election."

"What can we do? If we only had the 'Sonnyblabs' DVD."

Bob listened to the conversation and felt bad that he was involved in the lost disc and said, "Longshot, the FBI has Ginger's laptop. Can Johnson make a call to his FBI buddies so I can take a look at it?"

"Why?"

"I don't know, maybe she's got something in there that we could use against Sonny. We're desperate."

"You're right. Jade, have Johnson call his FBI contacts and ask them to release Ginger's laptop to Bob."

"Why?"

"I don't know. Bob wants to peek at the files. Just do it. We're running out of time."

Jade spoke with Johnson, who called the FBI, who called Bob at the radio station in less than ten minutes. They gave Bob the address to their office, and he took off at once. Within the next thirty minutes, he was back at the station sniffing around her laptop files, looking for anything that could help.

Fat pulled up to Scratch's house and noticed his parked car in the driveway. He turned to Toni and said "Listen, Scratch is embarrassed about his sexual preference. He might feel awkward if we show up at his door with you. Why don't you go in by yourself? We'll call Scratch in an hour or so to see how he's doing."

Toni said "Okay. Poor sugar. I hope he wants to see me."

Sticky said, "Oh, he will, Toni. I'm sure of it."

Toni got out of the car, and Fat drove away. Once they got out of sight, they parked the car and ran around to the back of the house. They looked in the window, and saw Scratch lying on the couch watching *The Godfather*. The back door was still open. Toni stood at the front door for a few moments, fixing his hair and straightening out his wrinkled clothes as a result of the three-hour car ride from Key West. Once presentable, he knocked on the door.

Scratch had been at the beach earlier in the day, followed by an early dinner, and downing a few hundred beers at a local sports bar. He was phasing in and out during the movie when the knock sounded from the front door. He grabbed his gun, carefully motioned over to the door, and yelled, "Who is it?"

Toni responded, "Sugar, it's me, Toni. Open the door."

Scratch was totally confused. He opened the door, and standing in the dusk of the setting sun was Toni. He said, "Ooh. I like the beard and long hair doo. Can I come in?"

Scratch said, "What are you doing here? In fact, how did you know where I live?"

Toni said, "Well, I heard all about your breakup with your old girlfriend from your friends, Freeman and Sticks. They told me how depressed you were, and how you missed me. Is it true Sugar? Did you miss me?"

Scratch said, "Who the hell are Freeman and Sticks?"

Just then, Fat and Sticky oozed into the living room like puss leaking out of a nasty cut. They emerged from the opened back door, pointing their handguns at Scratch. Fat said, "Sugar, it's us. We knew you weren't like most guys, and we felt bad for making fun of you, so we decided to bring your lover to you."

Sticky said, "That's right, Scratch. We always thought you liked guys, but when we saw your video, well, we had to bring you two love birds together." Scratch looked at the DVDs and saw the broken "Sonnyblabs" disc in the corner of the room.

Fat said, "Scratch, drop your piece, NOW!"

Scratch dropped his gun. Toni was trembling, demonstrating that he had been mentally ambushed by Scratch's unforeseen enemies.

Sticky said, "Sonny told us to finish your business, and we have. Sonny has access to the Ginger DVDs, so your services are no longer required. They'll be aired any day now. He also told us to take care of you. We planned on just wasting you, but when we found your homo DVD, well, why should we have all the fun. We wanted to get you two love birds back together, just to see the look on your face. Now we can release your video to all your friends. Fat, who do you think will try to kill Scratch first?"

"Oh man, who knows? It could be one of hundreds of people."

Toni's eyes were all blurred. Fat said, "Poor Toni. Hey, peckerhead, go take care of your lover boy. We'll use your camera here and take some pictures for your fans."

Toni said, "It was a long car ride, and with all this commotion...I have to use the bathroom."

Fat said, "Sure thing princess. Go through the kitchen here."

Fat and Sticky snarled and snickered at Toni as he moved in their direction to use the bathroom. Scratch wanted to be put out of his misery and wished they'd just kill him on the spot. Fat kept his gun pointed at Scratch, and Sticky lowered his gun as Toni walked between them. Then, out of nowhere, Toni forcefully kneed Sticky in the crotch and swiped his gun away as Sticky bent over in pain. Fat, moving his huge body with the speed of a manatee out of water, had no time to react, and Toni thrust his fist into Fat's nose, resulting in a sickening popping sound as most of his cartilage was lodged into his frontal lobe. Toni leaped to the ground and grabbed both of their weapons. Toni then walked behind each of the kidnappers and hit each of them over the head with the barrel of the gun, knocking them both unconscious.

Scratch stood there in total disbelief, watching a super being rescue him from certain death. He said, "That was amazing. Where'd you learn to fight like that?"

Toni caught his breath and responded, "When I was growing up, I used to get beat up all the time from kids 'cause, well, I was different. My mom made me take self-defense classes. Now I teach self-defense courses in Key West for extra money. It's been a long time since I had to use it. Man, what a rush. I feel like banging something else."

Scratch said, "Easy, cowboy. One thug at a time. Hey, were you really trembling?"

Toni said, "Naw, I just had to let them think I wasn't a threat. Worked pretty good, huh?"

Scratch said, "Hell, yes. Remind me to never piss you off."

Toni said, "Now what?"

Scratch thought for a moment and said, "First things first," and he destroyed the DVD. "Now, let's reverse the tables. You feel like being in some pictures?"

Toni said, "To save your sorry ass? Sure."

They cleaned the blood off Fat's face and took off his and Sticky's shirts. They dragged them to the sofa and took pictures of them that went way beyond the term male bonding. Toni joined in some of the pictures, but his face was never revealed. After the brief photo session, Toni tied them up while Scratch downloaded the pictures to his laptop and printed them out on his color printer.

While they waited for the pictures to print out, Scratch told Toni about the Ginger DVDs, Blabs, and the entire election campaign with Sonny. At the end of the story, Toni said, "What are you going to do now?"

Scratch thought for a moment and said, "That son of a bitch Hoag used me and then tried to kill me. I can't kill him, but I could sure screw up his chance to become president."

Scratch packed up his belongings, including his fake passport. Then, he pinned several of the pictures to the thugs clothes, splashed some water on their faces to make them coherent and said, "Hi boys. Funny, isn't it? You came here to bury me as a homosexual, and now, you might just get buried with that same title. While you guys were under, I let Toni have his way with you."

Toni walked over to them and said, "You were both delicious."

Sticky was just about ready to throw up when Scratch said, "Oh, by the way, the police should be arriving here shortly and arrest you for breaking and entering. But before I leave, you should know that I have copies of your little love fest. I'm not sure what to do with my copies, but one thing's for sure…if Toni or I ever have any dealings with you or anyone like you, these pictures will be released to the wolves. Ta-ta, pecker heads."

They jumped in Scratch's car, and Scratch said, "I don't know where to go now."

Toni said, "You have a fake ID. Why not come and hide out in Key West for a while like the rest of us fugitives down there. Stay until you figure out what you want to do."

Scratch embarrassingly said, "Okay, but I need to make a call." He pulled out Johnson's card and called him.

"Johnson here."

Scratch paused for a second and said, "It's Scratch."

Johnson, with no surprise in his voice, said, "Who's trying to kill you? Sonny?"

"Yep," he replied, "But I'm safe for the moment. Listen. You asked me to join your team."

Johnson was quick to say, "Sorry bro, we have the bird and the DVDs are destroyed. Our team's full."

Scratch replied, "That's what you think. I was just paid a visit by two competitors who are working for Sonny. They said he'll be showing the Ginger videos right before the election. They got the videos from another source. I just wanted to let you know. That's the best I can do to try and help you nail that asshole Hoag. And one more thing. These two guys are currently tied up in my house. They tried to kill me, but it didn't happen. Can you arrange to have the police pick them up, and keep my name out of it? One of them has a nose stuck in his brain."

Johnson said, "Okay, I'll take care of it, but in the future, stay out of Ginger's business. Otherwise, I'll become your next nightmare."

"Yeah. Yeah, now go get that pig," and Scratch hung up. He turned his car south on I-95 and headed for a life of transparency.

At that moment, Johnson had no idea how to use the provided information from Scratch.

Bob weaved his way through a variety of folders on Ginger's laptop, hoping something of value would pop out at him other than a stimulating body part, but nothing came into view. After an hour of searching, he decided to look at her emails, and then call it quits. When her email opened, four new files were sitting in her in basket. Two of the files were sent from former clients, wishing her well on her marriage. One email had the subject "Protect America," which he proudly left in her in basket. The last email, which had been sent just over a month ago, caught his attention.

The email was sent from her Internet Service Provider in Omaha. It said that her Internet service was going to be interrupted for one hour so that a complete system backup could occur at a new storage facility in West Virginia. Service would be restored immediately after the change, and all files would then be accessible. Bob thought about this for a moment. "Hmm. All the files are saved at a separate storage facility. I wonder if..." At the bottom of the email was a tech support hotline number. He yelled out to Longshot who was across the room "Hey, Longshot. Call Jade and get Ginger's login ID and password for her website."

"Why?" replied Longshot.

"Not this again. Just do it." In a matter of minutes, Ginger indirectly relayed her sign-on information to Bob. Bob went to her Internet site, logged in, and discovered that her personal videos were still out there. "Longshot, come here, quick. I'm into Ginger's porn videos."

Longshot came over and said, "Partner, don't you think it's a little sick to be looking at her videos?"

"No man, don't you get it? She never changed her password or deleted the files. This is how Sonny is going to access her site."

Longshot said, "Quick, delete the files." Bob said, "Wait. This might be our chance to blindside the pig man."

He called the Internet tech support number, and after replying to a few security questions, a tech support person said, "How can I help you today?"

Bob said, "I understand that you back up all files at a remote storage facility. Is that correct?"

"Yes sir, we do."

Bob came back, "I accidentally deleted a file from my Internet folder. Can I retrieve it from your back up storage?"

"Absolutely." He was given simple directions on how to use the control panel and reacquire the lost file.

Bob hung up and then followed the directions. After a few searches, he discovered the Sonnyblabs.avi file. "Holy shit, Longshot. It's the Sonny video." He clicked on copy, and transferred the file to Ginger's Internet folder, and then to her own laptop. Then he turned to Longshot and said, "I bettcha $50 I can bring the pig man down."

Longshot laughed and said, "Bob, you've never won a bet with me, but this time, I'll take the bet and hope you win."

Bob said, "Call Jade and set up a conference call with the team." In a matter of minutes, Team Taylor, all of whom were packing to return to Las Vegas to vote, were set up for the conference call. Russell was on the campaign trail and unable to join in.

Bob kicked off the call. "Hi, guys. Listen. I don't have time to explain everything, but I have a plan to get the pig man."

"Who?" exclaimed Jade.

Bob, being annoyed by the response, said "Sonny! Who do you think? I recovered a copy of the 'Sonnyblabs' video." Team Taylor screamed and cheered, but Bob was on a roll. "Listen up, people. Jade, leak out a story to the press saying that Sonny never took the polygraph. Do it immediately. Then call ConFess security and have them set up the test for noon tomorrow, since we vote the day after that. Got it?"

"Yes," replied Jade.

"Next, Longshot, announce on your show tonight that the Honest Scorecard was never taken by Sonny, and all those Americans who donated money to submit their questions were ripped off due to Congressman Hoag's lie to take the test."

Longshot said, "Will do, partner."

"Okay. Now Jeff. I want you to call the pig man himself, and tell him that you'll quit the election race immediately if Sonny promises not to show Ginger's videos."

The entire team yelled "What?"

Bob said, "Don't worry, that pig won't keep his promise, and Jeff won't quit. Just tell Sonny that. I'm gonna try something out, and with a little luck and timing, we'll be partying in the White House next year. Now move."

Jade had built strong relationships with several news media organizations over the last few months, and she asked some of her most influential contacts why they never hounded Sonny about taking the polygraph. She made it appear like it was their oversight rather than her encouragement to hype the story. She also used her contacts to get the number of Sonny's campaign manager and left him a message saying Jeff Taylor needed to speak with him first thing in the morning.

Longshot was also in the midst of the plan, and during his last radio broadcast before the election, he asked his listeners how Sonny could have escaped the

Honest Scorecard, when all the other presidential candidates promptly completed the test. The press was listening to this broadcast, courtesy of Jade's media influence. Team Taylor missed the broadcast, as they were flying back to Las Vegas that evening.

Hole Number 18
Par 5

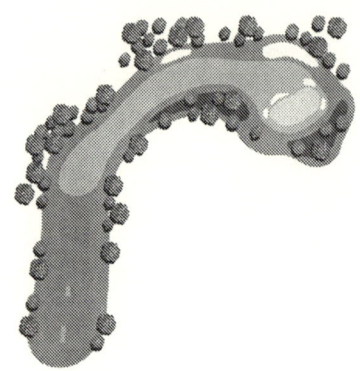

(**Course Notes:** An ace in the hole, or is it a hole in the ace? **White House synonyms** - clubhouse, whorehouse, penthouse, doghouse, nuthouse, outhouse, madhouse.)

Sonny's phone rang at 5:30 A.M., courtesy of his campaign manager. "Who the hell is calling me at Gad dang 5:30 in the Gad dang morning."

"Sonny, it's me, Blake Silver. It's all over the news. You never took the Honest Scorecard, and the press is having a field day with it. They want you to take the test today at noon."

"Son of a bitch. I thought we squashed this mess. Everyone forgot about it."

"Well, someone reminded someone, and your butt's on the line. You gotta take it."

Sonny screamed, "My schedule's booked! Hell, you booked it. I have my final press conference today at 1."

Blake said, "The test will only take a few minutes. You can take it at the police station right down the street from your campaign headquarters. I'll set up the test for noon, and have you back at your office in plenty of time for your final press conference. Sonny, you beat the polygraph, and you'll lock in the presidency. This could work in your favor."

Sonny said, "Someone from the Taylor camp must have leaked it out."

Blake said, "I don't think so. I had a message on my voice mail this morning that Jeff Taylor wants to speak with you on your private line regarding his leaving the race."

Sonny said, "That doesn't make sense." But then Sonny arrogantly figured that Jeff thought that he had the Ginger DVDs, and Jeff wanted to protect her, especially since he was about to lose the presidential race. "Blake, set up the phone meeting with Jeff Taylor. I think he's gonna pass his votes over to me."

Blake said, "Really, why would he do that?"

"Dammit boy, who do you think you're talking to? That bum has no business running for this office. He's got no Gad dag contacts, no experience, nothing. He's smarter to quit without being shamefully embarrassed at the polls."

Blake said, "Right you are, Congressman. I'll set up the call with Jeff and the polygraph test."

Sonny lay in bed with a sinister smirk on his face, knowing the election was his. His smirk, however, changed to the look of an old boiler heater ready to explode when he read the morning newspaper. The headlines read, "Hoag's Afraid to Take the Test." Sonny flipped on one of the national morning news stations, and one announcer came right out and said "Congressman Hoag. You're leading the polls, yet you've never taken the Honest Scorecard. What are you trying to avoid?"

"Gad dammit. The damn election is tomorrow. I don't need this shit now. This Taylor is a royal pain in the ass."

At 8:00 A.M., Blake Silver called Sonny. "Congressman, I just got off the phone with Taylor's press secretary. He'd like to speak with you at 11:30 this morning. I gave them your cell number. You can speak to him while you're driven over to the police station. I've rearranged your schedule."

Sonny said, "Blake, I'll speak with Taylor. But now listen closely, and take some damn notes so you don't screw up what I'm about to tell you."

Blake was extremely pissed to be treated like a no-brain loser rather than a successful campaign manager but swallowed his pride once again and said, "Shoot, Congressman."

Sonny continued. "I'm going to pass this test with ease, but I need you to do something for me to solidify the election. I'm going to forward an email to you with a link, user ID, and password. Have a PC set up in our campaign conference room, and be logged in to the link. Make arrangements to have the press set up some TV cameras pointed at the PC. After the polygraph, I'm going to comment on the polygraph results and then squash this nasty Taylor bug once and for all. It'll be candidate bashing at its finest. Don't screw this up. Got it?" Click.

Sonny hung up on Blake, and Blake was livid but followed through with Sonny's plan, knowing he'd be rid of Sonny once he won the election.

For the rest of that morning, Sonny worked out of his home office, taking care of last minute victory party preparations. At 11:25, his personal driver called him and said, "Congressman, it's time to go." Sonny's ego and confidence were at an all time high. He regally strutted out to the car. The driver said "Good morning, Congressman," opened the car door, and the king entered his motor coach without giving the driver any reciprocal comment or eye contact. As they drove off, Sonny said, "After tomorrow, you'll be saying good morning, Mr. President. Now close my damn privacy window." The driver raised the window that separated the front seat from back seat of the limo.

At precisely 11:30 A.M., Sonny's personal cell phone rang. "Yes?"

"Congressman? It's Jeff Taylor. You win." Sonny slouched into his richly leathered seat and smothered himself with those two words that projected ultimate victory. "The pressure got to be a little to much for you, huh, Taylor? I'm surprised you lasted this long."

Jeff seethed for making this call, but he knew it had to be done. "Congressman, we both know why I'm backing out of the race. I understand that you obtained illegal access to some personal video files that would be very embarrassing to certain parties. If you give me your word that you won't show them, I'll make an announcement later today saying that I'm quitting the race, and ask everyone to vote for you instead of me. Your landslide victory will be unprecedented."

Sonny gloated over this call and wished it could last for hours. "Taylor, you never really knew who you were dealing with. I own Washington. Everyone's in my pocket. In fact, I own most of the world. You and your slut wife were barely a thorn in my side. I must say I don't blame you for marrying her though. She sure knows how to pleasure a man. I know that for a fact. After I'm elected, I'll pay you to rent her services. She'd love Camp David. Oh, I'm sure you'll lose all those product endorsements once you lose the election. You'll be back to being a losing golfer. A nobody. Say, since you've been around golf courses, I'm sure I can get you a job cutting the grass around the White House. Yeah, that's it. You cut the grass, and I'll do your wife. At least you'll get to live in Washington. She's a fine looking whore you have there. It did cost me a pretty penny to set you up and force you out of the race. It shouldn't have taken this long. Anyway, you have my word. I won't show the videos, as long as you promise to share your bitch with me after the election. Deal?"

Jeff couldn't stand it any longer. He couldn't play the game and continue to let Sonny lay his skid marks all over him and degrade Ginger. Jeff shouted "No deal, Pig man."

Team Taylor was in the room with Jeff during the call and couldn't believe that Jeff was changing the plan, and with such emotional and destructive force. "I've changed my mind. You're going down, pig. You'll go down in history as the most pathetic and deceitful politician to ever be a Congressman. And when I'm elected, you're going to jail. And it won't be one of those country club jails. It will be the real deal. You'll redefine the word squeal."

Hoag started laughing on the phone while the limo pulled up in front of the police station. It was mobbed with the news media and spectators. Sonny condescendingly said, "Taylor, you must have been smoking the grass you played golf on. I can't lose. I'm showing Ginger to the world at one today. She's a whore, and you're a loser. The party's over Taylor."

Jeff took a deep breadth and said, "Think again, pig man. While you're taking your polygraph test, I'm showing your porn video to the world. That's right, asshole. I have a copy of your DVD. You can't pass the polygraph knowing that your fat, pompous ass will be making most of America puke. And oh, by the way, Ginger is not in the video, but her parrot is. In fact, that's who you made love to. Bestiality with Congressman Hoag, what a headline that will be. Enjoy your visit at the police station. You'll be spending a lot of time there real soon, pig man." Jeff hung up, and Team Taylor exploded in jubilation. Longshot shook Jeff's hand and said, "What a bluff. Remind me to never play poker with you."

Sonny started trembling nervously. *Could he really have a copy of that video? Did I really do it with a parrot?* He was sweating profusely, yet his mouth was as dry as a 2000-year-old Egyptian crypt. Sonny looked at his watch, and it was five minutes to noon. He heard people outside the car screaming, "Take the test. Take the test." The police barricaded the crowd away from the limo. His driver lowered the privacy window and said, "Are you ready to get out, Congressman?"

Sonny was in a blur. He didn't know what to do. The police kept shouting to have the Congressman exit the vehicle, as they weren't sure how long they could hold back the ready-to-riot crowd. Sonny's driver decided to push him along. He got out and opened the Congressman's door. Sonny looked up at him and said, "I don't know if I can do this."

His driver replied, "Oh sure, now you want to talk to me. You're on your own, Jack."

A police officer quickly approached the vehicle, yanked Sonny out, and pushed him inside the police station saying, "Sorry, Congressman. We had to get you out of there. We couldn't control the crowd much longer."

Sonny didn't say a word. Chief of Police Muldoon introduced himself, along with Deputy Hanley, the officer who would administer the test, and Elliot Connelly of ConFess Security. They escorted Sonny to a small olive green interrogation room that smelled musty. It had annoying lighting that cast awkward shadows, making it difficult for eyes to focus. This police department was an eventual recipient and promoting distributor of Johnson's "Protect America" chain email. As a result, they treated Sonny with the dignity and respect of a common criminal. With gentle force, they attached him to the sensors of the polygraph and described how the test worked. Elliott Connelly opened his briefcase and removed the test questions.

The last question was submitted by ConFess themselves. Based on Bob's recommendation, Jade gave them the option to ask one question to Sonny as a bonus for their fine work and suggested question eight. ConFess welcomed the suggestion and included it with the others.

"Congressman, we're ready to begin. Are you ready?"

Sonny said, "Could I have a glass of water and a few minutes to compose myself? It was quite hectic out there."

Elliott said, "Of course." After his water was delivered in a paper cup, they left the room.

Sonny pulled out his cell phone and called Fat, hoping he'd contradict Jeff's possession of the "Sonnyblabs" video, but all he heard was Fat's voicemail. The phone was, in fact, turned off, and stored in a secure locker at the Ft. Lauderdale Police Station while Fat was in recovery from having surgery to remove his nose from his brain under police guard.

Sonny then called his campaign manager.

"Hi Sonny. Is the test over already?"

"No, we're just getting started. I wanted to know if you're all set with the PC and login link?"

Blake replied, "Yes, Congressman. I looked at the video files, and understand why you'd like the press to see them. But, I won't be the one to click open the files, as I imagine they were acquired illegally, and I'm in no position to go to jail for this. I'll let you do it."

Sonny was glad to hear that the files were available for showing. He regained some of his attitude and said, "Listen, chicken shit. You're fired. You're deserting me when I need you the most, so hit the road. I'll do it myself." Sonny hung up the phone, took a deep breath and yelled out, "Come on. Let's get this thing started. I'm a busy man, dammit."

Deputy Hanley came in, double checked the polygraph and tape recorder, and said "Congressman. I'm going to ask you eight questions. Many of the questions submitted in the Honest Scorecard were repeated, so the questions were narrowed down to eight. The first two questions help to validate that the polygraph is working. Simply answer yes or no to each question. Are you ready?"

"Yeah, yeah, let's do this."

"Okay. Question one. Are you Congressman Hoag?"

"Yes."

"Question two. Have you ever cleaned the toilets in the Capital Building with a toothbrush?"

"No. Of course not."

Deputy Hanley said, "Good. According to the polygraph, you answered these known questions truthfully and the polygraph recorded them as such. Let's proceed.

"Question Three. While running for any past or current governmental positions, did you ever use any illegal or immoral activities in your campaign efforts to win?"

"No."

"Question four. Have you personally reaped any illegal financial profits or wealth during any of your governmental positions?"

"No."

"Question five. During your tenure as Congressman, did you leverage your position to benefit campaign contributors, specifically oil companies and car manufacturers?"

"No."

"Question six. Have you ever had any extra-marital relationships while in any governmental office?"

"No."

"Question seven. You voted to deploy our troops to a variety of missions around the world, resulting in many casualties. Have you, or any business that you are aware of, profited solely from any U.S. participation in war or military conflicts?"

"No."

"And now for the eighth and final question, 'Have you ever been involved in any porn videos?'"

Sonny screamed, "What? What the hell kind of question is that? This is bullshit! This whole damn lie detector test is a set up. I refuse to answer." Sonny ripped off the sensors and stormed out of the room. His shirt was still unbuttoned, and his huge stomach bounced around like a grotesque belly dancer with a hairy navel in desperate need of a shave.

The police dispersed most of the rowdy crowd outside police station, leaving only a few hungry news teams. The cameras easily captured Sonny bashing his way through the police doors and jumping into the backseat of his limo.

The driver was relaxing in the car, listening to the mellow sound of Marvin Gaye on the radio, until he was startled by Sonny's entry. "Get your black ass in gear, and get me the hell out of here."

The driver turned around and said, "What did you say to me, white trash?"

Sonny was overwrought with rage and plowed his way out of the backseat to attempt to thrash the subservient driver. He fell over the curb and floundered on the sidewalk like some rare mollusk found off the cold shores of Scandinavia. The driver locked the door, while Sonny jumped to his feet and banged furiously on the bullet proof glass screaming, "Open the door, Gad dag smart ass! I'm gonna kill you!"

Two police officers peeled Sonny off the limo and used necessary force to place him in a squad car that pulled up behind the limo. They held his hands behind his back, lowered his head to avoid clunking it on the car door, and cast him inside. The doors were locked so he couldn't escape, so he kept banging on the window of the squad car. The cameras caught all the action, using their zoom lenses to add a touch of Hollywood to the soon-to-be seen footage of an exploding Congressman.

After a few minutes of driving around town, Sonny calmed down and asked the police to drive him to his campaign headquarters. While in the back seat of the squad car, he made a quick call to his secretary. "Bernice. Has anything unusual been released on the news regarding me?"

Bernice replied, "Unusual? You mean like your ranting and raving like a maniac outside the police station?"

Sonny replied, "Well, no. Anything besides that?"

"No, Congressman. That's about it."

Sonny said, "Thank God, he was bluffing" and hung up the phone. It was fifteen minutes to one o'clock. He fixed his shirt, regained his composure, and demonstrated how a president can react under such adverse conditions by walking into his office like nothing had ever happened. The press was there waiting for him, but he asked them for five minutes before he answered their questions. During that time, the Chief of Police showed up with the results of the test.

Sonny went into the empty conference room, clicked on one of the Ginger files, and saw his saving grace to the election, as Ginger was in full view, engaged in acts uncommon for First Ladies. Sonny thought *The election is mine.* He closed the file and admitted the press corps into the conference room, projecting a renewed sense of confidence.

As the cameras were being set up, the Chief of Police walked over to Sonny and quietly said, "Congressman, I just wanted to let you know that, according to the polygraph, you answered all the questions truthfully. To be honest, I don't know how you did it, and I may never use a polygraph again."

Sonny looked at him and said, "Now I know why I didn't vote for you when you ran for office."

It was five minutes to one, and the press was drooling for the results, as well as some justification for Sonny's outburst outside the police station. As Congressman Hoag and the Police Chief stood shoulder to shoulder in the crowded room, Bob and Longshot were neck and neck, glaring into the computer. The rest of Team Taylor was pacing in different directions around the TV. They created designs similar to the artistry of a two year old fumbling with the dials on an Etch-a-sketch.

At one o'clock, the news came on. "Good afternoon. We're interrupting our normal television broadcast to take you live to the Sonny Hoag presidential campaign headquarters for an update on the Honest Scorecard."

The Chief of Police stood in front of the PC with Sonny, and spoke into a microphone first. "Good afternoon. I'm Chief of Police Muldoon. An hour ago,

Congressman Hoag underwent a polygraph test at our police station. He answered questions that were submitted by ConFess Security, in relation to the Honest Scorecard. The final test results demonstrated that Congressman Hoag truthfully answered the first seven questions. The last question was inconclusive. I'll read each question, along with the Congressman's response."

Several thousand miles away, Jeff yelled, "Dammit, that son of a bitch beat the test. I can't believe it." As the police chief read the results, Ginger's eyes were glued to the computer screen in front of Hoag and Muldoon. The worst part of her life was sitting on a computer, awaiting the world's eyes and judgments. Just as Muldoon came to question eight, the computer screen changed and reverted back to the login screen.

The Internet Service, for security purposes, automatically timed out a session and shut down after ten minutes of inactivity. When the login screen appeared on TV, Bob quickly logged in to Ginger's account. He went into each of the eighteen folders and deleted Ginger's files. Next, he placed a copy of the "Sonnyblabs" video file into each of the eighteen folders. When the copy complete message appeared, Bob and Longshot high-fived each other, and Bob logged out saying, "I don't have time to test each file. I hope they copied okay."

Meanwhile, the Police Chief was still the central focus for the news cameras and millions of Americans across the country. "Question eight. Have you ever been involved in any porn videos? Well, the answer to this question was inconclusive, as Congressman Hoag never actually answered it. This is when the fireworks started, and I'll let the Congressman take it from here. Congressman Hoag?"

Sonny politely pushed the Police Chief out of the eye of the camera, presented a winning presidential smile, and said "Good afternoon. As you all know, I'm Congressman Sonny Hoag, and I'm running for president of the United States. I'd like to make a brief statement before I address question eight. I believe the Honest Scorecard is a scam. Even though I clearly demonstrated that I answered all the questions correctly, the last question was inappropriately placed in there to discredit my reputation. In fact, I have PROOF that my campaign manager and personal driver were part of a larger conspiracy, attempting to remove me from the presidential race. After the test, when I entered my car, my driver harassed me and gave me further indication that the test was fixed, which certainly caused me to overreact. I'm sorry to announce and demonstrate to you that the pornographic conspiracy is actually headed up by my opponents... Jeff and Ginger Taylor."

The news personnel in the room, as well as the huge television audience nationwide, all gasped at the same time, including Team Taylor.

"I urge all parents to remove young children from the room, as what I'm about to show you is graphically explicit and not appropriate for children." Sonny slowly sauntered to the front of the podium, which increased the hype and tension of his lethal remarks. With a login screen in view of the world, he typed Ginger's user ID and password on the computer keyboard. Eighteen folders appeared on the screen. Sonny's heart started racing. He could already smell the fresh cut roses in the oval office. He clicked on the first folder, and a file displayed.

He was so obsessed with the feeling of winning, he didn't read the name of the file. His hand moved the mouse to the file name, and his finger throbbed in excitement, knowing that one light click of the mouse would guarantee his presidency. Sonny's mind was racing during that five-second time frame. "What band should I select to perform at my inauguration bash? Who will be my first presidential mistress? How rich will I become?" Then, he turned around to the cameras, smiling like a gladiator ready to kill his opponent with one final blow and said, "Ladies and Gentlemen, as your president, I will crush this, and all other conspiracies that stand in the way of Justice and America." He clicked on the file, and the news cameras began transmitting the crystal clear video, displayed on the high resolution flat panel monitor. The video file opened, along with the mouths of everyone watching, as...

...a small green and yellow parrot came into view standing on a wet mountain of fat flesh while singing, "You can't always get what you want. You can't always get what you want. But if you try sometimes, you might find...you'll get some bird seed."

The 19th Hole

In the early 1990's, Apratep and Zotpabat claimed their independence from Russian sovereignty. Neither country was larger than the state of Vermont. They were bordered by the Caspian Sea to the east, and the rolling hills of the mountains to the west. Both countries exploited their holistic spring waters and gentle climates as a means to attract tourism, but with little success. Apratep even created the first golf course in the area to further encourage vacationers to visit their new country. The course received great reviews for its scenic views of the sea and mountains, as well as its challenging layout but it was under played.

Over the years, a goat herder from Zotpabat complained to the local governments that the eighth putting green veered into his property, but officials from both countries were unable to determine accurate property boundaries, and both prospered from attraction of the course, so they made no actions to resolve his issue. One day, an errant tee shot injured one of the herder's prized goats, and he decided to resolve the conflict himself.

Several forgotten soviet tanks were stored in a hidden bunker on the herders land. The herder and his two sons were clever enough to study the operations manual they found inside one of the tanks, and taught themselves how to drive them. After making some minor repairs, they fueled the tanks and maneuvered them into battle to reacquire their perimeter area.

Meanwhile, several Japanese businessmen were taking golf lessons from the local golf pro. While the golf pro video taped the swing of one golfer for analysis, the roar of engines and clanking of moving metal rushed into view from behind a hill. The tanks rolled across their practice area and sped to the eighth green. They drove over the flag stick, and laid deep tank tread marks on the green, coming to rest on top of the golf hole. The golf pro filmed the battle scene, including the heroic victory party the goat herders held after they reacquired their land. They climbed out of the tanks shouting and cheering, took the keys, and went home feeling an extreme amount of accomplishment.

The pro quickly showed the video to the leaders of both countries. Tempers flared up by both leaders, and blamed each other for the act of war. Several days later, armies of both countries lined up along the eighth fairway, waiting for the order to attack.

Following their normal morning routine, Jeff and Ginger were enjoying each other in the tub when the phone rang. "Hi Jade. What's up?" Jade replied "Mr. President. We have a situation brewing between two of our new allies that could result in war. Are you done with your bath yet?"

"I am now. Your call sunk my battleship. I'll be right out." Jeff walked into the Oval Office, and was greeted by Jade, Russell, Johnson, and several members of his cabinet. He reviewed the video clip and started yelling "Oh man, look what that tank did to that golf green. I always wanted to play that course. It received great reviews. This war has to be stopped so the course is preserved. Tell each country leader not to engage until I speak with them. Now get the jet ready." Within the hour, the president and First Lady were boarding Air Force One. They were greeted by Gloria and Lourdes "Good morning Mr. President. Welcome aboard Madam President." Jeff said "Good morning ladies. We're off to stop a war today. How's your family doing Lourdes?" "Oh Mr. President, your job and technology initiative rescued them. Their computer consulting business is really taking off. You saved them and millions of Americans. Thank you." Jeff said, "Thank Russell next time you see him. It was his idea."

While en route, Johnson approached the presidential couple and said "Mr. President. Agents Hills, Sciani and International Golf Liaison Mastroe are already at the golf course and convinced the two leaders to hold off the war until you get there for peace discussions. Tyrone said each leader would rather avoid the conflict, as many of the troops are relatives of their so-called enemies. Also, it appears that a local goat herder is at the heart of the problem." Jeff said "A goat herder?"

When Air Force One landed, a helicopter transported the president and first lady to the country club. They were greeted by Don, Tyrone and Jack, as well as the country's leaders. President Taylor said "Bring the goat herder to me. Also, tell the soldiers to relax and hit some balls until we resolve this issue."

The goat herder and his sons were brought forward under heavy guard, frightened out of their wits. With the help of a translator, Jeff said "Hi guys. I'm Jeff Taylor. I'm president of the United States. I saw the video of your tank maneuvers. You guys were great at driving those things. Can you show me how? I always wanted to drive a tank. It looks so cool." The herders felt proud at Jeff's compliment, and they all went off to the eighth green. Jeff got in one tank, and Ginger got in another. Within the hour, they were playing army, and eventually drove the tanks back to their original home at the bunker. A cease fire was immediately called, relieving the troops' tension of shooting at their cousins.

Afterwards, Jeff inspected the damage to the green, and was amazed by the texture and radiance of the grass. He diplomatically arranged to have the herder become a government official of both countries, responsible for the evaluation and development of using goat manure for golf course fertilization. The herder gladly accepted the offer, in exchange for giving part of his pasture to the golf course.

After a few months of testing, the herder created an amazing new type of goat manure to fertilize the course, and irrigated the grass with the local mineral waters. Just Fore Golf did a special report on the turf, indicating it was the most pristine grass in the world to make a divot. The two countries were overwhelmed by golfers wanting to play on this special grass, and their tourism industry boomed.

Jeff's diplomacy averted the war and developed a new economic stream for the poor countries. In addition, the secret goat manure mixture was sold to a U.S. fertilizer company for millions of dollars. The two countries split the payoff with the herder, and used their proceeds to add a heath spa to the country club.

The spa was known world wide for its ability to bring new life to aging faces as well as grass. The herder concocted a variation of his goat manure as an anti-aging cream called Fleece Release. Basically, people spent $1500 a day to have goat shit spread on their faces. The recipients thought "This stuff must really work if it smells this bad" and felt rejuvenated after several applications.

* * *

Leo Scratchmore (a.k.a. Scratch) moved in with Toni at the Stiff Wind and assumed the responsibility of setting up breakfast and making drinks at happy hour. Everyday he concocted a new happy hour potion, using less toxic mixes than he had previously attempted. By using secret and more natural ingredients such as key lime, hibiscus flowers and frangipani tree extract, he developed an exotic rum punch that caused tourists and locals alike to stop by the Stiff Wind for the specialty drink called "Smooth Keys Breeze." Before too long, he began bottling the magic mix and started his first legitimate and booming business. The cruise ships were his largest customers, selling and serving his passion potion to on-board guests to help them maintain their island attitude at other ports-o-call.

It is not known if Scratch officially crossed over into Toni's world of sexual preference, but they have remained "close mates" to this day.

* * *

After Jeff won the election, he had to break most of his product endorsement contracts as he wasn't able to meet their obligations while in office. However, he did fulfill some aspects of the contracts, which resulted in the payout of several million dollars. He and Longshot split the total fees with their team members, much to their surprise and appreciation.

* * *

Longshot ended up breaking even with his bet to his followers, but signed a huge contract to air his show on satellite radio, as his popularity soared with his courageous bet and connection with Jeff. Bob, in addition to receiving his split from Jeff, followed Longshot's path and signed a substantial contract to produce his gambling shows. A year later "Up Your Odds" made its first television debut. Bob added some Vegas flare to the show by using glitzy show girls to jazz up the program. He ended up marrying one of the girls who was more of a plastic surgeons' creation than God's. Bob actually preferred the man-made element much to her obvious delight.

One of the show's sponsors was Royal Flush Eyewear, a company that launched a Longshot logo line of designer gambling sunglasses. They guaranteed that you'd bet and win with the confidence of a professional gambler. Longshot donated a portion of his sunglass contract proceeds to Gamblers Anonymous, knowing the sunglasses hid the eyes of losers.

* * *

Since banners, signage and advertising were not used in his Jeff's campaign, it was estimated that 78 trees are still producing oxygen as a result, and Americans were spared 724 hours of political TV ads.

Jeff's non-official campaign generated over 64 million dollars to an assortment of valid charitable organizations. There has been no official release of scientific medical breakthroughs or improvement to the quality of life based on these donations. The only measurement of success was the 798,228 thank you emails that were received and counted by Ellen Spackler's staff.

* * *

Johnson banked his split from Jeff, and came out of semi-retirement to work for Jeff as his personal security assistant. He immediately hired Tyrone and Jack to head up the Secret Service. Part of their responsibility of protecting the president and first lady was to destroy any and all ghosts that hid in their former closets. They found and eliminated anything that could equate Ginger with her past.

Fat, Sticky, and the two I-thugs were arrested and sentenced to a minimum of eight years of seclusion, potentially protecting Ginger through two terms. They also protected the pictures that Scratch took of Fat and Sticky, using that as leverage in case they decided to divulge any knowledge of Ginger's past.

* * *

Sonny's departure from office left the Swine Dine unprotected from his political guard. This gave the health department an open door to investigate the restaurant chain when several hundred cases of food poisoning were reported. Health officials ordered a variety of BBQ dinners to go, and had them analyzed. **Except** for beef, pork, and chicken, virtually every other type of animal, including some larger reptiles, were discovered in the food. Health officials didn't know that animal shelters located within a ten mile radius of any Swine Dine had the lowest rate of occupancy. In addition, road kill was virtually non-existent in those areas. Free meat-like sources generated a tremendous amount of revenue for Ashley's father, but he ended up filing for bankruptcy to pay his attorneys for the barrage of lawsuits that were generated.

He sold the chain of restaurants for a song to a Korean company that opened an all-you-can-eat Asian buffet called FuYu. Coincidentally, the animal shelters located within the proximity of the restaurants still continued to boast the lowest rate of occupancy.

* * *

The RGoodBandMan did play at the inaugural party. High Pops were not allowed at this event, but Reggie and the band members were seen drinking a mysterious punch, before, during, and after the concert. The bass player was seen giving some punch sips to a new member of the Secret Service. Romantic sparks were generated. They washed up on the shores of Bermuda several days later. President Taylor explained to her commander that she was doing a secret service for him, and that no reprimand was necessary.

Jade and the drummer, had little recollection of their previous High Pop fling, so no sparks were ignited during their brief White House encounter. However, Jade did acquire a large glass of the punch from Reggie, and offered some to a Marine General who was invited to the inaugural bash courtesy of Johnson. Early the next morning, local police discovered Jade and the General at the base of the U.S. Marine Corps War Memorial (Iwo Jima Statue) singing the USMC anthem. They were discreetly escorted to their respective abodes without fanfare or incident. Jade ended up dating the general during her successful career as White House Press Secretary.

* * *

During the first five minutes of the video, Sonny had a flash front (instead of a flash back). He foresaw the nightmare that would erupt based on the world's view of the video and quickly determined that his life was ruined. His campaign headquarters was filled with national news media and campaign volunteers, and they were all petrified and glued to the TV. During the congressman/bird duet, Sonny discretely acquired car keys from one of his dazed campaign volunteers and drove off unnoticed.

With one phone call, he arranged to have a private jet transport him to Maracaibo, a large Venezuelan city known for its rich oil fields. While traveling to the airstrip, he went through the drive-in window at a local Swine Dine and ordered and devoured a rack of ribs and four beers. Afterwards, he proceeded to the air strip where the jet was waiting for him. He quickly boarded. In flight,

Sonny became ill and figured he drank bad beer. He considered suing the brewery but fell asleep in thought.

When his plane landed, he was greeted by a confidant who presented him with his new South American identity: Senior Sanchez Paloma. Sanchez stayed at the villa of an influential oil-related friend until he purchased a hacienda among several hundred acres of jungle, known especially for its habitat of rare and exotic parrots.

Like those who travel outside of Las Vegas to fulfill their lustful fantasies at the Chicken Ranch Brothel, Sanchez created the Parrot Ranch. His brothel delivered sexually safe sex of a feathery nature, fulfilling the fantasies of Fortune 500 colleagues and dignitaries from around the world. Sonny spent two years on the equator's edge riding the wings of passion and forging the lust for revenge.

Sonny knew how fickle and downright stupid Americans could be when it came to voting for presidents. Americans could remember detailed sports statistics, nightly TV schedules, or the past spouses of major celebrities with ease. But, they didn't remember who ran for president, or even, in some cases, who won. Sonny, therefore, recouped in South America, and developed a plan to run for the presidency and even the score with Jeff, Ginger, and Blabs.

Two years before the next election, Sonny placed a call to the United States. After three rings, a voice on the other end of the phone said, "Hey, partner. This is Longshot. What can I do you for?"

Printed in the United States
200263BV00004B/184-189/A